T0291363

Vladimir Putin and Russia's Imperial Revival

Vladimir Putin and Russia's Imperial Revival

David E. McNabb

CRC Press
Taylor & Francis Group
Boca Raton   London   New York

CRC Press is an imprint of the
Taylor & Francis Group, an **informa** business

CRC Press
Taylor & Francis Group
6000 Broken Sound Parkway NW, Suite 300
Boca Raton, FL 33487-2742

© 2016 by Taylor & Francis Group, LLC
CRC Press is an imprint of Taylor & Francis Group, an Informa business

No claim to original U.S. Government works

Printed on acid-free paper
Version Date: 20150805

International Standard Book Number-13: 978-1-4987-1198-2 (Hardback)

Visit the Taylor & Francis Web site at
http://www.taylorandfrancis.com

and the CRC Press Web site at
http://www.crcpress.com

This book is dedicated to Dr. Gundar J. King, professor and dean emeritus of the Pacific Lutheran University School of Business and founding president of the Association for the Advancement of Baltic Studies.

Contents

List of Figures..xiii

List of Maps..xv

List of Sourcelines..xvii

List of Tables..xix

List of Boxes..xxi

List of Acronyms..xxiii

Preface..xxv

Acknowledgments..xxvii

Author...xxix

SECTION I A MILLENNIUM OF EMPIRE BUILDING

1 The Collapse and Rebirth of the Soviet Empire 3

    1.1   Introduction 3

    1.2   Rebuilding a Nation 5

            1.2.1   Russia Is Back 7

    1.3   Shaping Putin's Foreign Policy.............................8

    1.4   Rise of the Phoenix..9

    1.5   Regaining Status Lost......................................10

    1.6   Ending Ties with the West 11

    1.7   A Renewal of the Cold War?..............................11

    1.8   Resurrecting Relations with *Special-Interest* Neighbors..................12

            1.8.1   Regaining Respect 13

    1.9   Conclusion 15

2 Stages in the Building of a Russian Empire 17

    2.1   Introduction 17

    2.2   The Kievan Rus Empire....................................19

    2.3   The Muscovite Empire.....................................23

            2.3.1   Territorial Expansion 24

                    2.3.1.1   Expansion under Ivan IV 24

2.4   The Romanov Empire..25
        2.4.1   The Age of Catherine the Great 28
                2.4.1.1   Growth after Catherine...........................29
                2.4.1.2   Setback in the Crimean War....................30
        2.4.2   Consolidation under the Romanovs.....................31
2.5   The Soviet Empire 31
2.6   Conclusion 35

SECTION II   FROM UNCERTAINTY TO SUPREME CONFIDENCE

3   Russia's Foreign Policy in Transition 39
3.1   Introduction 39
3.2   Factors Shaping Post-Soviet Foreign Policy......................39
        3.2.1   Ideological Foundation Shift............................... 40
        3.2.2   Effects of Socioeconomic Crises 40
3.3   A New Role for Russia? 43
3.4   Rebuilding the State 45
        3.4.1   Recentralization of the Political System 46
        3.4.2   The Dictatorship of Law.................................... 46
        3.4.3   Souverenaya Democratiya 47
                3.4.3.1   Controlling Corruption 48
                3.4.3.2   Forging New Alliances..........................48
        3.4.4   Relations with Former Soviet Possessions...........50
                3.4.4.1   Rebuilding Russia's Armed Forces.........51
3.5   Russia, the EU and NATO..52
        3.5.1   Testing, Testing, Testing.....................................53
3.6   Conclusion 54

4   The Putin-Era Foreign Policy of Consolidation 57
4.1   Introduction 57
4.2   Evolution of the Consolidation Policy 57
4.3   Putin-Era Foreign Relations 58
        4.3.1   Relations with the West 59
        4.3.2   Relations with Former Republics 60
4.4   Foreign Policy Goals...61
        4.4.1   Regaining Superpower Status 62
        4.4.2   By Force If Necessary...62
        4.4.3   Against All Enemies..63
4.5   Russia's Use of Soft Power 65
        4.5.1   Building Friendly Networks................................68
4.6   Conclusion 70

5 Building Defensive Barriers 73
  5.1 Introduction 73
  5.2 Building Barriers in the West 74
      5.2.1 The Brezhnev Doctrine 76
          5.2.1.1 Changing Strategic Doctrines 77
          5.2.1.2 Russia's European Alliances 1970–1989 79
  5.3 Building Barriers in the East...79
      5.3.1 Strategic Aims in Central Asia 81
      5.3.2 Alliances in East, South and Southeast Asia........................82
      5.3.3 Maintaining Russia's East Asian Policy 83
          5.3.3.1 Economic Strengths 84
          5.3.3.2 Strategic Alliances 84
          5.3.3.3 Military Forces.......................................85
  5.4 Colonization and Deportation in the Conquered Territories 86
      5.4.1 Colonization in Muscovite Russia.......................87
      5.4.2 Colonization in the Romanov Empire.....................88
          5.4.2.1 Colonization for Economic Growth.................88
          5.4.2.2 Colonization for Security 89
  5.5 Conclusion 90

SECTION III   RUSSIA'S FOREIGN POLICY WEAPONS

6 Reforming and Rearming Russia's Military......................................95
  6.1 Introduction 95
  6.2 The Need for Reforms 95
      6.2.1 Military Budgets...96
  6.3 2000–2008 Military Reforms 97
      6.3.1 Objections to Proposed Reform 97
      6.3.2 Effects of the Chechnya Insurgencies 97
      6.3.3 Impact of the War with Georgia 99
  6.4 2008–2015 Military Reforms and Reorganizations 99
      6.4.1 Objectives of the Reforms..................................100
          6.4.1.1 Reorganizing the Russian Army....................100
          6.4.1.2 Command-and-Control and Organizational
                      Changes 101
          6.4.1.3 Land Forces Reorganization.........................102
  6.5 All-Forces Personnel Reductions..................................104
  6.6 Rearming the Russian Military 105
      6.6.1 The 2007–2015 Rearmament Plan 105
      6.6.2 The 2011–2020 Plan 105
  6.7 Conclusion 107

7 Russia's Undeclared Cyber Wars **109**
    7.1   Introduction 109
    7.2   Cyber Tactics.. 111
    7.3   2007: Cyber War with Estonia 112
    7.4   2008: Cyber War with Lithuania... 116
    7.5   2009: Kyrgyzstan under Cyber Attack 117
    7.6   2009: Cyber and Shooting War with Georgia........................ 118
    7.7   Cyber Wars with Ukraine... 119
    7.8   Conclusion 120

8 The Energy Weapon in Russia's Foreign Policy **123**
    8.1   Introduction 123
    8.2   State Control of Energy Resources... 124
        8.2.1   Decentralized Production 125
                8.2.1.1   Oil Production Areas 125
                8.2.1.2   Gas Production Areas............................. 125
    8.3   Control of Transit Routes and Modes..................................... 126
        8.3.1   Alternative Sources of Supply.................................. 127
        8.3.2   Southern Pipeline Proposals.................................... 127
                8.3.2.1   The South Stream Pipeline..................... 128
                8.3.2.2   The Trans-Caspian Pipeline 129
                8.3.2.3   The Turkmenistan–China Pipeline 129
    8.4   Means for Implementing the Energy Weapon 132
        8.4.1   Problems and Pitfalls... 133
        8.4.2   Employing the Energy Weapon 135
                8.4.2.1   The 2006 Gas Crisis.............................. 135
                8.4.2.2   The 2009 Gas Crisis.............................. 137
        8.4.3   2014 Cutoffs in Ukraine 139
    8.5   Acquiescence of Target Countries.. 139
    8.6   Conclusion 141

SECTION IV   RUSSIA'S FOREIGN POLICY IN ACTION

9 Russian Aggression in Ukraine: Empire Revival **145**
    9.1   Introduction 145
    9.2   History of Russian–Ukraine Relations 145
        9.2.1   The Orange Revolution.. 147
        9.2.2   Ukrainians Protest Russian Language Law 148
                9.2.2.1   The Maidan Protests 149
    9.3   Putin's Revenge 150
        9.3.1   The Importance of Crimea....................................... 151
        9.3.2   The Continuing War.. 153
                9.3.2.1   The Takeover of Crimea......................... 154

9.4 What Happens Next? 156
    9.4.1 Economic Warfare 158
9.5 Conclusion 158

10 Russian Intimidation in the Baltic and Nordic States........................159
10.1 Introduction 159
    10.1.1 NATO and Baltic/Nordic Defense 162
    10.1.2 The Arctic Theater...163
    10.1.3 Russian Aggression in the Baltic States 164
    10.1.4 The Importance of the East Baltic....................................167
    10.1.5 Post-Soviet Transition 168
10.2 Future Regional Security Scenarios 170
    10.2.1 Control of Regional Security..170
    10.2.2 Peaceful Gaining of Economic Control 171
    10.2.3 Creating Client States 171
    10.2.4 Territorial Expansion 172
10.3 Changes in the West's View of Post-Soviet Russia 172
    10.3.1 Policy Implementation 173
10.4 Conclusion 174

11 Russian Foreign Policy after Putin..175
11.1 Introduction 175
11.2 What Role for Russia? 175
    11.2.1 A Smaller, Weaker Empire 176
11.3 The Putin/Medvedev Power Vertical..177
    11.3.1 Putin's Strengths 178
    11.3.2 Putin's Weaknesses..179
11.4 Alternative Foreign Policy Strategies..180
    11.4.1 The Martial Arts Approach 180
    11.4.2 Economic Warfare Approach 181
    11.4.3 The Aggressive Diplomacy Approach 181
    11.4.4 The Friendly Neighbor Approach....................................182
11.5 The Recurring Foreign Policy Aim 182
11.6 Implications for the West..184
11.7 Russia's Relations with the West...186
    11.7.1 Relations with NATO...186
    11.7.2 Relations with Former Possessions 186
11.8 Scenarios for a Russia after Putin...187
    11.8.1 Status Quo...187
    11.8.2 The Path to the West...189
    11.8.3 Stalin Lite 189

            11.8.4 Chaos in Russia.. 189
            11.8.5 The Most Probable Scenario.. 190
      11.9 Conclusion 190

Appendix.. **193**

References **197**

Index **215**

List of Figures

Figure 1.1 Interrelated forces shaping efficacy of a foreign policy......................4

Figure 5.1 First-half 2014 trade values for Russia's major trading partners......83

Figure 6.1 Top 20 defense budgets in 2013..96

Figure 6.2 Regional distribution of Russian military districts after
reorganization 101

Figure 8.1 December 2014 spot prices for Brent (Europe) crude oil..............134

Figure 8.2 December 2014 spot prices for West Texas (US) crude oil 134

Figure 8.3 Eight-year price averages for oil and gas for Europe, all sources
of supply 137

List of Maps

Map 1.1   Eurasian Russia with major cities 4

Map 1.2   Independent states of the former USSR...............................13

Map 2.1   Kievan Rus: the first great Russian empire 20

Map 2.2   Viking river trade routes and first land of the Kievan Rus in the ninth century...21

Map 2.3   Mongol invasions of Central Asia and Kievan Rus in the thirteenth century...23

Map 2.4   The three partitions of Poland: 1772, 1793, 1795.............30

Map 4.1   Route of the Russian–German Baltic Sea natural gas pipeline 70

Map 5.1   NATO and Warsaw Pact countries in the Cold War.........................75

Map 5.2   East Asia with countries of geopolitical interest to Russia 80

Map 5.3   Map of the Caucasus and Central Asia.............................81

Map 7.1   Ukraine, including the Crimean Peninsula......................112

Map 7.2   Estonia and bordering states 114

Map 7.3   Lithuania and adjacent states 116

Map 7.4   Kyrgyzstan and bordering states 117

Map 7.5   Georgia with South Ossetia and Abkhazia......................118

Map 8.1   Route of the Nord Stream natural gas pipeline from Russia to Germany..128

Map 8.2   Route of the Trans-Caspian gas pipeline and connection to Azerbaijan and Turkey...131

Map 8.3 Route of Turkmenistan to China and other Asian gas pipelines to China...131

Map 9.1 Russia's *Special-Interest* States in North and Central Europe............146

Map 9.2 Russian map of Crimea...154

Map 10.1 Europe with all countries bordering on the Baltic Sea..................160

List of Sourcelines

Figure 5.1 From TV-Novosti (RT), Russia-China trade hits record
$59 billion in first half of 2014, available at http://rt.com
/business/197516-russia-china-trade-half-2014 (retrieved
January 5, 2014), 2015 83

Figure 6.1 From Young, A., Global defense budget seen climbing in 2014;
first total increase since 2009 as Russia surpasses Britain
and Saudi Arabia continues its security spending spree,
International Business Times (February 6), available at
http://www.ibtimes.com/global-defense-budget-seen-climbing
-2014-first-total-increase-2009-russia-surpasses-britain-saudi
(retrieved July 7, 2014), 2014..96

Figure 6.2 From http://en.wikipedia.org/wiki/Military_districts
_of_Russia#/media/File:Military_districts_of_Russia
_December_1st_2010.svg. 101

Figure 8.2 From NASDAQ, December 8, 2014 134

Map 1.1 From CIA.gov, Map of Russia, available at http://www.cia.gov
/library/publications/cia-maps-publications/ (retrieved August
19, 2014), 2013 4

Map 1.2 From Open Source maps..13

Map 2.1 From Dutertre, G., Historical map of Ukraine, available at
http://www.google.com/url?sa=i&rct=j&q=&esrc=s&source
=images&cd=&cad=rja&uact=8&docid=NSNmUCIHlm7m
GM&tbnid=2o8ee3B95WJQ6M:&ved=0CAQQjB0&url=http
%3A%2F%2Fgillesenlettonie.blogspot.com%2F2011_08_01
_archive.html&ei=U9eVU-r0G8TyoATgnoKQCQ&bvm=bv.68
445247,d.cGU&psig=AFQjCNGY_EcckYDe0HYFpxQ91MuN
qX0HvA&ust=1402415075217995 (retrieved June 9, 2014), 2011 20

Map 2.2 From Wikimedia Commons, 2014...21

Map 2.3   From Wikimedia Commons, 2014...23

Map 2.4   From Wikimedia Commons, 2014...30

Map 4.1   From Wikimedia Commons, 2015. 70

Map 5.1   From COSD, The beginning of the Cold War, (Canada), Online Learning Resources, available at https://eschoolbc.sd23.bc.ca /mod/book/view.php?id=23449&chapterid=9948 (retrieved June 10, 2014), 2014..75

Map 5.2   From CIA.gov, Map of Russia, available at http://www.cia.gov /library/publications/cia-maps-publications/ (retrieved August 19, 2014), 2013...80

Map 5.3   From http://www.usaid.gov/locations/europe_eurasia/car/................81

Map 7.1   From CIA.gov, Map of Russia, available at http://www.cia.gov /library/publications/cia-maps-publications/ (retrieved August 19, 2014), 2013 112

Map 7.2   From CIA.gov, Map of Russia, available at http://www.cia.gov /library/publications/cia-maps-publications/ (retrieved August 19, 2014), 2013 114

Map 7.3   From CIA.gov, Map of Russia, available at http://www.cia.gov /library/publications/cia-maps-publications/ (retrieved August 19, 2014), 2013 116

Map 7.4   From CIA.gov, Map of Russia, available at http://www.cia.gov /library/publications/cia-maps-publications/ (retrieved August 19, 2014), 2013 117

Map 7.5   From CIA.gov, Map of Russia, available at http://www.cia.gov /library/publications/cia-maps-publications/ (retrieved August 19, 2014), 2013 118

Map 8.1   From http://neftegaz.ru. 128

Map 8.2   From Thomas Bloomberg 2012 and Creative Commons.org...........131

Map 8.3   From Energygeopolitics, Wordpress.com, 2013.............................131

Map 9.1   From Ian.macky.net, PAT (Public Domain Maps of Eastern Europe)...146

Map 9.2   From Wikimedia Commons 154

Map 10.1 From CIA.gov, Map of Russia, available at http://www.cia .gov/library/publications/cia-maps-publications/ (retrieved August 19, 2014), 2013..160

List of Tables

Table 2.1 Soviet Territorial Expansion Imperial and Repression in Asia and the Middle East 33

Table 4.1 Countries Russians Most Consider Enemies, 2005–2013 (% of Respondents).. 64

Table 4.2 Countries Russian Residents Consider Friends, 2005–2013 (% of Respondents)..69

Table 5.1 WP Armed Forces in 1969...78

Table 5.2 East, South and Southeast Asian Countries and 2013 Population Estimates 82

Table 6.1 Changes in the Numbers of Army Officer Positions from 2008 to 2012 104

Table 6.2 Spending Distribution of SAP 2010 Budget Allocation.................106

Table 6.3 Force Share of SAP 2020 Rearming Plan with Equipment Examples 106

Table 7.1 Comparison of Cyber Warfare in Post-Soviet States...................... 110

Table 8.1 Russia's 2014 Oil Production by Region (Thousand Barrels per Day)... 124

Table 8.2 One-Day High and Low Spot Prices for European Brent Crude, November 2013–October 2014 126

Table 8.3 Average World Prices for Oil and US Price for Natural Gas, 2012–2015 136

Table 8.4 Dependence upon Imported Energy for EU and Selected Nations, 2004–2012 (%) 138

Table 9.1 Russian and Ukrainian Military Comparisons in 2013.................. 155

Table 10.1 Selected Sources for Russia's Interests in the Baltic State Region...166

Table 10.2 Average Voter Turnouts in European Elections, 1999–2009 170

Table 11.1 The Population of the Soviet Union by Region and Ethnicity, 1989 176

Table 11.2 Population of Russia, the United States, China, India and Ukraine 1980–2012 179

List of Boxes

Box 1.1 Underlying themes: Démarche over Putin's revanchist policies.............9

Box 2.1 The coronation of Ivan IV of Moscow.................................18

Box 2.2 Death of the last, greatest Russian empire.........................32

Box 3.1 Colonization in the late Russian empire 49

Box 4.1 Russia's use of soft power in Europe to influence public opinion 66

Box 5.1 The combination of deportation and collectivization:
An Estonian example...87

Box 6.1 Russian military reforms include more missiles and
nuclear submarines. 103

Box 7.1 Weapons in the cyber war arsenal 113

Box 7.2 Hackers hit US businesses over Ukraine standoff.....................120

Box 8.1 2014 European Energy Security Strategy.............................130

Box 8.2 Turkey's role in the Russia–EU gas wars 140

Box 9.1 Ukraine's Orange Revolution of 2004 148

Box 9.2 NATO's reaction to Russian aggression in Ukraine.................... 157

Box 10.1 Nordic–Baltic security cooperation 161

Box 10.2 Russia's aggressive military exercises threaten the
Nordic–Baltic region 163

Box 10.3 Russia's ongoing threat for the Baltic and Nordic regions..............168

List of Acronyms

AC	Atlantic Council (1996)
APEC	Asia-Pacific Economic Cooperation (1998)
CBSS	Council of Baltic Sea States (1992)
CCD COE	Cooperative Cyber Defense Centre of Excellence (NATO) (2008)
CC (C2)	Military command-and-control systems (n/a)
CES	Common Economic Space (2006)
CFI	Connected Forces Initiative (NATO) (2014)
CICA	Conference on Interaction and Confidence-Building Measures in Asia (1999)
CIS	Commonwealth of Independent States (1991)
CMEA	Council of Mutual Economic Assistance (1949)
CRDFCA	Collective Rapid Deployment Force for Central Asia (2001)
CSCE	Helsinki Conference on Security and Cooperation in Europe (1995)
CSTO	Collective Security Treaty Organization (2003)
CURBK	Russia, Belarus, Kazakhstan Customs Union (2009)
EAS	East Asian Summit (2011)
EDB	Eurasian Development Bank (2006)
EEAF	East European Allied Forces (1999)
EIA	Energy Information Administration (US) (1977)
ESPA	Eastern Siberia–Pacific Ocean Oil Pipeline (2nd stage) (2012)
EurAsEC	Eurasian Economic Community (2000)
FA	Federal Assembly (Parliament of Russia) (2000)
FEFD	Far Eastern Federal District (2000)
NAC	National Anti-Terrorism Committee (2006)
NATO	North Atlantic Treaty Organization (1949)
NORC	National Opinion Research Center (1941)
NRC	NATO–Russia Council (2002)
NRF	NATO Response Force (2013)
OPEC	Organization of Oil-Exporting Countries (1960)
OSCE	Organization for Security and Cooperation in Europe (1975)
PCC	Political Consultative Committee (first formed in Poland) (1940)
RA	Resettlement Administration (1896)

RF	Russian Federation (1991)
RFE	Radio Free Europe (US) (1949)
SCO	Shanghai Cooperation Organization (2001)
SFD	Siberian Federal District (2000)
SS	South Stream (Black Sea gas pipeline) (2012)
WTO	Warsaw Treaty Organization (1955)

Preface

This book is not only about the end of an empire—what Strayer (2001, 376) called "that grand meta-narrative of world history, the fall of empires." But it is also about the early stages of the rebirth of another empire—at least the first clumsy, rough-shod steps in that process. In addition to this preface, this book includes 11 chapters that focus on one or more aspects of the historical and present empirical foreign policies followed in building the Russian Empire in the shapes that it has taken since it emerged out of what is today Ukraine.

In the chapters that follow, I address the antecedents of the Russian and Soviet Empires and the imperial rebirth emerging from the aggressive, expansionist foreign policy of Russian President Putin. Although Russia is a long way from reclaiming its position as one of two global superpowers, it is still a nuclear power with a long history of depending upon armed diplomacy to achieve its foreign policy objectives. Russia is slowly but surely reforming its armed forces to meet local threats even while it maintains a nuclear power, with it modernizing its military and coming to terms with the reality of the failure of its dependence upon an army of one-year conscripts. It has tested its nearly quarter-century focus on fighting a land army with massed armor and found it inappropriate in the new reality of small wars fought in its borderlands. Vestiges of the military doctrine of a first-strike rocket nuclear war remain among senior officers of the army and navy. Still, Russia's new-found will to aggressively threaten its smaller neighbors and annex their territories has been enough to bring all but very few NATO countries to continue to increase their annual defense budgets.

The discussion is divided into four related parts. Section I, *A Millennium of Empire Building*, includes two chapters that introduce aspects of Russian foreign policy from the twelfth century to the dissolution of the Soviet Union. Chapter 1 describes the framework followed for analyzing the factors behind the show of force that continues to appear in the foreign policy of Russia and its relations with the rest of the world. Chapter 2 is an overview of the early progression through the four central manifestations as an empire.

Section II, *Russia's Post-Soviet Foreign Policy*, includes three chapters dealing with the author's interpretation of the geopolitical and economic events that have shaped the Russian Federation's foreign policy since 1991. Chapter 3 describes the evolution of Russia's foreign policy from the presidency of Yeltsin to that of Putin. Chapter 4 describes the elements of the policy of imperial consolidation implemented by Putin and Medvedev that emerged from the foreign policy vacuum that came with the elimination of the Communist Party and the loss of pride and self-esteem brought about by the loss of the Soviet Empire. Chapter 5 examines several policy tools employed by the Romanov and Soviet Empires to grow and defend their imperial positions from the 1880s to roughly the 1950s. These include the use of internal colonization and deportation and the barrier-building defensive networks of the post-World War II foreign policy of the Soviet Union.

Section III, *Russia's Foreign Policy Weapons*, contains three chapters that describe the tools that Russia's leaders are using to achieve their twenty-first-century foreign policy goals. Chapter 6 reviews the rebuilding of Russia's military capacity after the decline that the military has suffered through since the heady days of its victory in the Great Patriotic War (WWII). Chapter 7 describes the way Russia has employed cyber warfare as an aggressive tactic designed to destabilize security and governance institutions of its enemies, to intimidate its present and past territories and as a weapon in its real and threatened armed aggression. Chapter 8 examines the examples of Russia's use of its vast energy supplies and its power over captive markets for Russian oil and gas as weapons in the aggressive foreign policy that it employs toward nations that contest its bullying of its neighbors and former possessions.

Section IV, *Russia's Aggressive Foreign Policy in Action*, brings the discussion from its elements and antecedents to two examples of Russia's exercise of these and other weapons of aggressive foreign policy to achieve its will over smaller and weaker neighbors. Chapter 9 focuses on Russia's past and present aggression in Ukraine, from withholding that nation's near-total dependence upon Russian oil and natural gas to armed aggression that culminated in annexation of the Crimean Peninsula and the continuing support of Russian separatists in Ukraine's eastern and southern districts. Chapter 10 is a discussion of Russia's threatening stance in the strategically important Baltic Sea states of Estonia, Latvia and Lithuania and the Nordic states of Finland, Sweden, Norway and Denmark. Chapter 11, the final chapter in this book, summarizes the author's and other Russia watchers' conceptions and interpretations of the shape and future direction of Putin-influenced foreign policy.

Acknowledgments

The author once again acknowledges the debt he owes to Dr. Gundar J. King, Latvian patriot and dean emeritus of the Pacific Lutheran University School of Business. Many thanks are also due to senior editor Lara Zoble and the editorial and production staff at CRC Press. Those highly supportive and talented people can never be thanked enough for their consistent support and guidance throughout the writing of this book and previous works. Finally, I convey my sincere gratitude to Pacific Lutheran University for their many years of support for this book and my previous academic endeavors.

A policy analysis of this type is overwhelmingly dependent upon the works of the many different researchers and policy analysts that have devoted themselves to the study of the Russian empires from their earliest beginnings. I have done my best to ensure that their contributions are recognized in the text and references. Any error of omission or commission is mine alone.

Author

Dr. David E. McNabb is a professor emeritus at Pacific Lutheran University, an adjunct professor at Olympic College, Bremerton, Washington, and a recent consultant for an agency of the federal government. He has gained extensive experience teaching and researching in Europe and several former Soviet satellites, having been a visiting professor at the Stockholm School of Economics–Riga, the American University of Bulgaria, the University of Maryland–University College (Europe) and a regional business education program in Northern France. He has also taught in the Masters of Public Administration program at Evergreen State College, Oregon State University, the University of Washington–Tacoma and several community colleges. He earned his PhD at Oregon State University, an MA at the University of Washington and a BA at California State University, Fullerton. He served as director of communications for a caucus of the Washington House of Representatives and as director of economic development for the city of Fullerton, California. He is the sole author of 10 books, joint author of 2 others and author or joint author of nearly 100 articles and conference papers. Much of his research has been on the transformation of government institutions both here in the United States and in the Baltic states. The first edition of his first book, *Research Methods in Public Administration and Nonprofit Management: Quantitative and Qualitative Approaches* (M.E. Sharpe, 2003), received the Grenzebach Prize for Outstanding Published Scholarship in Philanthropy. He is, or has been until recently, a member of the Academy of Management; American Marketing Association; American Society for Public Administration; Association for Slavic, East European, and Eurasian Studies; Association for the Advancement of Baltic Studies; American Political Science Association; Midwestern Political Science Association; the American Statistical Association; and the American Academy of Political Science.

A MILLENNIUM OF EMPIRE BUILDING

1

Chapter 1

The Collapse and Rebirth of the Soviet Empire

1.1 Introduction

The *glasnost* (openness) and *perestroika* (restructuring) policies that Soviet Union President Mikhail Gorbachev introduced in the 1980s triggered the release of internal forces, which, by December 1991, split the Soviet Union into 15 independent republics and indirectly led to the rise to power of Vladimir Putin. Gorbachev's foreign policy was aimed at kick-starting the stagnant Soviet economy while reducing the influence of the Communist Party. Except for the war years but including the years of the Great Depression, from 1920 to 1960, the Soviet economy grew at rates higher than most of the nations of the West. However, after 1960, growth rates steadily declined, sinking to flat or negative rates by the 1980s. In an effort to rekindle growth in the Soviet Union, Gorbachev adopted policies of retrenchment in both domestic spending and foreign relations. He cut military spending, removed missiles from Eastern Europe, ended financial support to communism movements and pushed for greater regional cooperation. In a move with major repercussions, in 1988, he adopted a policy of noninterference in Eastern Europe satellites by renouncing the Brezhnev Doctrine, thereby freeing the Warsaw Pact countries to proceed on their own. His strategy involved using foreign policy that included rapprochement with the West and disarmament primarily to advance perestroika. The shift culminated in his decision to not contest the removal of the Berlin Wall in November 1989, finally concluding with the end of the Union of Soviet Socialist Republics (USSR) in 1991 (Snyder 2005). The elements of a workable foreign policy are in Figure 1.1.

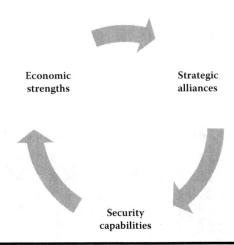

Economic
strengths

Strategic
alliances

Security
capabilities

Figure 1.1 Interrelated forces shaping efficacy of a foreign policy.

What was left after the collapse of the USSR was the remaining rump of Soviet heartland and Siberia—still geographically the largest nation on the globe and one of the richest in terms of natural resources, the Russian Federation (RF). What was left was large in territory, but it was no longer one of the two global superpowers. Gorbachev's plan failed; the economy sank deeper into free fall. The reduced RF found itself no longer able to directly control the politics and economies of the republics that chose to leave the USSR. Map 1.1 shows the geographic extent of Eurasian Russia, its major cities and its relation to neighboring nations. This book is about the policies and actions taken by Putin to return Russia to its lost glory as an empire and global superpower.

Map 1.1 Eurasian Russia with major cities.

Despite the dissolution of the Soviet Empire and loss of superpower status, Russian foreign policy continues to employ the use of aggression and intimidation in its efforts to control the politics and foreign policies of its former republics and any nation it considers to fall under its *special interest* mantle. The tactics employed since 2000 are not new; they have characterized the foreign policies of Russia for as long as there has been a Russian Empire. Even while Russia lures potential friends in the East and West with long-term, low-price contracts for the delivery of oil and gas, it continues to sponsor civil unrest and aggressive actions and spying in what it considers its regions of special interests and enemies of the state. These include Ukraine, the Baltic states and other former republics, the European Union (EU), North Atlantic Treaty Organization (NATO), the United States and anyone else who gets in its way. Russia continues to test the responses of nearby nations with incursions into the coastal waters of the Nordic states, holds threatening invasion maneuvers in the Baltic Sea and sends its long-range bombers into the airspace of Western European nations. A suspected repeat in 2014 of an earlier threatening incursion was the suspected test landing of Russian special forces personnel from a submarine onto the coast of Sweden. A similar incursion occurred in 1981 when a Russian submarine became stranded inside Russian waters close to a major Swedish naval base (Pollard and Scrutton 2014). A report nine days earlier from Finland accused the Russian navy of interfering in an unarmed Baltic Sea research vessel nearing Swedish waters, while Finland was conducting a regular monitoring of the conditions of the Baltic Sea. The Russian Defense Ministry refused to comment (Rosendahl 2014).

The aggressive use of armed diplomacy and display of Russia's military muscle faded with the 1991 collapse of the Soviet Union. The traditional centralized control and autocratic leadership appeared to be a thing of the past with the election of Boris Yeltsin as the country's first elected president. Yeltsin sought a rapprochement with the United States, outlawed the Communist Party and, after a bitter fight with the new Russian legislature in 1993, pushed through a new constitution that gave the Russian president supreme power. Over the next eight years, his battles with legislators resulted in failure to carry out the transition from the Communist Party autocratic government to a Western-style democracy. Since 2000, Presidents Putin and Medvedev turned into an autocratic state ruled by a strongman with a legislative body that endorses without question his every action.

1.2 Rebuilding a Nation

Collapse of the USSR in 1991 made it necessary to replace the Soviet-era constitution with one that reflected the shrunken state of the remaining RF. Included in the new constitution was the establishment of the office of an elected president. A newly reorganized Russia's lower house of parliament, the *Duma*, voted in March 1991 to adopt the new constitution—thereby sanctioning the establishment of the new post. An elected president would run the country; a prime minister named by the president but approved by parliament would run the legislative branch. Boris Yeltsin was elected Russia's first elected president in June 1991. A brief, failed coup in August of that year aimed at reversing Gorbachev's policy of changing the Soviet system ended with Gorbachev's resignation. The new president then began reducing the power of the Communist Party.

Most of the republics quickly announced their independence. Yeltsin then dissolved the Soviet Union, replacing it with the weak Commonwealth of Independent States, which included Russia, Belarus and Ukraine. He set about solidifying his power by appointing his own supporters to positions as all district governors and other important administrative posts (Vasudevan 1993).

The system as established by Yeltsin and enforced by his appointed successor Vladimir Putin has included the following characteristics: bureaucratic capitalism managed and regulated by the state, an authoritarian political system dominated by bureaucrats and oligarchs, a social welfare system wholly dependent upon the state with little if any involvement by a vibrant civil society and a foreign policy that fluctuates between willingness to partner with the West and vilification of the West as enemies out to curtail Russia's role as a world leader. If it is possible to summarize the Yeltsin legacy in a single statement, this statement by Lilia Shevtsova (2007a, p. 894) may come close:

> [The chief legacy of Boris Yeltsin's presidency is] the hybridization of economic, political, social and foreign policy, reflected in adherence to mutually exclusive principles such as market and bureaucratic control, authoritarianism and democracy, paternalism and social Darwinism, and anti-western and pro-western trends ... further shaped by the replacement of any coherent ideology by 'pragmatism' [and] the adoption of a policy of imitation that allows the system to adapt to new realities without rejecting traditionalism.

The story of Yeltsin's reputation as Russia's first elected president is told by many critics as the man who sought power without possession of the necessary vision and purpose. In short, he was described as "perhaps the wrong man at the wrong time for Russia" (Gidadhubli 2007, p. 1820). He apparently believed in greater economic and political cooperation with the West but was not trusted enough by his parliament to be able to implement a foreign policy of rapprochement beyond cosmetic changes. His victory in his subsequent war with the parliament resulted in creation of a strong presidency and a weakened parliament and democratic tradition.

The question of what foreign policy role Russia was to take after dissolution of the USSR emerged early in the presidency of Boris Yeltsin (Matz 2001). In 1990, while still chairman of the Duma, Yeltsin announced that Russia was not interested in becoming the center of any new empire and would not seek any advantages over any of its former republics. In 1992, a few weeks after the formal breakup of the USSR, Andrei Kozyrev, President Yeltsin's foreign minister, echoed those sympathies, asserting that relations with the family of former republics were then conducted as between equals; Russia did not seek any special position in the family. In February 1993, however, that spirit of equality was becoming shaky. Kozyrev announced a new policy when he reminded the West that Russia continued to have an interest in all armed conflicts in the territories of the former USSR. He then added that Russia retained a special responsibility in the region and called for all international organizations, including the United Nations, to grant Russia special powers as a guarantor of peace and stability in all former Soviet territories.

The immediate post-Soviet era found many Russians asking themselves such questions as, Who are we? Are we Western? European? Euro-Asian? Or are we something unique? If unique, how so? Does being unique mean being Russian? If so, what does it mean to be *Russian*? Did unique historical and cultural characteristics create something totally different? (Gorenburg and Gaffney 2006). Exemplifying that quest for a new national identity is this comment by Eduard Shevardnadze, one-time KGB (Committee for State Security) and Communist Party official, Russian foreign minister from 1985 to 1990 and president of Georgia until 2005:

> The belief that we are a great country and that we should be respected for this is deeply ingrained in me, as in [every Russian]. But great in what? Territory? Population? Quantity of arms? Or the people's troubles? The individual's lack of rights? In what do we, who have virtually the highest infant mortality rate on our planet, take pride? It is not easy to answer the questions: Who are you and who do you wish to be? A country which is feared or a country which is respected? A country of power or a country of kindness?
>
> **J. Matz**
> *Constructing a Post-Soviet International Political Reality, 2001*

These questions were typical of the type being raised in the determination of which foreign policy best reflected the new political reality facing Russians before Putin took office. Since then, however, Putin's foreign and domestic policy pronouncements provided an answer for that appears to have satisfied a majority of the Russian political elite. That answer is, apparently, Russia is first and last *Russian*. Russian foreign policy is formed with an eye to how that policy will affect Russia's self-interest (Lo 2003; Kuchins and Zevelev 2012).

1.2.1 Russia Is Back

Commenting on the recent return of Russia as a force on the geopolitical scene, Lilia Shevtsova (2007b), senior associate at the Carnegie Moscow Center, said, "It's true—Russia is back. But it has only returned to the past." She concluded that Russia is retreating from the moves to establish closer ties with the West that characterized Russian foreign policy during the days of Gorbachev and instead is adopting a foreign policy that is clearly anti-Western. This attitude has become the national consensus:

The Russian political elite have long dreamed of finding a national idea capable of rallying the people. Former Soviet leader Mikhail Gorbachev tried to consolidate the country with his idea of socialism 'with a human face.' Former President Boris Yeltsin roused the people around anti-communism. And President Vladimir Putin came to power under the unofficial slogan: 'Let's put an end to the Yeltsin-era chaos.' Now the elite are pushing a new national idea to rally the nation. It can be stated as follows: 'We will protect the country from external enemies and establish a new global order to replace the one that so humiliated Russia in the 1990s.' To put it more simply, Putin's motto is: Russia is back!

L. Shevtsova
The Moscow Times, 2007b

1.3 Shaping Putin's Foreign Policy

Under Putin's presidency, it has become increasingly important for the current political elite to reach an agreement on a national idea that will preserve the gains that the country has achieved over the years of his administration. Casting the West once again as Russia's principal enemy has apparently turned out to be the idea that the public is most willing—and apparently most eagerly—to accept. Shevtosova also said, anti-Western sentiment has become the "new national idea and national revival has taken the form of revisionism."

What's behind Russia's brand of aggressive foreign policy and rejection of democracy? Is it a deep, driven quest for regaining the lost glory of an empire? Or is it because of hurt pride and a concomitant longing to once again be respected as one of the players with the big boys? Is it a reaction to centuries-old fear of invasion from the West? Or is it simply a feeling of low esteem, a way of compensating for a feeling that other nations look upon Russians as just modern-day Huns? Or is it just habit, a way of behaving extant for so long that Russia's leaders do not know of any other way to interact with other nations. The terms used in describing policy are included in Box 1.1.

Clearly, the answer to why Russian foreign policy manifests itself in the way it does is not an easy one to answer. In the following pages, four of these possible causative forces will be looked at: the ingrained habit of centuries of being larger, stronger and in many ways better than those who would contest its right to an empire; preempting the ingrained fear of modern-era invasion from the West; a reaction to low self-esteem generated by loss of its empire, reputation for bullying smaller neighbors, and recognition that its once globally touted political–economic system was, from the beginning, a failure; and simply an effort to regain the lost pride that comes with being considered a global superpower.

**BOX 1.1   UNDERLYING THEMES:
DÉMARCHE OVER PUTIN'S REVANCHIST POLICIES**

Among other definitions, a *démarche* may refer to a typically false assertion by a government leader or diplomat, often in protest of accusations of wrong or illegal actions expressed by another leader, nation or nations. It is the character of Putin's railings against the West and his avowed rationale for annexing Crimea, as well as the increasing numbers of other vengeful behaviors against Russia's borderland states. It characterizes nearly every statement about Ukraine made by Putin since Russia's annexation of Crimea and earlier revanchist actions against former Soviet republics.

Revanchism is the term used since the 1870s to describe the actions taken by a state to regain territorial losses it incurred, often following a war or separatist social movement. A *revanchist* is an advocate or supporter of a political policy of revanche, especially in order to seek vengeance for a previous military defeat. A revanchist foreign policy is a foreign policy aimed at revenge or the regaining of lost territories or the desire or support of such a policy. The twenty-first century foreign policies followed by Russia under President Putin clearly appear to be revanchist.

Russia had a good cause to feel ignored. With the West having *won* the Cold War, throughout the 1990s, US and EU leaders unceremoniously shunted Russia off the main track of world leadership. The Russian Bear was dead, so the victorious West could go on with the serious business of governance. For Russia, the Cold War loss was devastating: it lost an empire, its status as a global leader and nuclear power to be reckoned with and its identity as the Socialist nation's titular leader; the Cold War loss also resulted in the loss of well-being at home (Merritt 2001).

When Russia objected to such threatening moves as bombing their long-time Serbian allies in the former Yugoslavia and the expansion of NATO into Eastern and Central Europe, those objections were ignored. Russia was no longer considered a force to really be counted as having a voice in world leadership. Russia was simply ignored during the 1990s. Western leaders simply assumed that Russia's days as a great power were over, and no attention had to be paid to its interests when important foreign policy decisions were to be made (Kanet 2010b).

1.4 Rise of the Phoenix

Like the mythical bird that never dies, Putin is set on bringing about the rebirth of a strong, powerful and globally respected Russia. The West's ignominious ignoring of Russian concerns after 1991 had to be rethought when, in the 2000s, the Russian Bear arose from the dead. Yeltsin's handpicked successor Vladimir Putin began to aggressively reassert Russia's role in world affairs. The West is living with the wages of that reassertion today, as the following statement asserts:

> One major result of Moscow's redefinition of Russia's role in world affairs during the decade [of the 2000] has been Russia's emergence as a revisionist power committed to rolling back some of its geo-political losses that occurred after the collapse of the former Soviet Union and to returning Russia to the status of a major world power. This has involved Moscow's reasserting its position as the dominant actor in former Soviet space, in the areas of Russia's privileged interests, as President Medvedev noted soon after Russia's military intervention in Georgia in August 2008.
>
> **R. E. Kanet**
> *International Journal on World Peace, 2010b*

After undergoing a decade of economic disasters, rampant corruption and political dissolution during the presidency of Boris Yeltsin, Russia under President Vladimir Putin first brought its own house more or less under control. Putin and Medvedev–led Russia succeeded in building a political system and resource-based economy that enabled the Russian heartland to regain a position of perceived regional strength. This, in turn, has enabled the RF to engage in unhindered armed aggression against its smaller neighbors and one-time subject nations. Another one of these incursions occurred in Ukraine in 2014.

In the opinion of *The New Yorker* correspondent John Cassidy, Putin's March 12, 2014 speech in Moscow can be interpreted in two different ways. The optimistic interpretation is that Putin's revanchist actions and verbal attacks on the West are a traditional way of covering Russia's weakness and the pitiful state it still finds itself two decades after the collapse of the Soviet Union. The pessimistic view is that his essentially bloodless annexation of Crimea is the onset of the "chauvinistic and expansive Russian nationalism that goes back to the tsars" (Cassidy 2014). A reading of the many books and articles on Russia's behavior under Putin suggests a reading that is a composite of both interpretations. It is apparent that Putin is following a revanchist foreign policy to regain lost territories, counter NATO moves into areas over which he believes Russia has a special interest and, in the process, regain Russia's reputation as a world power with the power and strength to be a source of influence in the affairs of the world.

1.5 Regaining Status Lost

Russia in a post-Soviet world appears to once again be aggressively undergoing a campaign for what it believes is its natural place in the world: an equal geopolitical partner with the United States, China and the EU in a multipolar world. In seeking to achieve its one-time superpower status, it has engaged in calculatedly belligerent activities seen by outsiders as questionable and controversial but which many Russian citizens looked upon with favor. That policy of aggression included two overly aggressive wars against its own citizens in Chechnya and military interventions in Moldova, Tajikistan, Georgia and Ukraine (Motyl 1999; Baker and Glasser 2007). The apparent first step is to regain its superpower status, beginning with distancing itself from ties with the West.

1.6 Ending Ties with the West

Immediately after the implosion of the USSR, it appeared as if Russia under Boris Yeltsin would achieve the announced goal of establishing closer ties with the West, even going so far as to be considered for a membership in NATO. However, under Putin before and after the presidency of his self-appointed predecessor Medvedev, Russia has undergone a retrenchment in its foreign policy aims. Russia has apparently returned to its former anti-West, anti-US and anti-NATO foreign policies. This book is about that change. It addresses what appears to be Russia's calculated use of aggression as a tool of diplomacy in achieving the aims of its long-functioning foreign policy. The alternative policy of rapprochement with the West that emerged under Gorbachev and Yeltsin began to fade in Yeltsin's controversy-laden later years. Under Putin, that shift accelerated.

1.7 A Renewal of the Cold War?

If, indeed, as some foreign policy analysts suggest, Russia's exercise of aggressive expansionism signals a renewal of the Cold War, a good starting point for an analysis of Russian foreign policy might be George Kennan's 1946 "Long Telegram," published in *Foreign Affairs* in 1947 as "The Sources of Soviet Conduct." Although the collapse of the Soviet Union brought an end to much of the ideological bases upon which early communist foreign policy was based, a number of ideological points remained valid. Kennan summarized the key points of communist ideology: (1) the manufacture and exchange of material goods determined the character of society; (2) the capitalist system invariably results in exploitation of the working class and failure of the system to equitably distribute manufactured goods; (3) the capitalist system will inevitably fail due to its own shortcomings, with power going to the working class; and (4) imperialism, the peak phase of capitalism, results in war and revolution; hence, aiding global revolution to halt imperialism was morally necessary.

Lenin asserted that self-determination was the right of all people. However, the Marxist–Leninist state of Russia must expand to abet and guide the revolution and protect the ensuing socialist society. Ensuring long-term conformity to the socialist system demanded the control of society by a strong central state. These core tenets changed slowly in the years following World War II (WWII) to eventually be rejected during the openness policies by Gorbachev. The brief rapprochement with the West during the Yeltsin years ended with the failure of Yeltsin's economic policies to bring about improvement in the economic well-being of most Russians. After being appointed president during the last days of Yeltsin's second term, Vladimir Putin would bring Russia's experiment in democratic governance to a close. The hallmarks of Putin's first two terms of office would be a return to a strong, central government with political and economic control of all important functions of the state. In his third term as a president, these were combined with a new assertive push to regain global power status. Putin showed the world that he would no longer meekly accept Western dictates or policies he considered to be aimed at encircling Russia. The actions taken in the smaller states on Russia's borders would be the target of that new foreign policy.

1.8 Resurrecting Relations with *Special-Interest* Neighbors

A quarter century after the disintegration of the USSR, the independent nations of the former soviet Union fall into three distinct peripheral categories. The first is a group of mostly southwestern Eurasian nations; it include Georgia, Armenia, Ukraine and Moldova. The second is a group of northeastern European countries; it include Estonia, Latvia, Lithuania and Belarus. The third is a large group of former Soviet republics in central and southern Asia; it include Azerbaijan, Kazakhstan, Kyrgyzstan, Tajikistan, Turkmenistan and Uzbekistan. These are all regions for which Russia holds a special interest.

The special interest element of Russian foreign policy was made public in an August 31, 2008 television interview of President Dmitry Medvedev in which he stated the last of the five principles of Russian foreign policy.

> As is the case of other countries, there are regions in which Russia has privileged interests. These regions are home to countries with which we share special historical relations and are bound together as friends and good neighbors. We will pay particular attention to our work in these regions and build friendly ties with these countries, our close neighbors.

> **D. Medvedev**
> *Interview given to Television Channel One, 2008*

At the core of these three groups is the Russian heartland—the Great Russia of the Muscovite era. The heartland is administered by 85 quasi-decentralized districts

Map 1.2 Independent states of the former USSR. (1) Armenia; (2) Azerbaijan; (3) Belarus; (4) Estonia; (5) Georgia; (6) Kazakhstan; (7) Kyrgyzstan; (8) Latvia; (9) Lithuania; (10) Moldova; (11) Russia; (12) Tajikistan; (13) Turkmenistan; (14) Ukraine; (15) Uzbekistan.

that make up the RF. Included in the 85 districts are 22 republics. Upon election to the presidency, one of Putin's first acts was to do away with the practice of local elections for district governors; they are now all appointed by Putin.

The sovereign states that were once Soviet republics are what Russia considers its space of *special* or *privileged interest* (Map 1.2). These states are ones for which any erosion of that special interest by the West is perceived by Russia as an act of aggression against Russia itself. The most recent example of this policy action was Russia's 2014 annexation of the Crimea in retaliation for Ukraine's desire for closer economic, political and security ties with the EU and NATO. This was clearly a demonstration that Russia is willing to use military action to protect and maintain its sphere of special interest and that this principle is one that underlies much of Russia's twenty-first century foreign policy. The series of aggressive acts designed to stabilize Russia's special position in its borderlands are also designed to influence outsiders of Russians, progress on the return to geopolitical status.

1.8.1 Regaining Respect

States such as Armenia, Georgia, Ukraine and Moldova are characterized by high levels of antipathy toward Russia. They are also where Russia has exercised armed aggression through support of independent enclaves, ostensibly to protect Russian minority subjects remaining in the regions. Such northern and eastern European former USSR republics are hobbled by legacies of their communist past and large ethnic Russian minorities. They seek to implement social democratic systems similar to those of the Nordic countries of Finland, Denmark, Norway and Sweden but lack the economic resources to do so.

Many of the Central Asian states enjoy considerable energy resources, but some remain under control of political despotic leaders. Having joined with Russia in forming a customs union patterned after the EU, Belarus and Kazakhstan are the two former Soviet republics with the closest remaining ties to Russia. Russia maintains control of a small Bering Sea coastal district of some 431,000 citizens between Poland and Lithuania known as the Kaliningrad Oblast. Kaliningrad has no land connection with Russia.

Russia's borderland states—what Russia used to refer to as its *near abroad*—tend to include large public sectors, high levels of female participation in government and the economy and fluctuating, uneven economic growth and inflation. Many fall into what the Russian public perceives as Russia's greatest enemies. Three small Baltic states fall into this category and suffer the same problems as the other states in this category: low levels of public trust in government and low investments in social welfare programs and social capital. A US State Department survey in Russia in 2000 said they believed relations with Estonia to be Russia's most difficult (Merritt 2001; Fenger 2007).

The governments of these strategically important nations found themselves struggling with enormous difficulties as they sought to develop and build and maintain adequate governance institutions and public services in the face of economic and geopolitical problems exacerbated by the steep recession of 2008–2010 and the aggressive expansionist actions of their former overlords (Fenger 2007).

Finally, the postcommunist Soviet Bloc or Warsaw Pact European countries such as Bulgaria, Croatia, the Czech Republic and Slovakia (formerly part of the central European state of Czechoslovakia), Hungary, Poland and Rumania are characterized by economic, political and social systems that reflect conservative elements of EU countries such as Austria, France, Germany and Greece. Regaining direct Russian control of this group of Soviet Bloc states is more difficult than that of its former republics. However, Russia has at its disposal an exceptionally powerful soft power tool: these and other European states still depend upon Russia for much of their oil and gas. As a result, they are slow to offend Russia by criticizing its aggressive diplomacy actions. That reluctance to reach was shaken somewhat in reaction to the 2014 annexation of Crimea and continuing support of aggression by ethnic Russians within Ukraine. As a result, Russian President Putin's *empire project* has taken on a new direction, placing greater emphasis on the exercise of hard power tactics. NATO expansion eastward, economic sanctions coupled with steep drops in oil and gas prices, renewed gun battles with insurgents in Chechnya and other pressures have contributed to a rebirth of Russia's feelings of being beset by enemies at home and abroad. This was reveled in the tone of Putin's December 2014 speech to the Federal Assembly. Rather than the upbeat tone common in earlier addresses, in this speech, Putin stressed a need to defend against these and other Western-instigated aggressive actions. Exemplifying this shift was noted in a quote from his address that was included in a December 4 (2014a) issue of *Stratfor*: "This year Russia faced trials that only a mature and united nation and a truly sovereign and strong state can withstand. Russia has proved that it can protect its compatriots and defend truth and fairness."

Annexing Crimea can be seen as proof that Putin is in the early stages of rebuilding the Russian Empire.

1.9 Conclusion

Beginning in the 1980s, the Eurasian expanse of the world underwent a remarkable change. By the second decade of the twenty-first century, the Soviet multiethnic system changed from its position as a nuclear-armed superpower competitor to what has become a truncated but still hostile center of instability and belligerence. Following the collapse of the Soviet Union, many of the former Soviet satellites have transformed themselves into independent nation-states of genuine but fragile stability, Euro-Atlantic integration and economic dynamism. According to the Atlantic Council, this transformation was by no means predestined; rather, it was the result of what the council described as "skillful execution of policy in Washington, the Nordic-Baltic countries, and beyond" (Nurick and Nordenman 2011, pp. 67–71). Yet, not much has changed as it may seem.

The series of aggression actions by Russian forces and Russian-backed ethnic Russian civilians in former Soviet territories have signaled a renewal of Cold War competition. Russia's policy of rapprochement apparent after the collapse of the Soviet Union has morphed into a policy of aggressive, armed diplomacy designed to reestablish Russia as a military and political force to be reckoned with. It was common practice during the Communist era for the Soviets to expand their territory by what Professor Mosely described in 1948 (p. 209) as "by coming with superior force to the defense of 'oppressed' groups within neighboring states."

The Atlantic Council's objective of a "Europe whole, free, and at peace" emerged after the collapse of the Soviet Union and two world wars that were unprecedentedly destructive of human life and property in the first half of the last century and the ever-present threat of a nuclear war from 1950 to the last decade of the century. In the second decade of the twenty-first century, new threats have emerged to threaten world peace and the Euro-Atlantic partnership.

Donaldson and Nocee (2005) described Russia's Soviet and Putin-era foreign policy as a continuation of the balance of power policies common among European nations in the nineteenth century. However, the balance of power argument was only part of the foreign policy scene over the past 200 years. Russia's aggressive and expansionist foreign policy direction went further back than this. The salient feature of Russian foreign policy since the twelfth century has been protection of the heartland by conquering and controlling smaller states on its borders. The product of expansion over the past 600 years has been the establishment of four Russian empires. The story of those four empires is presented in Chapter 2.

Chapter 2

Stages in the Building of a Russian Empire

2.1 Introduction

Since the founding of the Romanov dynasty in 1631, Russia has employed a mix of external and internal foreign policy strategies while amassing and defending the security of the Russian Empire. From the Muscovite era on, a key force shaping the external foreign policy and tactical approaches of Russian tsars was the constant amassing and maintaining of a secure, albeit difficult to administer, empire. To gain the security it needed, it was evident that its objectives included forming a defensive barrier with the neighboring territories that it was able to collect. Expansion could thus function as a barrier to invasion from the west, contribute to the economic well-being of the state in the center and provide living space and farmlands for its growing population in the newly acquired rich-soil steppes to the south and east.

Russia's strategy of internal defense included such weapons as colonization, deportation and Russification to absorb and develop the territories conquered into a unified and integrated state. Once a territory was acquired, populating it with people that could be trusted and spoke the common language became important. This chapter looks at Russia's use of both the foreign policy aimed at acquisition of an empire and the subsequent internal growth and pacification policies in territories for maintaining an aggressive defense.

Transition from one political framework to another while building an empire is not a new phenomenon for Russia. This chapter traces Russia's rise and fall through four different imperial iterations, concluding with its present policy of creeping reimperialization. A suggested definition of imperialism once applied to the fifteenth-century Russia's foreign policies applies equally to the policies followed since the beginning of the twenty-first century: imperialism is the policy and actions followed by one nation to acquire more territory, impose its culture and language on a neighboring state or otherwise gain control over the people of another state, or for the purpose of achieving its own end, be it military, political or economic (Backus III 1954).

Beginning in the tenth century, the western reaches of the Asian continent were collected by Russia's first great empire, Kievan Rus. In the second expansionist period, the Muscovite Empire solidified its imperial standing by territorial accretion from the twelfth to the seventeenth centuries. Midway through the period, Ivan IV (Ivan the Terrible) became one of the first Russian rulers to call himself *Czar of all Russia and Autocrat* (supreme ruler); the elements of his coronation ceremony making this point are included in Box 2.1. The title *czar* (or *tsar*) was a Russianized allusion to Caesar, a reflection of Muscovite Russia's obsession with the Byzantine Empire.

The third empire-building period began in 1721 when Peter I (the Great) became the first Russian ruler to make specific reference to Russia as an empire. This period continued until it was brutally ended with the murder of the last of the Romanovs in the early twentieth century. It was during the Romanov period that the Russian Empire's expansion into the East accelerated, and its tentative experiment on the North American continent ended with abandonment of small outposts in California and the sale of Alaska to the United States.

BOX 2.1 THE CORONATION OF IVAN IV OF MOSCOW

On January 16, 1547, Ivan IV became the first tsar and autocrat of all Russia. In a ceremony in the Kremlin Church of the Dormition, before an assemblage of the imperial family, princes and boyars and the clergy, Metropolitan Makarij anointed the 17-year-old Ivan and invested him with the regalia of office.

The ceremony of 1547 had much in common with earlier Muscovite princely coronations. Following Orthodox theocratic tradition, it also echoed Byzantine imperial ideas and rites … After prayers for the ruler by the metropolitan and the whole assemblage, Ivan and Makarij mounted the dais to their thrones. The metropolitan sat down, while the young tsar-to-be stood before him and announced that all his ancestors were grand princes of Vladimir, Novgorod, Moscow and all of Russia and that he too wished to be recognized as such. Makarij recognized his claim, crowned him "with our ancient titles," blessed him with the cross and seated him. Then, Ivan again addressed Makarij, claiming that in addition, he wished to be "anointed and crowned Tsar according to our ancient custom." Makarij assented, saying "now thou art crowned and anointed and title Grand Prince Ivan Vasil'evič. God crowned Tsar and Autocrat of all great Russia" (Miller 1967).

The fourth period began with the 1917 Russian Revolution and the ascendancy of Communist Party domination. In this period, the Soviet Union reached its peak of imperial expansion by absorbing the former Russian states that had achieved independence in the 1920s, parts of Germany and Poland, and by setting up a chain of puppet buffer states in Eastern Europe. The Soviet Union continued in power until 1989 when it imploded. A wave of democratic leaders in the republics opted out of the USSR, many of them moving closer to the West.

The disestablishment of the Soviet Union in 1989 does not mean that the Russian people have seen the last of the country's imperial ambitions. This section briefly describe the empire expansionist policies followed in each of these periods to set the stage for a more detailed examination of Russia's current foreign policy. A number of policy analysts are already alluding to Russia under Putin as being in the early stages of a new Russian empire. Alexander Etkind, for one, held no punches as he described the events in Soviet Russia following World War II (WWII):

> After World War II, the growth of the Muscovite state continued when other western empires disintegrated. Even when the USSR collapsed, the loss of territory was smaller than what the western empires experience with their decolonization. With surprise, the twenty-first century is watching the imperial resurgence of post-Soviet Russia.

> **A. Etkind**
> *Internal Colonization: Russia's Imperial Experience, 2011*

The underlying aim of Putin's revanchist foreign strategy for Russia is to be able to, as far as he can and in any way possible, rebuild the empire. Aggressive acts of Russia reveal that an accepted way to achieve this goal is by reannexing elements of sovereign states that were once integral parts of the Soviet Union or to gain control of those states without their actual annexation. In the process, Russia is on the path toward regaining its position as one of the world's most influential and powerful states. The official Russian Federation biography of President Putin explains that achieving world leadership status has already been accomplished, whereas the Biography Channel identifies Putin's occupational status as *World Leader* (Biography.com 2014). Sections 2.2 through 2.5 follow the pathways taken by Russia in establishing its past empires.

2.2 The Kievan Rus Empire

Russia's first great empire was the Kievan Rus, who ruled from their capital in Ukraine from about 880 and lasted to the middle of the thirteenth century and became servants of the Mongol invaders until the fifteenth century (Curtis 1996; Freeze 2009; Kaplan 2013). An approximation of the extent of Kievan Rus is shown in Map 2.1. The central city of Kiev was one of a series of towns that controlled trade along the Dnieper River between Scandinavia and the Byzantine Empire. That connection would be important in the conversion of Russian Slavs to Orthodox Christianity in the tenth century (Spinka 1926).

The first leaders of the ruling family that became the Kievan Rus were probably Viking (Varangian) chieftains who travel on the Folkhov River and Lovat River north–south trade route from the Gulf of Finland (Map 2.2). Early invasions had concentrated on raids for the sole purpose of plundering Slav villages and eventually as far south as Constantinople. However, by the 800s, the more powerful leaders had become princes over groups of Slav villages. They took up permanent residence and peacefully collected tribute from the same villages they once plundered. The Scandinavian Rurik was the most successful of these

Map 2.1   Kievan Rus: the first great Russian empire.

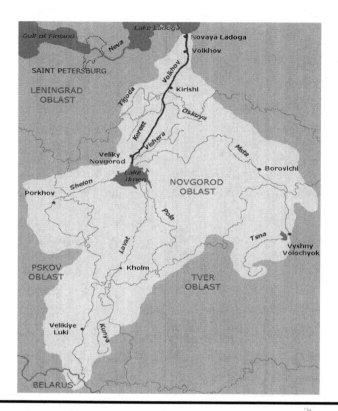

Map 2.2 Viking river trade routes and first land of the Kievan Rus in the ninth century.

princes. He was able to stop the internecine warfare between warring princes, including his two brothers, and became sole ruler of the region, with Kiev his capital. After his death in 879, a regent, Oleg, ruled for Rurik's infant son Igor. Rurik, Oleg and Igor continued to expand their territory to the south and Caspian Sea. From Kiev, Rurik's descendants ruled the growing empire until the Mongol invasion in 1237–1240. For the next century, Kievan rulers were subject to Mongol (Tatar) rule. By the mid-fifteenth century, the practice of *partible inheritance* (dividing ownership or rule of lands among all sons) had cut the former Kievan Empire into a number of smaller fiefdoms whose princes were constantly jostling among themselves for dominance. Also by the mid-fifteenth century, the capital had been moved first to Novgorod and then to Moscow, where the beginning of the next empire, the Muscovites, would take place.

During the ninth and tenth centuries, there were two non-Russian societies functioning in Kievan Russia. Both focused on trade rather than agriculture. One, Khazars, who resided west of the Caspian Sea and used the rivers flowing into that sea as their major trade routes (Kaplan 1954; Longworth 2005). The other was the

Scandinavian Vikings who used river routes from the Baltic to the Black Sea and Constantinople. In this way, the Khazars developed commercial traditions in the south, whereas the Varangians did so in the north.

The Khazars taxed and protected trade on the Don and Volga rivers from their capital city near what became Stalingrad. They mostly traded in products produced by Slavic people to the north, concentrating on animal skins and furs, honey and beeswax. They traded these with the Byzantines, Arabs, Persians and Central Asian Mongols. Their lands at one time had extended as far west as Kiev but by the tenth century had retreated to their traditional lands east of the River Don.

As the Varangians extended their trade southward from their chief center of Novgorod, they met and eventually intermarried with Eastern Slav tribal farming groups expanding north and west into what became Ukraine. In addition to the products traded by the Khazars, the Varangians traded weapons and Slavic slaves in Constantinople for precious metals and spices.

These trading societies contributed to the growth in the tenth century of a Slavic people, the Kievan Rus, to establish the beginnings of a Russian with its capital at Kiev. The Rus extended their control of the river routes into the adjoining hinterlands in search of more fertile farmlands. The majority of that expansion was westward as the eastern regions were controlled by steppe nomads. In this way, a tradition of territorial expansion was nurtured. That tradition has been a hallmark of all subsequent Russian empires.

The Swedish Varangians had established their first capital at Novgorod, near present-day St. Petersburg. Oleg, Rurik's grandson, became a key early figure in the history of Kievan Rus expansion. As he conquered more lands to the south, Oleg expanded control over East Slavic tribes and eventually besieged Constantinople itself. He negotiated a trade treaty there that gave power and impetus to the growth and wealth of Kievan rulers who followed. Two other important Rus leaders were Vladimir the Great (980–1015) and his son, Yaroslav the Wise (1019–1054). During this golden age, two imperial developments stood out: Christianity became the established religion, and the first East Slavic legal code was written. After these great leaders, however, internecine warfare and disruption caused by Mongol rule drove apart the loosely established empire. Trade with the Byzantine Empire began to dry up as Constantinople lost its importance. In place of that fading trade, Rus commercial connections with Europe increased.

As migration to the west and north increased, Moscow, Smolensk, Novgorod and other more central and northern cities became commercially important and more powerful than Kiev. The final blow to the Kievan Rus Empire came with Mongol invasions in the thirteenth century (Van der Oye 2010). The Mongols sacked Kiev in 1240 before moving west into Poland and Hungary. One branch of the Mongol Horde established itself on the lower Volga River, where they ruled the Kievan Rus and then the Muscovite Rus principalities through appointed princes and tax collectors until the middle of the fifteenth century.

2.3 The Muscovite Empire

When the Mongol invasion began in 1237, Moscow was a small trading post settlement, too small to be worthy of Mongol plundering. Daniel Aleksandrovich, a descendent of Rurik, inherited the principality, which was then under control of Mongol overlords. His son, Ivan I, was eventually granted the title of Grand Prince of the region by the Mongols. Ivan collected tribute in the region and from other principalities for the Mongols and maintained peace throughout the region. In the process, he was able to establish control over a growing territory (Map 2.3). His position in history was secured when in 1327, the metropolitan of the Orthodox Church (i.e., the bishop of a region's most important town) transferred his post from the city of Vladimir to Moscow. By the thirteenth century, the Muscovite princes began the process of gathering nearby lands that would enable them to officially establish a Russian Empire. This was not achieved until the sixteenth century, when Muscovite claims to the mantle of *Byzantine–Kievan Imperial Inheritance* would be officially recognized (Pelenski 1983)—Byzantine because of the movement of the Orthodox Church to Kiev from Constantinople after the city's fall in 1453.

The principality of Moscow was transformed over the fifteenth and sixteenth centuries to the Russian Empire (Martin 1983). Acquisition of lands in the forming

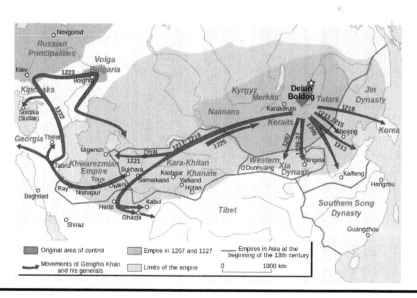

Map 2.3   Mongol invasions of Central Asia and Kievan Rus in the thirteenth century.

of the empire was given a major boost under the leadership of Ivan III (Ivan the Great), who ruled from 1462 to 1505. Muscovy was relieved of its Mongol yoke in 1480, after which time the ethnic Russian lands were united under the control of Moscow. Ivan had captured the old Varangian capital of Novgorod in 1478 and went on to capture the next important principality north of Moscow, Tver, in 1485. He inherited lands to the south and east and competed with Lithuania for some of the lands to the west that had been independent during the Kievan period. Overall, during Ivan the Great's rule, Muscovy tripled in size (Curtis 1996).

2.3.1 Territorial Expansion

Growth by expansion and annexation of neighboring lands became the theme of Russian foreign policy after Ivan IV, who was reborn under Peter the Great, and reached its acme during the reign of Catherine the Great. Although territorial expansion was an element of Muscovite foreign policy in the fourteenth century, expansion was generally limited to only the smaller estates of boyars near the central core of the empire. Annexation on a vastly larger scale only occurred with Ivan's victories over Tatar overlords in the mid- and late sixteenth century.

2.3.1.1 Expansion under Ivan IV

The expansionist policies that kicked off the empire-building process began after Ivan IV was crowned as tsar of Muscovy in 1547. From then to his death in 1584, his foreign policy focused on eliminating Mongol incursions of and tribute payments to the Tatar Khans to the east and south of Moscow and on acquiring an outlet to the Baltic Sea. Both Ivan and Peter would follow the policies of conquest and annexation, although Ivan's mental aberrations later in his reign made it impossible for him to achieve much success in unifying the conquered territories. That would have to wait for the ascendency of Peter for an effective and efficient centralized system for administering the acquired territories with their ethnically diverse populations (Bushkovitch 2009).

Ivan IV's first big success was conquering the Volga Tatars of the Khanate of Kazan in 1552. The Muscovites had been at war with Kazan since at least the 1430s. The Khanate city of Astrakhan controlled the mouth of the Volga, restricting trade and exacting tolls and tribute. The loosely organized Khanate of Sibir (Siberia) was conquered in 1558 by a small Cossack army employed by Ivan. These victories resulted in the acquiring of the vast tracts of Central Asia land and eliminated the need for collecting and paying tribute to the descendants of the Golden Horde.

The vacuum of leadership caused by regional princely competition for power helped make the loss of Kiev to Mongol invaders in the thirteenth century. With Kievan Rus without leadership, control of the empire moved to the northeast where a small city had been established in 1147. This was the beginning of the Muscovite Empire. From that time until what is known as the *Time of Troubles* from 1604 to 1613, the new Russian Empire continuously expanded from its new center, Moscow. The first substantial control of the Muscovite empire fell to Ivan I.

Growth by expansion of neighboring lands and improving relations with European powers became the prominent aims of Russian foreign policy beginning with Peter the Great and reached a high point during the reign of Catherine the Great. Although territorial expansion had been underway as a distinct element of foreign policy since at least the late fifteenth century, it only became the central focus of most Muscovite tsars with the ascendancy of Peter the Great in the late seventeenth century. Peter, officially Peter I, ruled from 1689 to 1725. During that long reign, Peter brought Russia under the influence of European thought, science and engineering. He formed a strong navy, maintained one of the largest-standing armies of the era, built the new capital of St. Petersburg, defeated the Swedish army of Charles XII, in the Great Northern War, and absorbed into his realm what eventually became Estonia and Lithuania. He changed the name of the country to the Russian Empire and was the first to call himself emperor of Russia (Donaldson and Nogee 2005).

2.4 The Romanov Empire

The Romanov dynasty ruled Russia from the end of the decade of the Troubles in 1613 until deposed in 1917. The dynasty can be divided into three distinct periods: (1) from 1613 to 1681, the age of Peter the Great, when the focus was on southward expansion; (2) from 1682 to 1796, the empire expanded to the west and north, eventually acquiring the eastern lands of the Polish–Lithuanian Commonwealth; and (3) from 1796 to 1917, expansion shifted to the East; this period stopped only with the outbreak of the First World War and the Russian Revolution.

Under the Romanovs, that empire would last three centuries, only ending in revolution in 1917. At the time of Peter's accession to the Russian throne, Russian territory consisted of a total of 265,126 square miles, divided into 79,345 square miles in Europe and 185,781 square miles in Asia. By 1870, the empire has acquired an additional 124,185 square miles of territory, including Poland and Finland. Comprising something like one-ninth of all the dry surface of the globe, the empire was geographically the largest ever assembled (Michell 1872).

During the first period, the old Muscovite territories continue to expand out from the core around Moscow, eventually adding vast regions of the central plains to its control. On its western boundary, it met resistance from the joint Polish and Lithuanian Empire. On the south, it expanded to various Cossack lands, including those in Ukraine, Crimea and in the old Tartar lands on the Volga River. Eventually, expansion to the vast open steppes on the east would take the empire into the land of the Siberian Khan.

Two major geopolitical events in Russian and Ukrainian history occurred during the era of the Muscovy Empire. The first was the invasions of the Mongols from Central Asia and the formation of their empire. The second was the expansion of the empire that continued until the end of the sixteenth century. During this period, grand princes of Muscovy led by Ivan III acquired neighboring lands of ethnic Russians after the Mongols were finally defeated in 1480. By 1500, all of what was considered to be *Great Russia* was united under the Muscovite tsars. The formal proclamation of the Russian Empire then followed in 1721.

The first period of expansion during the Romanov dynasty began with Peter the Great (1682–1725) and ended with the death of Catherine the Great in 1796. Peter is considered to have been the most effective of the dynasty's rulers, beginning the long history of successful territorial expansion and westernization for which the Romanovs would be recognized (Hughes 1998). A significant achievement in the establishment of the first official Russian empire was the military victory of Peter I's eighteenth-century victory over the armies of Swedish King Charles XII and his Ukrainian allies. Peter's expansion of the Russian Empire by conquest would later earn him the sobriquet of Peter the Great. Russia's first official annexation of Ukraine was thus a consequence of war—the taking of the spoils of war by right of conquest. The more modern taking of Crimea occurred as a coup by ethnic Russian civilians and armed forces guided, armed and supported by Russian forces and local secessionists.

The changes contemplated by Peter of Muscovy were more complex, expansive and very expensive in terms of men and money. In Central Europe, Sweden was forced to operate over long supply lines in an unfamiliar environment and with unreliable allies. These investments and two decades of royal struggle gave Russia a new position in the European balance of power. Several aspects of this new empire are parts of our discussion of Peter's empire and innovations in the following.

Peter gained long-coveted western borderlands, whereas Charles XII of Sweden lost what was *de facto* an undeclared Nordic empire that at its peak stretched from Ingermanland on the Neva River to Stralsund in Germany. Peter lost major battles at Narva and Riga and minor, the almost separate conflicts during the Great Northern War, possibly because he did not consider the abilities or intentions of his adversaries, losses that may have been averted by better intelligence.

Having survived touchy political moments in his early life, Peter was also a cruel risk taker who knew his own and his enemy's strengths and weaknesses. He committed his last resources (even mortgaging his wife's jewels) to build, train and test his armies. Consisting mostly of uneducated serfs, the soldiers under Peter needed to be trained and retrained at an enormous cost to fight under the new battlefield conditions then taking place. He knew his allies, the Ukrainian nationalist and Jesuit-educated Cossack Hetman (military and later political chief) Ivan Mazepa, and well enough to use his and Crimean Tatars' help to conquer Livonia and the Sankt Petersburg area. In achieving, Peter gained control of Estonia, Livonia (part of today's Latvia) and the strategically important lands between the Gulf of Finland and Lake Ladoga.

Temperamental and brutal, Peter also ordered Mazepa's headquarters, supply base and town destroyed to prevent Mazepa from switching his resources to help Charles. Such an alliance would have allowed Charles to dominate much of Central

Europe. Physically and intellectually more powerful than his opponent, Peter was also an *innovator's innovator*. Peter eventually won his wars and his borderlands, thus ensuring the long-term existence of a new Europe. Peter negotiated for weak coalitions and short-term agreements and used many Baltic German nobles in his armed forces and in state administration.

Absolutely bent on building the empire he declared in 1721, Peter picked the smaller, least-defended lands first. He let Charles chase the Polish king and Saxony's ruler Augustus all over Lithuania and Poland, while he trained his Russians. He had lost and won battles and in the process learned how and when to trust and distrust strangers, including the companion of Charles and later Peter's lieutenant, General Balthasar von Campenhausen. To calm his rages, Peter trusted only one person: his second wife, the Empress Catherine, the former Lithuanian Martha Skowronska, a Livonian war captive from Pastor J. Ernst Glueck's household.

Peter learned to trust only a few selected Russians in high positions; many were officers from abroad or from the borderlands. His tactics were simple but expensive in terms of men and materials. Peter picked his conquests, avoiding controversial campaigns and questionable military engagements. His troops devastated Livonia and the smaller Ingermanland before taking them over for his future empire.

Peter's empire was not a democracy. Like all tsars, he had his select aristocracy, his adventurers for empire building and a virtually unlimited mass of peasants for his armies; all were subject to the autocrat's call and orders. Well aware of a need to combine his and his allies' strengths, he incessantly organized coalitions against Charles. Eventually, his organizational skills resulted in a victory at Poltava on July 8, 1709 in what is now in eastern Ukraine.

Having suffered through an especially harsh Russian winter of 1708–1709 and starved as a result of Peter's scorched earth policy, at Poltava, the hungry and decimated 20,000 veterans of Charles almost won over twice the number of Peter's victorious army. Charles fled the battle with just some 500 followers, whereas 19,000 of his soldiers surrendered to the Russian forces. Charles was granted sanctuary in Constantinople for four years. He never again added any land to his Swedish empire. Praised later by Voltaire in Paris, the warrior king fought for another decade after Poltava. In 1718, Charles was killed by a bullet fired by either a friend or foe of Sweden at the Fredrikshald fortress in Norway.

After his victory at Poltava, Peter used his partnerships and alliances to expand his influence and territories in Europe and Asia. Following the example of the early Byzantine Empire, Peter gained a good understanding of what it took to become an imperial ruler. Moreover, he was well aware of functioning European empires of the British, Danish, Dutch and French expansion through trade, war or both. He brought new Western schools and science to Russia. He built two navies, one for service in the Black sea and another for the Baltic. Russia's sphere of interest again extended from the Baltic Sea to the Black Sea (Foucher 1999).

More than simply acquiring more territory, historians have concluded that Peter's long-range goal for Russia was to "create a modern, absolutist, bureaucratic state with the ultimate purpose of advancing the cultural and economic level of the Russian populace and placing Russia in the ranks of the leading European powers" (Donnelly 1975, p. 202).

Peter's goal of acquiring a permanent position on the Baltic Sea was the cause for his long wars with Sweden. However, he was also interested in gaining control of two other seas, the Black and the Caspian. Control of the Black Sea and victory over the Ottoman Empire would give him unrestricted naval access to the Mediterranean and beyond. Control of the Caspian and the lands that border on the sea was key to become the dominant power in the Caucuses, Persia, Central Asia and even India (Donnelly 1975).

In addition to the important territorial acquisitions, the reign of Peter the Great (the Petrine Age) saw the beginning of the forging of a unified nation out of the multiethnic imperial territories that had been acquired since the days of Ivan IV. Adoption of Western administrative and reforming diplomatic processes and procedures was as important in Peter's nation building as was his importing European military technological advances (Bohlen 1966).

2.4.1 The Age of Catherine the Great

Catherine the Great was one of several women who ruled Russia after Peter's death. Peter's widow, Catherine I, his half-niece Anna and his daughter Elizabeth together ruled Moscow for more than 32 years (Longworth 2005). Catherine II, a German princess, married Elizabeth's son Peter in 1745. The marriage was not a success. After Elizabeth's death in 1761, her son Peter became tsar. His relations with his wife Catherine were never easy. He planned to have her killed so he could have his mistress help him in governing Russia. However, Peter was overthrown and murdered six days later, many believe in a coup orchestrated by Catherine II, who was then to rule Russia for the next thirty years. A large portion of the territorial expansion to the west occurred during Catherine's time. Most of that expansion occurred at the expense of Poland and Lithuania. The disintegration of Poland occurred in three steps during the reign of Catherine.

The first of the three partitions of Poland occurred in 1772, the second in 1793 and the third in 1795 (LeDonne 2009b). Catherine took for Russia what had been the farthest northeast reaches of the Polish eastern expansion. This meant adding Polish Livonia, including the major town of Dinaburg (the Latvian Daugavpils), as well as most of Belarus. A victor in the war with Poland— ostensibly over Poland's mistreatment of Orthodox Russians living in the eastern part of the country—Catherine gave large portions of western Poland to her allies Prussia and Austria. Russia's share included the cities of Polatsk, Vitebsk, Orsha, Mogilev and Mstislavl—adding approximately 1.6 million people to her empire. Prussia's share added 900,000 people, whereas Austria's acquisition of the province of Galicia meant an increase of 2.5 million citizens (Troyat 1980; Madariaga 1990).

Catherine's armies were also victorious in two wars against the Ottoman Empire in 1769 and 1790. As a result, Russia gained lands on the western shore of the Black Sea, the strait between Crimea and the northeast shore of the Black Sea and freedom to become a naval power in the Black Sea. The peace treaty also required removal of Ottoman troops from Crimea, thus making it possible for Catherine to annex Crimea in 1783 under the pretext of protecting Orthodox Christian residents.

The second partition of Poland consisted of much more territory than the first partition, also extending Russia's western boundary farther to the West. The second partition resulted in annexation of the portion of Ukraine on the right bank of the Dniester River, including Kiev. This added another 3 million people to Russia.

The third and last partition of Poland under Catherine saw the western boundary of Russia extended as far as the Baltic, including Lithuania, much of what became Latvia and the rest of Ukraine, including Poltava, the site of Peter I's historic victory over Swedish troops. While Catherine was annexing this last part of Poland, Prussia and Austria were once again dividing the rest of the once-large Polish Empire between them. By 1796, Poland no longer existed as a state. However, acquisition of Lithuania, Latvia and Ukraine brought Russia closer to Europe (Lewitter 1958).

2.4.1.1 Growth after Catherine

By the end of Catherine's reign in November 1976, Imperial Russia had become a major European power. The empire's borders extended as far west as the Habsburg Empire of Austria, whereas the empire's possessions included all lands that bordered on the eastern shore of the Baltic Sea and ran as far to the north of the Barents Sea and the Arctic Ocean. It shared its southern borders with Manchuria, Mongolia, China, Afghanistan and Iran (in the third period that began with the short reign of Catherine's son Paul [1796–1801]). Russian fur traders crossed the Bering Strait to set up permanent posts in Alaska and from 1812 to 1842 at Fort Ross in Northern California. Paul also ended Russia's war with Persia and withdrew troops from the plan to conquer Georgia, Armenia and other Caspian Sea lands.

Armenia and Georgia were distinct in their religious differences with much of the southern lands added to the empire. Armenians and Georgians had adopted Christianity in the fourth century, whereas most people of other southern lands had adopted Islam. Islands in the Islamic world, Christian Armenians and Georgians were drawn voluntarily into the Orthodox Russian Empire. Portions of Armenia were taken by Russia in a war with Persia in the early nineteenth century, with the rest absorbed into the Ottoman Empire. In order to escape being taken over by Persia, Eastern Georgia became a vassal of Russia in last years of the eighteenth century and in 1801 was officially incorporated into Russia (Pipes 1964).

The Romanovs maintained a large powerful army and were in the early stages of becoming an international naval power. The empire maintained naval bases from the Baltic Sea to the Pacific Ocean and included bases on the Black and

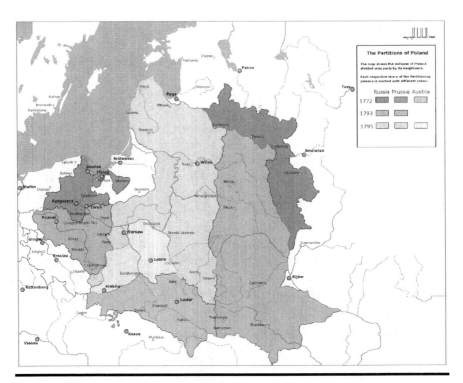

Map 2.4   The three partitions of Poland: 1772, 1793, 1795.

Caspian Seas. Expansion south occurred at the expense mostly of Persia and the Ottoman Empire; expansion west targeted Swedish and Polish lands; and expansion East and Central Asia occurred against former nomadic tribes of the Siberian steppes and the Chinese. Treaties with China in 1858 and 1860 extended the Russian boundary to the Amur River. The regions and periods of accession are seen in Map 2.4.

2.4.1.2 Setback in the Crimean War

The Empire's peasant armies suffered their first setback in over 100 years when they were defeated in the Crimean War (1853–1856). Fewer large territorial expansions occurred after that defeat. The war began after Turkey, with French support, rejected Russian demands that the Russian Orthodox rather than the Catholic Church be granted the right to protect Christian sites and Christian people in the Holy Land. Russian troops were victorious initially, successfully invading Ottoman Romanian territories and defeating the Ottoman fleet. When European armies joined the fight, they eventually captured the Russian naval base at Sevastopol resulting in Russia's capitulation and ending the war. Philip Longworth described the aftermath of the loss in his 2005 book:

For the first time in a century Russia had failed at arms, and it paid the price in the ensuing settlement. Its frontier was moved away from the Danube, and it was barred from the Black Sea, as were Turkish warships. Russia's advance in the west had been halted, its primacy as a European land power ended, and it sustained a grievous blow to its prestige. It paused to take stock ... it was recognized in St. Petersburg that the roots of the Empire's problem lay in an inadequate transportation system, underdeveloped industry and an antiquated social system based on serfdom.

P. Longworth
Russia's Empires: Their Rise and Fall from Prehistory to Putin, 2005

2.4.2 Consolidation under the Romanovs

Expansion of the empire during the third period resulted in an empire that included a wide variety of people, languages, religions and lands. During the peak pre-revolutionary and postwar years of the USSR, three main groups formed what was recognized as the Russian Nation: the *Great Russians*, the Ukrainians and the Belarusians (the *White Russians*), along with a number of other, smaller groups of *Russified* or assimilated ethnic groups. All others that were non-Russians were never part of the Russian nation but were associated regions that became the formal republics of the USSR. They included Estonia, Latvia, Lithuania, Moldova, Azerbaijan, Georgia, Armenia, Kazakhstan, Turkmenistan, Kirghizstan, Tajikistan and Uzbekistan. In the 1920s, the Soviets recognized 194 different ethnic groups; by 1930, Russification and administrative action had reduced this number to just 108 different language groups (Sorokin 1967).

The geographical expansion that resulted in the creation of the Russian Empire after the victories of Peter the Great was a product of Russian fears of encroaching armies of the Tartars and other Central Asian nomadic tribes. Two-thirds of that empire lay in Asia, with more than half of the empire's population non-Russians; a good estimate of the size of the empire at this time is the current borders of the Russian Federation (Box 2.2).

2.5 The Soviet Empire

By the end of the nineteenth century, 350 years of continued expansion had produced a Russian empire that stretched from the Baltic Sea to the Pacific Ocean. Table 2.1 lists the dates of Soviet expansion to 1946. The end of the Romanov dynasty did not bring an end to the expansionist policies of the leaders of their replacement. If anything, expansionist policies were enhanced under the Soviet

BOX 2.2   DEATH OF THE LAST, GREATEST RUSSIAN EMPIRE

In his superbly written 2005 analysis of the rise and fall of Russia's empires, Longworth (2005) described the end of the Soviet Union; thus,

> At midnight on 31 December 1991 the Soviet Union ceased to exist. The satellite states had gone their separate ways two years earlier, but now the Baltic states regained their independence and Ukraine, Belarus, Kazakhstan and all the other constituent republics started out on a new existence as sovereign states. The red flag with the hammer and sickle was run down the Kremlin flagstaff, and a blue, red and white tricolour was run up instead ... Russia had again been shorn of empire.

P. Longworth
Russia's Empires: Their Rise and Fall from Prehistory to Putin, 2005

However, events in the rise of Russia under Vladimir Putin suggest that a pause might be appropriate in the reading of his earlier statement: "The fourth, and greatest, Russian empire was gone, never to be resurrected."

system. Expansionism was granted a near-holy justification for its goal was not overtly aggrandizement; rather, it was promoted as the means to hurry the collapse of capitalistic imperialism and the victory of a socialist hegemony.

The Soviet Union's territorial expansion just before, during and after WWII occurred mostly in Europe (East 1951). Annexation of large portions of Finland took place after wars with that small neighbor in 1940 and again in 1947; 400,000 Finns were forced to migrate from the three large areas ceded to the Soviets. After their brief fling with freedom from 1920 to 1941, the Baltic states of Estonia, Latvia and Lithuania were annexed and made full-fledged Soviet Socialist republics. In addition to the territory taken from Finland, after 1945, the USSR took lands from Germany, Poland, Czechoslovakia and Rumania. Together, this added some 190,000 square miles of territory to the Soviet Union. Including the residents of Ukraine and Belarus republics, the acquisitions added close to 24 million people to the USSR. Acquisition of the Baltic states as Soviet republics and lands taken from Poland for the Belarus and Ukraine republics after WWII moved Russia's boundary with Poland some 200 miles closer than it had been just six years earlier. Soviet Moldavia was formed from lands ceded by Czechoslovakia and Rumania.

In the Far East, the Soviet declaration of war against Japan in the last days of WWII gave it the right to reclaim the Kurile Islands and all of Sakhalin Island. After Japan's victory in the 1904 war with Russia, the south half of the island had been awarded to Japan; in 1945, total control was given to the USSR. The

Table 2.1 Soviet Territorial Expansion Imperial and Repression in Asia and the Middle East

Region	Activity	Year
Georgia	Independence declared 1918; Red Army invasion followed by Soviet annexation	1921
Armenia	Independence declared 1918; Soviet annexation	1921
Azerbaijan	Independence declared 1918; Soviet invasion and annexation	1920
Kazakhstan	Kazakh nationalist government Kazakh Soviet Republic established USSR troops quell Basmachi revolt	1917 1918 1923
Tadzhikstan	USSR troops quell Basmachi revolt	1917
Tannu-Tuva (northeast Mongolia)	Independence declared 1921; Soviet annexation	1944
Afghanistan	Communist coup led by Soviet-trained officers USSR invades; new Soviet puppet leader imported	1968 1979
Uzbekistan	USSR troops quell Basmachi revolt	1917–1923
Turkistan	USSR troops quell Basmachi revolt	1917–1923
Azerbaijan, Iran and Gilan	USSR-supported Persian Soviet Socialist Republic established Soviet occupation USSR forms Azerbaijan and Kurdish Republics (both crumble on attack by Iran army)	1920 1941 1945–1946

Source: Paksoy, H. B., "Basmachi": Turkistan national liberation movement 1916–1930s, in Paul D. Steeves, ed., *Modern Encyclopedia of Religions in Russia and the Soviet Union*, Vol. 4. Gulf Breeze, FL, Academic International Press: 5–20, 1991; and other noncited sources.

Note: Basmachi revolts refer to revolts in Russia's Asian territories after announcement in 1916 of the first conscription for military and labor service in Tsarist Russian armies of Muslim recruits.

USSR and China negotiated an agreement after the end of WWII in which China gave up its claims to Outer Mongolia. A plebiscite approved the region's independence under USSR guidance along with recognition of its *special interests* in Manchuria.

Russian foreign policy since 1989 has been as influenced as were Soviets by the traditional Leninist view that defense against imperialist Western capitalism must always be "unchangeable expansionist and aggressive" (Wallander 1996, p. 5). Hence, it was the duty of the socialist states to come together to counter capitalist aggression. *Coming together* would mean centralized leadership of Moscow and, eventually, central control or annexation.

The Soviet Union's foreign policy after 1945 focused on building a dependable series of barriers to a repeat of invasion from the west through cementing its political and military dominance in the ostensibly independent states occupied during Soviet armies' march to Berlin. By the end of 1945, Soviet army forces occupied Bulgaria, Romania, Hungary, Poland and Eastern Germany. By 1949, Russian control of the Eastern marches of Europe included bilateral treaties of friendship and cooperation with four of these states and Czechoslovakia. Soviet Russia built its modern structure of allies as a result of its defeat of Nazi invaders in WWII.

However, traditional means of territorial acquisition were rendered less feasible after the war. Changes in geopolitical conditions influenced by the possibility of massive retribution with atomic weapons reduced the opportunities and strengthened the potential penalties. Until the end of the nineteenth century, territorial expansion was possible through several different paths (Dinerstein 1958). As Catherine the Great, Prussia and Austria dismembered Poland in the eighteenth century, and Soviet Russia and Nazi Germany did so again in the twentieth century; one way to acquire new territory was by combining with a potential enemy in the dismembering of a weaker state. The agreement in advance eliminated the threat of retaliation by the greatest possible opponent. Another method was through the waging of a limited war, as Soviet Russia carried out in the two wars with Finland. A third has been to weigh the possible penalties and decide to take over neighboring lands without any declaration of war. This approach was followed successfully by Hitler in Czechoslovakia, by the Soviets when they kept the Baltic states after *liberating* them in 1940 and by Russia when it annexed Crimea in 2014. No war followed as a consequence of any of these adventures. A third approach is what Dinerstein called annexation by ultimate—the real or implied threat of violence toward another country unless it gives in to demands or backs off from a course of action. An example was the implied threat by the Soviets to Great Britain and France during the Suez Canal crisis.

Herbert Dinerstein (1958) cited three major changes that have resulted in the growing impossibility of growth by any of these traditional methods. First, the world today does not constitute the same playing field; there are no longer any weak or backward large regions available for partial or total conquest. China, India, Africa and the Ottoman Empire, for example, are no longer opportunities that are relatively easy to pluck. Central Asia was already under Soviet control. Second, acquiring territory was easier because the world was not characterized by two ideological camps competing with each other for world influence. Any gain by one side was a challenge to the other that had to be met. In the great days of imperial expansion, this divide did not exist; no power was strong enough to bar expansion in areas considered open. Third, the nature of war was changed by the threat of mutual mass destruction. The penalties and costs of a large-scale war are too great.

Soviet postwar successes in territorial acquisition and internal influence in satellite states began to crumble after 1950, ending by the end of the 1980s in a complete collapse of what was the world's largest empire. Some observers believe that since the turn of the century and accession to power of Vladimir Putin, Russia is on the road to reacquiring the territorial and influence status it once enjoyed. Although written in 1951 as the Cold War was building to a climax, W. Gordon East warned the world that the tradition of creating a defensive *cordon sanitaire* by attack and annexation of neighboring territories was a trait that was forever ingrained in the minds of Russia's rulers. Nearly 65 years and political implosion later, the foreign policies of its long-time president Vladimir Putin are proving Gordon East to have been prophetic. The post-Soviet Russian Federation appears to once again be focused on territorial expansion as a means of defending foreign invasions.

2.6 Conclusion

The pattern of outward expansion that has characterized the foreign policy aims of the several versions of a Russian empire was disrupted in 1989, but it was not extinguished. Under the presidency of Putin, many foreign policy analysts believe that the dream of the empire has been resurrected. That empire may not take the form it has built over the past millennium, but the idea of a multiethnic empire with Greater Russia as its central core has not changed. The opportunities for acquisition of additional territories in the twenty-first century are few. However, the building blocks are already in place: they are the former USSR borderlands. Regained unassailable influence and global respect rather than acquisition are the objectives of Putin's foreign policy. Attaining those objectives in this geopolitical environment can be achieved by rebuilding the Soviet empire from within—an internal empire composed of friendly and dependent former republics.

Putin has employed both soft and hard power tactics in his empire-rebirth project. His most influential soft power weapon is reminding Russians of their heroic past history as one of two global superpowers, along with the common cultural heritage of ethnic Russians and Russian language speakers. He has employed hard power in several different degrees, beginning with threats and support of Russian minorities in the Baltic states and cyber warfare against recalcitrant borderland states, progressing through the stopping of deliveries of natural gas and oil, to the waging of small wars in such former satellite states as Georgia, supporting separatists' revolts, to the ultimate tactic of annexing foreign state territories. The underlying message of all these policy actions is that Russia is still a power with the ability and willingness to use that power to coerce smaller borderland states in following the dictates of Moscow. In Chapter 3 are the author's interpretation and reaction to Russia's foreign policy actions in the two decades of the Putin/Medvedev presidencies.

FROM UNCERTAINTY TO SUPREME CONFIDENCE

II

Chapter 3

Chapter 3

Russia's Foreign Policy in Transition

3.1 Introduction

In nearly 25 years since the breakup of the Soviet Union, leaders in the West have seen the successor state the Russian Federation (RF) evolve through a variety of foreign policy iterations as it struggled to find its way in the rapidly changing political–economic world. Throughout the decade of the 1990s, Russia first appeared to be moving closer to the West. During this period, the formation of Russian foreign policy suffered without leadership from one crisis to another. By the end of President Yeltsin's second term, it was clear that that approach was dead, displaced by a policy that replaced cooperation with confrontation and renewed nationalist fervor. Encouraged by Putin, renewed nationalism has helped form, legitimize and bind together a coalition of neo-communist elites, former KGB, industrialists, intellectuals and the military (Snyder 1996). This coalition applauds Putin's policies designed to reestablish Russia as a global great power.

3.2 Factors Shaping Post-Soviet Foreign Policy

At least five different policy-shaping forces have been examined in some detail by analysts of Russian foreign policy: (1) shifts in ideological foundations, (2) regime change, (3) leadership politics, (4) interest group influence and bureaucratic politics and (5) the effects of external actions and reactions. Two of these are particularly appropriate for this analysis of post-Soviet Russia's foreign policy. The first is the Marxist–Leninist ideological traditions that have exercised a dominant influence upon Russia's politics and foreign policy since 1920. The second is the influence of a series of socioeconomic crises that followed the disintegration of the Soviet Union.

3.2.1 Ideological Foundation Shift

For more than 70 years, the Soviet Union was an ideological invention, founded in the core precepts of Marxist–Leninism, among which were the right to self-determination, a core professional revolutionary party to lead workers in the violent destruction of capitalism and imperialism, from which a proletarian class would eventually emerge. The West, with its tradition of empires, was identified as the enemy blocking the march to the eventual unification of all people; the economic and military rise of the United States saw it added to the leading position on the official list of enemies. After the revolution, solidarity of the proletariat would be the glue holding together the diverse people and cultures of the old Russian Empire. To assure that social needs were met, the guiding party would be formed to replace the imperial government (Comey 1962; Lenin 1963; Tishkov 1991). After the collapse and dissolution of the Soviet Union in 1989, a new ideology was needed to justify the new quasi-democratic government and to hold the diverse ethnic groups together.

3.2.2 Effects of Socioeconomic Crises

During the early years of the breakup of the former Soviet Union, neither Presidents Gorbachev nor Yeltsin was able to cope with a host of socioeconomic crises that characterized the apparent disintegration of the Soviet Union and directly influenced foreign policy. Those crises included an inability to

1. Achieve a new post-Soviet identity and a sense of purpose that could guide the nation through the challenges of surviving in a new political reality;
2. Develop an economic base that was not overwhelmingly dependent upon commodity energy (oil and gas) exports while gaining maximum long-term benefit from high-priced oil and gas exports;
3. Reshape the dysfunctional political system that existed at all levels, and that, in turn, was driving a nearly universal distrust of government and civil society in general while bringing together an internal consensus on policy priorities and legitimate internal power sharing that satisfy enough rival groups while also curtailing efforts by various power brokers to gain personal wealth and power over competitors;
4. Control the corruption rampant throughout society, including government and business;
5. Find a mutually beneficent policy for dealing with its former republics while also forging new alliances and partnerships in the wake of a disintegrated

empire of subject republics and increasing unipolar global action of the United States;

6. Reestablish a once powerful military/industrial establishment—including replacing or destroying a huge, deteriorating nuclear missile stockpile that threatens Russia's own survival.

Boris Yeltsin resigned as president of Russia in 1999, appointing Vladimir Putin as acting president. His appointment became official with his victory in the election of early 2000. Putin was reelected to a second four-year term of office in 2004. Dmitry Medvedev, Putin's elected replacement, appointed Putin to the post of prime minister in 2008. Putin was then elected for a third term as president in 2012.

Russian foreign policy took a distinctly revanchist, outward-looking turn with the ascendency of Putin. Shortly after he began his second term of office, Putin signaled his plans for returning Russia to its Soviet-era great power status in a speech given in Europe:

> We very often—and personally, I very often—hear appeals by our partners, including our European partners to the effect that Russia should play an increasingly active role in world affairs. In connection with this, I would allow myself to make one small remark. It is hardly necessary to incite us to do so. Russia is a country with a history that spans more than a thousand years and has practically always used the privilege to carry out an independent foreign policy. We are not going to change this tradition today.
>
> **V. W. Putin**
> *Speech at the 43rd Munich conference on security policy, February 10, 2007*

Vladimir Putin, over his first two terms as president of the RF, and a small band of former KGB and Federal Security Service (FSB) power elite, a number of whom were with Putin in the St. Petersburg security forces, attempted to address each of the Yeltsin-era crisis points. In the process, they also took significant first steps in an effort to reestablish Russia's reputation as a geopolitical superpower. Moreover, the very high prices for oil and gas exports that have existed for a number of years have helped make it possible for Russia to make giant strides toward reestablishing Russia as a geoeconomic superpower, including upgrading and rearming its military. In this paper, we will examine some of the themes in Putin's 2014 foreign policy that have been used to justify Russia's actions in Ukraine and other former Soviet regions and that should be taken as severe threats to their continued sovereignty.

One of the objectives for this book was to help rekindle what I perceived to be a reduction in the academic attention given to the foreign affairs of Russia since the end of the Cold War. A large proportion of the recent US scholarly research on Russia has focused on domestic affairs, particularly on sociocultural, economic and political issues. This research, albeit important to the understanding of the New

Russia, has to some degree neglected Russia's changes at the international level. Ambrosio (2005) cautioned that the study of Russia as a global force ought not to be delegated to the stagnant world of academic researchers; the changes that have taken place and are continuing to occur continue to be extremely important. Russia holds a predominant strategic location that spreads from the eastern flank of Europe across Central Asia to the Pacific Ocean. Events in Georgia and Ukraine bear witness to the importance of the study of Russian affairs.

It is manifestly apparent that Russia's several centuries of expansionism and world power influence have not been shelved. Moreover, the West has finally come to realize that expansion has been the policy aim of choice since the first election of Vladimir Putin. Not the least factor crying for greater attention to be paid to Russia's foreign policy is the existence of the thousands of nuclear warheads and the weapons to deliver them that remain in Russian hands. Along with completely rebuilding the nation's military forces, President Putin has announced proposals to rebuild much of its aging nuclear arsenal.

A number of related socioeconomic and sociopolitical factors have contributed to the aggressively revanchist Russian foreign policy followed by the Putin administration. Their interdependence is considered to be a key element in any foreign policy: international, government and internal conditions and contexts interact, thereby shaping the course and outcome of a nation's foreign policy (Wendt 1998; Matz 2001; Cordell and Wolff 2007; Ministry of Foreign Affairs [MFA] of the Russian Federation 2013). This is certainly the case in the Russia of the early twenty-first century.

Constructionist foreign policy theory builds on two fundamental principles. First, the structures of international politics are *social* rather than strictly material (e.g., regaining the respect of the international community is as important or more important for Russians than economic parity with the European Union [EU] or United States). Second, these structures shape nations' identities and interests rather than just their behavior (Wendt 1998). When the leaders of a nation are able to build on a set of existing and widely shared norms, they are able to choose otherwise unpopular courses of action that reflect and reinforce the importance of the shared norms. The social structures that influence and shape foreign policy have three shared ingredients: shared knowledge, material resources and practices (processes). First, social structures are defined by shared understandings, expectations or knowledge among the actors involved in shaping foreign policy. A shared national identity and a common external enemy are examples. Second, social structures involve material resources such as valuable resources, currency reserves and modern armaments. These, of course, have meaning when they become part of the shared knowledge and understandings. Third, social structures exist not on the actors' heads nor in capabilities but in the actions taken and the practices and processes that are manifestations of the shared knowledge and understandings. The lesson for constructionist foreign policy analysts, then, is to look at actions, not assertions. Russia's recent wars with its former subjects are actions enough for this analysis.

3.3 A New Role for Russia?

The question of what role Russia was to take after dissolution of the USSR emerged early in the presidency of Yeltsin (Matz 2001). In 1990, while still chairman of the Duma, Yeltsin announced that Russia was not interested in becoming the center of any new empire and would not seek any advantages over any of its former republics. In 1992, a few weeks after formal breakup of the USSR, Andrei Kozyrev, President Yeltsin's foreign minister, echoed those sympathies, asserting that relations with the family of former republics were then conducted as between equals; Russia did not seek any special position in the family. In February 1993, however, that spirit of equality was becoming shaky. Kozyrev announced a new policy when he reminded the West that Russia continued to have an interest in all armed conflicts in the territories of the former USSR. He then added that Russia retained a special responsibility in the region and called for all international organizations, including the United Nations, to grant Russia special powers as a guarantor of peace and stability in all former Soviet territories.

Writing near the end of Boris Yeltsin's second term of office, Chafetz (1996) described three fundamentally different political ideologies then competing among the political elite for dominance in the new Russia after the collapse of the Soviet Union. Whichever approach survived the confusion that characterized Russia among the early years of democracy would shape Russia's position in the global political sphere for the next century. The liberalist followers of Yeltsin believed that the right approach to follow would bring Russia closer to Europe; the second, a statist identity, would see a reduced Russia going its own independent way in the world; the third, authoritarian approach, would see Russians retreating to the historically combative and empirical orientation.

Political leaders who supported Yeltsin adopted a liberalist identity that was based on the conviction that Russia's destiny was tied with Europe, NATO, and the United States. For them, Russia was European. They were convinced that success in international relations was based on mutually accepted roles and norms. Within this view, it was deemed possible to resolve problems between nations and regions through diplomacy. Yeltsin based his foreign policy on the belief that the West did not pose a military threat to Russia. He was, therefore, able to make great cuts in defense spending, cutting the 4-million-man army to less than 1 million. Thus, Yeltsin and his liberal supporters saw Russia as a "modern, liberal state and part of the civilized society of similar states—a member of the club" as it were (Chafetz 1996, p. 675).

A somewhat middle-of-the-road political philosophy was that held by the second group jousting for leadership in post-Soviet Russia, the statist group. This group placed a greater reliance on the ability of the uniquely Russian cultural and historical achievements to base a post-Soviet identity for the nation that remained after the dissolution of the Soviet Union. In a *Foreign Affairs* review, Mandelbaum (2014, p. 156) identified the attraction of this approach: "People are generally more willing to be governed by those with whom they share an ethnicity, a religion, or a language than those with whom they regard as foreigners, and they are prepared to fight for the political system they prefer." Supporters of this identity believed that Russia was inherently different from both the West and the East. Therefore, Russia should go its own way in global affairs, exploiting the rich resources of its geographic vastness to fuel economic growth and military power, always placing its own interest before those of any global community of nations. The core ideology of the group was the belief that international relations among nation states that shared common values were anarchical rather than communal. In this light, Russia's role in the world would be to function as a counterbalance to power centers in the West and East, benefiting from either or both but aligned with neither.

The third group competing for defining Russia's identity in the post-Soviet period had its roots in the Communist authoritarian approach to international relations without advocating a return to the Soviet system. Authoritarians were convinced that Russia should never allow its foreign policy to be controlled by the European Union or NATO. Strongly anti-Western in general, this group based its conception that the right post-Soviet identity for Russia was that of again being a global superpower: one of two with the United States as the second or one of three with China as the third. For authoritarians, anarchy was the nature of world politics. Vehemently opposed to liberals, they pushed for reversing the movement toward democracy and a free market economy (albeit without reversing the privatization of Soviet-era economic institutions). Themes in their domestic propaganda that aimed to rebuild the people's commitment to a strong, stable government included anti-Semitism; racism; and fear of outsiders of any race, religion, or social norms different from their own. The final goal of authoritarians was to establish what Chafetz (1996, p. 679) described as a "new Russian imperialism based on pan-Slavism, racism, and fear of the West."

By 2008, the end of Vladimir Putin's second 4-year term as president, the authoritarians were well on the way to overpowering the rapprochement with the West-leaning of the liberals in government while enlisting many statists in their cause. After having himself appointed prime minister under his personally selected new president, Putin remained in a position to shape the country's foreign policy as it slid deeper and deeper into the murky sea of authoritarianism and centralized power over all aspects of the Russian government. Godzimirski (2008) has described how the power elite under Putin built a new identity for Russia by focusing on three themes: historical achievements, imperial expansion, and xenophobia. The historical achievement they focused on was reminding the public of the victories gained during the Great Patriotic War (WWII) as the Red Army drove the Nazis out of Mother Russia. From this came the respect gained from their achievements in science and industry, including nuclear energy and space exploration. Russians were justifiably proud of being citizens of a nation able to compete politically, economically, and culturally with the United States. The Putin regime sees promoting Russian language education in the former republics as an essential sociocultural identity device (Zamiatin 2008).

The authoritarian's answer to the special question was a reaction to having been forced to accept the loss of all 14 peripheral republics when the Soviet Union died. Russia was pared down to no more than it had been during the early reign of Peter the Great. Putin has emphasized the importance of regaining influence in those lost territories. Areas of special interest are as follows: they are being coaxed to return to Russia voluntarily as associates, they supported militarily breakaway regions with ethnic Russian majorities of independent states;, or, most recently, outright territorial annexation. In this way, Putin and Russian authoritarians are working to rebuild some semblance of the Russian Empire as it existed at its peak under the Soviets.

Answering the third post-Soviet identity question has been most difficult for Russia particularly in light of the apparent empire revival while existing as a multiethnic aggregation of people of different religions, languages, and long-term political aspirations (Shlapentokh 2013). Russia finds itself much in the same situation as the Ottoman Empire in the late nineteenth and early twentieth centuries. The Turkish core of that empire was being pulled apart by three competing political ideologies: an all-inclusive philosophy of young military officers. In Putin's Russia, the parallel is the reinvigorated security agency of the reinvented KGB. Thus, a military/paramilitary unit's members believed that the way to save the Ottoman Empire and reconstitute the Russian Empire was (1) to follow a policy of Ottomanism in which all people in the empire would have equal rights and privileges regardless of religion or ethnicity; for Russia, it was the early attempt to bring all former republics together under the Commonwealth of Independent States. (2) For the Ottomans, it was a diverse nation tied together by a common religion, Islamism, in which Muslims hold superior status in all endeavors; for Russia, it is the unifying force of orthodox Christianity. (3) A Pan-Turk nation that embraced all persons of Turkish ethnicity regardless of region or territorial location was attempted; in Russia, a Pan-Slav movement was an attempted unifying device. Neither of those approaches to imperialism was able to help the Ottoman Empire survive; only time will tell whether Putin's decision to create an authoritarian/statist Russian identity will embrace all people in the Asian–European still vastness of post-Soviet Russia.

3.4 Rebuilding the State

Russia's relations with the EU and the United States changed dramatically after Putin's second term of office began. Russia embarked on a very pronounced shift from what was considered to be the chaotic but open-mined political environment under Yeltsin. President Putin announced plans designed to rebuild Russia as a strong state based on three key objectives: (1) a recentralization of the political system, (2) the dictatorship of law, and (3) a *Souverenaya Democratiya*.

3.4.1 Recentralization of the Political System

If Putin will go down in history for only one accomplishment, it may be his success in turning a fractured political system of powerful, competing political elites jousting for the right to steal what they could for their personal interests to something that more closely resembles a Western democratic state. The first task taken on by Putin upon taking office in 2000 was to strengthen the authority of the central government.

The recentralization of the Russian political system has been accomplished. What is difficult for Western critics of Russia to accept is that this recentralization means placing as many of the reins of government, the security forces and the economy as they can collect into the hands of a group of former KGB and FSB (the post-Soviet KGB successor once led by Vladimir Putin). According to the *Economist* (2007a), individuals from the former FSB and related security organizations control the Kremlin, the government, the media, large sections of the economy, the military and all security organizations. Three out of four senior Russian officials in office in 2007 were at one time associated with either the KGB or other security and military operations.

It should not be forgotten that at the time of the breakup of the Soviet Union, there were thousands of KGB operatives functioning in Russia or abroad. The failure of the 1991 KGB-led coup against Mikhail Gorbachev did not erase their feelings of betrayal at the Communist Party's inability to retain the Soviet Union's position as a global superpower. However, that sense of betrayal has passed. Today, their control of all arms of the economy, together with the cornucopia of cash made possible by high prices for oil and gas, has placed members of former security agencies into positions of power and money in the Russia of 2007 greater than ever before in the history of the country. Alexei Kondaurov, a former KGB general and now a member of the Russian parliament, was quoted in an *Economist* (2007b, p. 25) review of the neo-KGB state: "Communist ideology has gone, but the methods and psychology of its secret police have remained."

3.4.2 The Dictatorship of Law

As a plank in his program to reorganize the Russian political system, Vladimir Putin announced during his 2000 presidential campaign that Lenin's concept of a dictatorship of the proletariat would from then on be replaced with a dictatorship of law, promising that this change would be a primary objective of his presidency. Lenin dismissed the rule of law in 1917, calling it a "bourgeois sham, designed to perpetuate the domination of capital over labor" (Hosking 2007). Thus, the concept of a civil society of honest, stable and effective government was replaced by the authoritarian rule of the Communist Party—only ending in 1990. Under Stalin, the substitution of a society based on laws with authoritarian rule resulted in "The re-enserfment of the peasants in collective farms, the virtual destruction of the Orthodox Church and other religions, the impoverishment of the public media and the nation's cultural life, the 'great terror' of 1937-8 and the mass deportation of whole nationalities" (Hosking 2007, pp. 5–6).

During a pre-electoral speech, Putin promised to bring a stable and predictable legal environment to Russia, emphasizing the role of the state as a guarantor of law enforcement. At the time, public reaction to the promise was mixed; they feared that he meant a return to a Soviet-style dictatorship. A Carnegie and MacArthur foundations–funded *Program on New Approaches to Russian Security* memo at the time noted, "While optimists openly associate their hopes for a revival of the Russian economy and society with the emergence of a law-bound state, pessimists fear the rise of a police state in Russia, bearing in mind Russia's autocratic traditions and Putin's KGB background."

Many Russians equate the chaotic, insecure time of the decade before Putin with the failed attempt at introducing a democratic society. They look back at that period with justifiable dread of poverty, unemployment, disease and widespread criminal activity through which many suffered. They long for a return to the stability of the past and are, therefore, willing to allow Putin to substitute a dictatorship of law for a rule of law. Accordingly, Putin has tried to reform the judiciary but without relaxing state control. He has instituted a simplified tax system but exercised the power of the state to ensure that taxes are paid. He has made ownership of land and facilities more stable but allowed many former KGB and FSB officers to acquire or retain properties gained at artificially depressed prices. Putin's presidency is clearly the most stable Russian administration to appear in decades (Derluguian 2006). What remains to be seen is what will happen after Putin. He was elected for a third term in 2012 and is expected to seek reelection again in 2016.

3.4.3 Souverenaya Democratiya

The concept of a sovereign, democratic, rule- or law-based state with the absolute right to exercise power over its branches and divisions is the third theme of the Putin administration. This state sovereignty theme first aired when the RF declared its sovereignty on June 12, 1990. In 1994, June 12 was officially declared the "Day of the Adoption of the Declaration of Russia's State Sovereignty." Unofficially, this is referred to by some as Russian Independence Day.

The absolute or sovereign right to express control within its boundaries is reflected in Russia's rejection of US and EU criticism of Russia's human rights record and other internal decisions. Putin considers Western objections to the severity of the repression in Chechnya and other rebellious states to be meddling in things that are purely an internal affair of Russia. In Russian eyes, this is simply dealing with extremist terrorists. Tasks high on the Putin list were controlling corruption, forging new alliances to replace the lost Soviet-era partnerships, reestablishing influence in the former Soviet republics and rebuilding Russia's armed forces.

3.4.3.1 Controlling Corruption

During the heady days of privatization under Yeltsin, corruption ran rampant. According to *Transparency International*, the Berlin-based organization monitoring global corruption, Russia and many of her former republics remain some of the most corrupt nations in the world. Each nation is assigned a *corruption perception index* (CPI) score based upon the degree of corruption seen by business people and country analysts (Transparency International 2014). The scores range from 1 (highly corrupt) to 100 (very clean). Countries are then ranked from 1 (most clean) to 177 (most corrupt) of all the countries in the 2013 ranking. Russia received a score of 28 out of 100 and was ranked 127 out of the 177 total, placing it very high on the corruption perception scale. Other former Soviet Union associates and republics with very high corruption index scores included Armenia (CP score 36, rank 95); Azerbaijan (28 score, rank 127); Belarus (29 CP score, rank 123); Kyrgyzstan (24 score, rank 150); Tajikistan (22 score, rank 154); Turkmenistan and Uzbekistan (tied with scores of 17 and ranks of 168); and Ukraine with a score of 25 and a rank of 144.

3.4.3.2 Forging New Alliances

Vladimir Putin has not been content to admit that during the 1980s and 1990s, the world evolved from two relatively equal superpowers competing through a system of alliances and spheres of interest for geopolitical supremacy to a unipolar stage where the one remaining superpower could and has acted unilaterally. Anyone wanting a clear indication of Russia's worldview in 2007 should read Putin's February 19, 2007 speech at the 43rd Munich Conference on Security Policy. He opened by stating that the unipolar model of a single superpower is not only politically unacceptable but also impossible to sustain because of the growing power of collections of states such as China and India (together with a gross domestic product [GDP] larger than the United States), and the BRIC (Brazil, Russia, India and China) countries, which together have a GDP greater than the United States. He also railed against extending NATO eastward to take in former Russian republics. He then accused the United States of acting irresponsibly in Afghanistan, Iraq, Kosovo, Ukraine and Georgia, warning of the dangers inherent in such actions. The key elements of Putin's speech are seen in Box 3.1.

President Putin also attacked the Bush administration for the December 2001 decision to back out of the 1972 ballistic missile treaty. In announcing the withdrawal just three months after the September 11, 2001 terrorist attack on the United States, President Bush said that the Anti-Ballistic Missile (ABM) treaty hindered the country's ability to develop ways to protect the nation against terrorist attacks

BOX 3.1 COLONIZATION IN THE LATE RUSSIAN EMPIRE

The scope and scale of the wave of colonization that occurred from roughly 1880 to 1936 have been described by Sunderland (2000):

> Colonization in late imperial Russia unfolded on a giant scale and produced gigantic effects. Between 1871 and 1916, over nine million settlers resettled within the Russian empire, with five of these nine million resettling in just the two decades before the end of the old Regime. While the Russians had been colonizing for centuries, this scale of settlement was completely unprecedented in Russian history. The vast majority of settlers moving at this time (well over 90%) were Russian and Ukrainian peasants who were leaving areas affected by land shortages, failed harvests, and/or famine in central Russia and Ukraine and moving to "open" lands in the "east," that is in Siberia, the Kazakh steppe, the Far East, and, to a lesser extent, Central Asia and Transcaucasia....Depending on where they settled, peasant colonists displaced nomads, semi-nomads, and earlier agricultural settlers; they cut down forests, plowed up steppes, dried up swamps, planted new plants, and imported new animals; agricultural production skyrocketed in certain regions...and the ratio of Slavs to non-Slavs in the eastern borderlands generally increased.

or rogue state missile attacks; the United States would renew its development of space-based anti-missile system.

During his Munich speech, Putin used several arms reduction treaties to make a further dig at the United States—the 1992 and 1993 Strategic Arms Reductions treaties (START I and II) between the United States and the post-Soviet–era states of Russia, Belarus, Kazakhstan and Ukraine and the 2002 Strategic Offensive Reductions Treaty (SORT). In a reaction to US withdrawal of the ABM treaty, Russia announced on June 14, 2002 that it would no longer be bound by its START II commitments. Under the five-party START agreements, the nations agreed to make *deep reductions* in the numbers of strategic offensive nuclear weapons and agreed to verification procedures. The United States had ratified the original START II agreement in January 1996 but never ratified a 1997 protocol extending an implementation deadline or modifications to the ABM treaty. President Putin signed the treaty in 2000, but the US Congress never voted to ratify the complete package.

Under the SORT agreement, the United States and Russia agreed to reduce their strategic nuclear warheads to a level of 1700 from 2200 by December 31, 2012. In a backhanded slap at the integrity of the Bush administration, President Putin took the Munich 2007 speech opportunity to have the United States recognized for its agreement to the treaty:

Russia intends to strictly fulfill the obligations it has taken on. We hope that our partners also act in a transparent way and will refrain from laying aside a couple of hundred superfluous nuclear warheads for a rainy day. And if today the new American Defense Minister declares that the United States will not hide these superfluous weapons in a warehouse or, as one might say, under a pillow or under a blanket, then I suggest that we all rise and greet this declaration standing.

He then added that Russia would continue to strictly adhere to the arms reduction treaties and intended to also adhere to the Treaty on the Non-Proliferation of Nuclear Weapons—agreements that have a *universal character.*

3.4.4 Relations with Former Soviet Possessions

One of the trouble spots of Russia's current foreign policy for the 15 years since the breakup has been deciding on what attitude to adopt toward its former republics, particularly the Baltic states (Estonia, Latvia and Lithuania), Georgia, Moldova and Ukraine. During the Yeltsin presidency, much of the country's foreign policy involved forging new ways for coming to terms with new relationships with these borderland states. Yeltsin administration policy makers also focused on dealing with instabilities in the north and southern Caucasus regions while also building new relations with the United States and Europe. The Caucasus includes the post-Soviet states of Georgia, Armenia, Azerbaijan plus such Russian political hotspots as Chechnya.

After the independence of the former Soviet republics that occurred during the Yeltsin presidency, the attitude of the new states fell into two categories. The first group included the states that remained suspicious of Russia and believed that it would try to regain control of their countries through overt or covert means; this particularly applied to the Baltics, Georgia and Ukraine. The second category included those states that were not ready for independence and therefore retained strong economic ties to Russia. Among the second group are Azerbaijan, Belarus, Moldova and, to a degree, Georgia. During the Yeltsin presidency, Russia attempted to move the former group toward the second by emphasizing its economic power, control over energy resources and pressures on their large Russian minorities residing in the Baltics.

As the twentieth century came to a close, there were still more than 25 million ethnic Russians living in the 14 former Soviet republics (Hopf 1996). After Russia's annexation of the Crimean peninsula and armed support of ethnic Russian separatists in the border regions of Georgia, Ukraine, Moldova and elsewhere, the question that lingers in the minds of the non-Russian leadership in the other republics when and under what conditions will Russia announce the fate of the Russians in their states has become an issue of Russian national security. Therefore, armed intervention to *protect* the Russian minorities is necessary and justified. In 1996, Hopf (p. 147) warned of the "horrific consequences for Russia, Russia's neighbors, and the West if a Russian leader opted for a military resolution of this question." Putin has, of course, already opted for such action, each time with little or no reaction, other than cosmetic *sanctions* from NATO, the EU or the United States. The remaining states bordering Russia are right to worry.

Russia took issue with Latvian and Estonian citizenship laws, which they charged discriminated against ethnic Russians living within their borders. When the three Baltic countries joined NATO and the EU, the situation became even more exacerbated. Russian appeals to the EU resulted in some easing of the citizenship laws, thus easing tensions somewhat.

Despite the weakened shape of the Russian military, there is no doubt that Russian armor can still roll almost unmolested across the borders of all her former republics. This is particularly true of the borders with the three small Baltic states. However, threatening these smaller nations apparently has earned Russia fewer internal payoffs than flexing its muscles at the United States and NATO. Rather than verbally attacking small, non-threatening countries, President Putin and his fellow political elite have found the West, and especially the United States, to be a far more politically advantageous enemy. Promoting an anti-Western rhetoric helps the ruling elite turn the attention of the Russian people away from the very real problems facing the nation and gives the people an attractive ideology by providing an easy, well-recognized target upon which to vent their very real frustrations.

3.4.4.1 Rebuilding Russia's Armed Forces

In late August 2007, President Putin joined the leaders of China and the other members of the six-nation Shanghai Cooperation Organization (SCO) to observe the last stage of joint military maneuvers then underway in Russia's Chelyabinsk region. Some 6500 troops and more than 100 aircraft were involved in the war games. Also on hand as observers were officials from India, Pakistan, Iran and Mongolia. One of the primary goals of the SCO, according to Ivan Safranchuk (2008), Moscow director of the World Security Institute, is to boot the United States out of Asia. The SCO clearly wants the United States to leave Central Asia; that's a basic political demand. That's why the SCO holds military exercises. Russia and China want to demonstrate their capability to take responsibility for stability in Central Asia.

At an August 2007 SCO summit in Kyrgyzstan, prior to traveling to view the joint maneuvers, the president emphasized that, while Russia was not seeking to build a Cold War style military bloc, he did see the SCO expanding from its original purpose as an economic association to become more of a military association. President Putin then added that the SCO is on the way to becoming a major force in ensuring security in the region of Eurasia. The SCO countries favor a multipolar international system providing equal security and development potential for all countries. He then added that the SCO ensures that any one nation's attempt (obviously alluding to the United States) to solve global and regional problems alone has no future.

3.5 Russia, the EU and NATO

Russia's reaction to the May 1, 2004 admission of ten new members to the EU and the admission of many Eastern European nations to NATO reflects its return to a highly aggressive approach to foreign policy. This expansion brought the EU to the borders with Russia as new members included the Czech Republic, Estonia, Hungary, Latvia, Lithuania, Poland, Slovakia and Slovenia. Accordingly, Russia feels that this eastward expansion of the EU and NATO forces her once again on the *geopolitical defensive* (Kuchins and Zevelev 2012). In reaction to this perceived encirclement, Russia has begun to modernize and rearm its military.

From more than 15 years since the breakup of the Soviet Union, EU relations with Russia were centered on two objectives (Kempe 2007). The first was working to construct a market-based economy in Russia. The second was using enlargement of EU into former Soviet territories as part of a plan to encourage democratic transition within the former Soviet republics in Eastern Europe.

During his speech at the Munich Conference on Security Policy, President Putin stated Russia's attitude regarding NATO expansion. He began by asking why NATO countries have not signed the 1999 Treaty on Conventional Armed Forces in Europe. In the seven years since the treaty was accepted, it has only been signed by four nations, one of which is the RF. He added that Russia is resolving the barrier holding back signing by many NATO countries—the retention of Russian bases in Georgia and Moldova. The Russian Army is leaving Georgia, and the 1500 troops still in Moldova are protecting Soviet-era weapons and ammunition. He called the NATO policy of placing 5000-man flexible forward bases in the former Soviet-bloc states tantamount to establishing a *cordon sanitaire* around Russia:

> It turns out that NATO has put its frontline forces on our borders, and we continue to strictly fulfill the treaty obligations and do not react to these actions at all. I think it is obvious that NATO expansion does not have any relation with the modernization of the Alliance itself or with ensuring security in Europe. On the contrary, it represents a serious provocation that reduces the level of mutual trust. And we have the right to ask: against whom is this expansion intended? And what happened to the assurances our western partners made after the dissolution of the Warsaw Pact? ... And now they are trying to impose new dividing lines and walls on us—these walls may be virtual but they are nevertheless dividing, ones that cut through our continent.

Russia's 2014 intervention in Ukraine may have been triggered as early as 2008 when NATO approved Ukraine's decision to join with Georgia in applying for NATO membership (Kanet 2010b). NATO's reaction was enthusiastically positive toward the proposed accession, as this official communiqué of the April 2008 NATO summit in Bucharest clearly indicates (emphasis added by Smith 2010, p. 117):

NATO welcomes Ukraine's and Georgia's Euro-Atlantic aspirations for membership in NATO. *We agreed today that these countries will become members of NATO.* Both nations have made valuable contributions to Alliance operations. We welcome the democratic reforms in Ukraine and Georgia and look forward to free and fair parliamentary elections in Georgia in May. A Membership Action Plan (MAP) is the next step for Ukraine and Georgia on their direct way to membership. *Today we make clear that we support these countries' applications for MAP.* Therefore we will now begin a period of intensive engagement with both at a high political level to address the questions still outstanding pertaining to their MAP applications.

3.5.1 Testing, Testing, Testing

Russian military airplanes and submarines have once again been seen testing the response capabilities of its European neighboring states. Aircraft have intruded into Georgian airspace, *accidentally* dropped a bomb on a small village some 30 miles from Tbilisi, the Georgian capital, and caused British fighters to scramble in late August 2007. In October 2014, a suspected Russian submarine encroached into Swedish coastal waters and was suspected of landing Soviet spies. Michael McFaul (2007b), a Russian scholar at Stanford University and senior associate at the Carnegie Endowment for International Peace, was asked in a national public radio (NPR) interview to respond to the question, "Is Russia again becoming a bully, using military force to try to intimidate its neighbors?" He answered with an unequivocal yes. McFaul added that the real problem behind these moves, however, is that the leadership in Moscow does not see itself as joining the West, nor do they see Russia as a member of the democratic community of nations. Thus, ensuring that your neighbors are aware of your military strength is a legitimate foreign policy activity. In place of placating Europe and their former republics, Russia is again becoming autocratic—a state of affairs where a little saber rattling should be expected. "I don't think it's just an accident that they're using their power in a more coercive way vis-à-vis countries (such as Georgia, Ukraine, and Belarus)," McFaul added.

Russian saber rattling has been supported by announcement of plans to spend US$11 billion immediately on defense improvements and plans to spend another $200 billion over seven years from its oil and gas export revenue to rebuild the Russian military (Strategypage.com 2013; Weir 2007). Most of the $11 billion to be spent in 2008 on new weapons is earmarked for nuclear weapons systems, including missile-carrying submarines and new ICBMs. For the first time in 15 years, the Russian army has been provided the funds to purchase new and refurbished equipment, including a new armored tank (the T-90), BMP-3 infantry vehicles, new radios and anti-aircraft missiles, new field uniforms, protective vests, new small arms and rocket-propelled and conventional grenades and, most importantly, the money to purchase supplies and ammunition for use in training. The tactical air force that supports the army is getting new bombers, ground attack aircraft, fighters and helicopter gunships.

On August 17, 2007, Putin ordered the Russian Air Force to resume strategic bomber patrols in both the Atlantic and Pacific oceans; thousands of Russian and Chinese troops conducted joint military exercises in 2007, and on August 21, Putin opened the largest air show in post-Soviet history (MAKS-2007) at which Russian military aircraft were displayed and offered for sale. In the first eight months of 2007, Russia signed contracts to export some $2.5 billion of Russian-made military aircraft, with civilian airlines projected to purchase another $600 million on Russian civilian aircraft (Smolchenko 2007).

Russian Admiral Vladimir Masorin announced in 2007 that the Russian Navy was to receive six new nuclear-propelled aircraft carriers over the next 20 years as part of the planned expansion and modernization of Russian naval power. Three of the carriers and their escort vessels are to go to the Russian Pacific Fleet and three to be assigned to the Northern Atlantic fleet. He also called for reopening Russia's former naval base in Syria to serve a permanent naval presence in the Mediterranean. Editors of the European weekly new publication *New Europe* concluded in 2007 that these plans for a stronger Russian Navy appear to be serious and not just a status announcement. However, the domestic economic crises that followed Western sanctions for Russia's annexation of Crimea and steep decline in oil and gas prices have forced shelving of the reform plan until a later date.

3.6 Conclusion

Cast adrift in the world after the 1989 collapse of the Soviet Union, leaders of the once-formidable global superpower had to learn how to build a truncated Russian state out of what was the largest empire the world has known. They suffered through a brief and nearly bloodless counterrevolution. The foreign policy statements issued by the Russian Ministry of Foreign Affairs in 2013 identifies Russia's perception of the dangers facing the country prior to the Ukrainian crisis, annexation of Crimea and world energy price free fall in 2014.

In a 2013 foreign policy statement, Russia expressed Putin's dissatisfaction with the continuing expansion of NATO closer to Russia's borders and the welcoming of former Soviet satellites into closer ties with the EU and the United States. The statement included a subtle recrimination of the United States and its NATO allies for their military actions against former Soviet allies such as Serbia, Iran and Iraq in the following terms: "There is a growing perception that no state or a group of states are able to solve any acute international problems alone and that current problems, including conflict resolution and crisis management, cannot be solved by force" (MFA 2013). The policy statement also included a proposal for creation of a regional security organization to take the place of NATO. The new organization's membership would include the European nations and RF affiliates. Its charge would be to develop and monitor an Atlantic-wide security policy and oversee the formation of a collective security system that could end economic and political ideological differences and the practices of the Cold War.

A year later, Russia annexed Ukraine's semi-autonomous Crimea—by force. Results of a December 2014 opinion poll by the Associated Press and the University of Chicago's National Opinion Research Center for Public Affairs Research showed that Putin enjoys an 81% approval rate among Russian citizens.

Chapter 4

The Putin-Era Foreign Policy of Consolidation

4.1 Introduction

Using conventional weapons with an armed force of around 1 million men, Russia today can only be overtly aggressive toward smaller and weaker opponents such as her former republics and satellites. The only way the core of the old Union of Soviet Socialist Republics (USSR) could take on a larger enemy is by using the very large arsenal of nuclear weapons it retains. The willingness to use tactical nuclear weapons is included in the defense policies of Russia. The problem with that is that others have nuclear retaliatory capabilities, and this is not going to change in the very near future. Putin has had to find other avenues for achieving his aim of regaining substantial influence, if not outright control, in the breakaway states of the former Soviet Union. As a result, since he became president, Russia has included a mix of hard power tempered with soft power wherever possible to achieve its foreign policy aims of consolidating the lost republics into a new federal association of like-minded states on the pattern of the European Union (EU).

4.2 Evolution of the Consolidation Policy

Vladimir Putin succeeded Boris Yeltsin as the president of Russia for two four-year terms. He then sat out as prime minister for four years and in 2012 was elected for a third term as the president. During that period, the once-promising move to a democratic society in the early 1990s has evolved into a government by autocratic home rule coupled with aggressive attempts to reclaim a lost global power position and consolidate lost territories into a larger federation of states favorable to Russia's position as a global leader. Subsequent events clearly indicate that an aggressive effort is underway to reestablish Russia as a global great power. Putin wants a Russia that is capable of forcing its will on any or all of its former Soviet empire territories. It is apparent that Russia has embarked on a path of imperial revival (Motyl 1999). Moreover, Russia has no reservations over the use of hard power to enforce its will and to subdue defiance in the small neighboring states on its borders.

More than one policy analyst has considered the Russian president's third four-year term as the president of Russia to be "apparently until 2024, Putin has one overriding objective: the creation of a … post-tsarist, post-soviet Russian empire" (Tisdall 2011). To achieve this goal, Russian foreign policy under President Putin has been moving from one crisis to another—and another, and another, and… This has brought the world closer to, if not to another Cold War, at least to what has been described as a *cold wave* (Arbatov 2007).

The new Russia being built by Putin and his close advisors is expected to be neither pro- nor anti-Western. Rather, it will be and do whatever it takes to remain *Russian*. The term *derzhavnichestvo* ("Russia is a great power or it is nothing") exemplifies this opinion held by many of the Russian elite including its president (Shevtsova 2007a, p. 892). On the other hand, Putin has not been reluctant to say that Russia is and will always be anti–United States and anti–North Atlantic Treaty Organization (NATO).

Under Putin's presidency, it has become increasingly important for the current political elite to reach agreement on a national idea that will preserve the gains that the country has achieved over the years of his administration. Casting the West once again as Russia's principal enemy has apparently turned out to be the idea that the public is most willing—and apparently most eagerly—to accept, because of the Russian government's authoritarian identity and where revision of history has long been common. It is also hinted at in Russia's 2014 foreign policy statement.

4.3 Putin-Era Foreign Relations

A constant theme underlying Russia's foreign relations is the quest for world recognition of Russia's supremacy in world affairs. In support of this theme, Putin continues to emphasize Russia's status as a sovereign, democratic, rule- or law-based state with the absolute right to exercise all necessary power over its neighbors and areas considered to be of vital interest.

Putin's foreign policy has clearly changed from what it seemed to be in his first two terms as Russia's president. Then, he appeared to be willing (if not eager) to negotiate with the West in the quest for a peaceful solution to the issue of how to exist amicably with the former republics in a greater Europe. This has been replaced in his third term with what seems to some analysts as a revival of Russian imperialism, the product of which was the annexation of Crimea and continued support of separatists in Ukraine's eastern provinces. With no real justification of the shift to aggressive foreign policy available, Putin often falls back on his view of the superiority of Russian culture as reason enough to his actions, as this 2014 *Foreign Policy* opinion piece suggests:

THIS IS THE CENTER OF PUTIN'S IMPERIAL VISION

The pragmatic political fixer of the 2000s now genuinely believes that Russian culture is both exceptional and threatened and that he is the man to save it. He does not see himself as aggressively expanding an empire so much as defending a civilization against the "chaotic darkness" that will ensue if he allows Russia to be politically encircled abroad and culturally colonized by Western values at home… This notion of an empire built on the basis of a civilization is crucial to understanding Putin.

M. Galeotti and A. S. Bowen
Foreign Policy, 2014

4.3.1 Relations with the West

Russia's reaction to the May 1, 2004 admission of ten new members to the EU and the admission of many Eastern European nations to NATO reflects its return to aggressive approach to foreign policy. This expansion brought the EU to the borders with Russia as new members included the Czech Republic, Estonia, Hungary, Latvia, Lithuania, Poland, Slovakia and Slovenia. Accordingly, Russia feels that this eastward expansion of the EU and NATO forces her once again on the *geopolitical defensive* (Kuchins and Zevelev 2012). In reaction to this perceived encirclement, Russia has begun to modernize and rearm its military.

During his speech at a Munich conference on security policy, President Putin stated Russia's attitude regarding NATO expansion. He began by asking why NATO countries have not signed the 1990 Treaty on Conventional Armed Forces in Europe (CFE). In the years since the treaty was accepted, it has only been signed by four nations, one of which is the RF. The United States and its NATO partners have refused to ratify the CFE until Russia complies with weapons limits and the commitments it made during the treaty negotiations. Also blocking the ratification is the US and NATO desire that the four new NATO members, Estonia, Latvia, Lithuania and Slovenia, be included in the agreement. There are no provisions for new membership in the original treaty. He added that Russia is resolving the barrier holding back the signing by many NATO countries (ACA 2012). Putin called the NATO policy of placing 5000-man flexible forward bases in the former Soviet-bloc states tantamount to establishing a *cordon sanitaire* around Russia:

It turns out that NATO has put its frontline forces on our borders, and we continue to strictly fulfill the treaty obligations and do not react to these actions at all. I think it is obvious that NATO expansion does not have any relation with the modernization of the Alliance itself or with ensuring security in Europe. On the contrary, it represents a serious provocation that reduces the level of mutual trust. And we have the right to ask: against whom is this expansion intended? And what happened to the assurances our western partners made after the dissolution of the Warsaw Pact? ... And now they are trying to impose new dividing lines and walls on us—these walls may be virtual, but they are nevertheless dividing, ones that cut through our continent.

V. W. Putin

Speech at the 43rd Munich conference on security policy, February 10, 2007

4.3.2 Relations with Former Republics

Russia's turbulent relations with its sister republics did not start with Vladimir's presidency. This assertive and sometimes aggressive behavior emerged in the open at least as early as February 1993 when in a speech to a group at the Civic Forum in Moscow, President Yeltsin called for the UN and other international organizations to recognize that Russia retained a special interest in guaranteeing peace and stability in all regions of the former USSR (Hill and Jewett 1994). The Russian political and military leaders of the time espoused the idea that Russia's centuries of experience in maintaining order in those regions made it rational that it should continue to do so. In repeating their justification for Russia's probable interference in the internal affairs of the former republics, Hill and Jewett (1994, p. 2) explained that this was and would continue to be the underlying rationale for its relations with the former Soviet republics:

> It should be stated at the outset that Russian involvement in the republics of the former Soviet Union is not surprising; historically, Russia has defended its perceived geostrategic objectives in the region and consistently sought to safeguard them by whatever means it has at its disposal. In the past—from Peter the Great to Stalin (and now Putin)—the annexation of territory or the creation of satellite states has been the preferred option. Russia's geostrategic objectives in the region has also remained essentially constant throughout its modern history, no matter what type of regime or ruler is in power.

Russia's relations with the former Soviet republics since the collapse of the Soviet Union are essentially the same as they were for the several centuries preceding their breakaway in the early 1990s. Among the key underlying policy objectives during those centuries were gaining and holding on to warm, ice-free ports in the Baltic and Black seas; building a barrier to invasion from the West, the East, and the South; maintaining influence in the foreign, economic, and political affairs of the annexed territories; establishing control over the production and distribution of the territories' natural resources; and maintaining control of defense facilities, operations, and a reservoir of potential military personnel.

Although fundamentally with the same objectives that shaped relations before the breakup, Russia's relations with its sister republics after their secession have not been the same as they were before their change in status. In the post-Soviet era, its relations with the republics differ in their geographic proximity to the Russian heartland. The republics with which Russia appears to be most concerned are those closest to the Russian heartland—the inner ring of states. They include Belarus, Kazakhstan, Kyrgyzstan, Tajikistan, Turkistan, and, for defense and economic relations, Armenia. All these states have large Russian minorities, in some as large as 40% of the total population. All are heavily dependent upon Russia, making their mutual relations most favorable of all former republics. The second group of former republics—the outer ring—includes Georgia, Ukraine, Uzbekistan, Azerbaijan and Moldova. Russia's relations with this ring are almost all bad. Russia has aided breakaway efforts in several states and annexed territories in others. Although several states have large oil or natural gas resources, they depend upon Russia for pipeline distribution and other services.

The third group is the Baltic states of Estonia, Latvia, and Lithuania. The Baltic states have moved farthest from their association with Russia, although all of them maintain trade ties with Moscow and depend upon Russia for oil and gas. All three are members of the European Union and of NATO. The three states gained their independence in 1920 but were forcibly annexed again by Russia in 1939 (King and McNabb 2009). That memory colors the tone of their relations with Russia, although in general, they maintain harmonious relations with Russia. For Estonia and Latvia, one reason for this is that both have large ethnic Russian minority populations—colonized there by the USSR during the Communist years. Russian intervention to ostensibly protect the Russian minority population is always perceived as a threat. For Lithuania, which also maintains a nonconfrontational stance with Russia, the smaller size of the Russian minority is less of a threat. Rather, as a requirement tied to removal of Russian military after 1991, Lithuania has been forced to permit Russian forces access to its Baltic Sea enclave of Kaliningrad through Lithuanian territory.

4.4 Foreign Policy Goals

The unofficial translation of Russia's official statement of its 2014 foreign policy lists nine basic goals, beginning with ensuring the security of the country and reasserting its position as a major global political player and an alternative to its unstated competitor, the United States. Other primary goals include maintaining economic growth while ensuring human rights and freedoms, promoting internal peace, developing bilateral relations with foreign states and interstate associations, strengthening global trade, promoting the Russian language and strengthening its use in the world and enhancing accord with regions of other cultures and religions. Goals that appear to conflict with Russia's overt foreign policy actions in Ukraine and elsewhere include "promoting good-neighborly relations with adjoining states and helping to overcome existing and prevent potential tensions and conflicts in regions adjacent to the Russian Federation," and "ensuring comprehensive protection of rights and legitimate interests of Russian citizens and compatriots residing abroad, and promoting, in various international formats, Russia's approach to human rights issues" (MFA 2013).

4.4.1 Regaining Superpower Status

The second section in the Russian foreign policy document begins with statements that reflect Russian opinion of its own role in a changing geopolitical spectrum. The section asserts that global power positions are changing from one superpower or great power to a polycentric system—one that includes Russia and China as well as the United States and the EU. The shift of global power from the West to the Asia-Pacific region has resulted in growing instability in international relations. In Point 15, the policy statement makes a not-so-subtle criticism of the US and NATO actions in Iraq and Afghanistan by citing risks to world peace caused by attempts to "manage crises through unilateral sanctions and … armed aggression outside the framework of the UN Security Council." Section II, Point 15 continues with this statement:

> There are instances of blatant neglect of fundamental principles of international law, such as the non-use of force, and of the prerogatives of the UN Security Council when arbitrary interpretation of its resolutions is allowed. Some concepts that are being implemented are aimed at overthrowing legitimate authorities in sovereign states under the pretext of protecting civilian population. The use of coercive measures and military force bypassing the UN Charter and the UN Security Council is unable to eliminate profound socioeconomic, ethnic and other antagonisms that cause conflicts. Such measures only lead to the expansion of the conflict area, provoke tensions and arms race, aggravate interstate controversies and incite ethnic and religious strife.

4.4.2 By Force If Necessary

After stating a position against the use of armed force to settle international problems, the 2014 Putin foreign policy begins its next policy section with the assertion in Point 27 that the use of force is clearly a permissible option. The use of armed force is as legitimate as political and diplomatic, legal, economic, financial and other tools resolving foreign policy issues. The selection of which tool should depend upon the issue's significance for Russia's foreign interests. The policy statement then adds in the next point that Russia's foreign policy is aimed at creating "stable systems of international relations based on international law and principles of equality, mutual respect and non-interference in internal affairs of states." The citizens of Ukraine and Georgia may need to have explained to them how this point balances with the Russian military occupation of their lands.

The priorities established in the foreign policy document spell out Russia's intentions relating to international law and its foreign relations. Two of the six positions specifically identified in the single point have particular interest for Russia's close neighbors. Subpoint B states Russia's intent to forcibly counter efforts of "certain countries or groups of countries" to arbitrarily or for politically motivated reasons reinterpret aspects of international law in ways to their interest. Included are international laws and norms such as non-use of force or the threat of force. Obviously, Russia's intentional occupation of Crimea by Russian military forces is deemed permissible in this humanistic assertion.

An extremely important statement that the leaders of all the lands adjacent to Russia should pay close attention to is that all those lands were legally members of affiliates of the Soviet Union. As this Putin-approved foreign policy priorities statement in the policy document clearly asserts, Russia intends to exercise control in the lands lost during the collapse of the Soviet Union.

> Russia intends to... work to finalize the international legalization of the state border of the Russian Federation as well as boundaries of the maritime zone over which it exercises its sovereign rights and jurisdiction while ensuring the unconditional observance of Russian national interests, primarily those related to security and economy, with a view to build up trust and cooperation with adjoining states.
>
> **Ministry of Foreign Affairs of the Russian Federation (MFA)**
> *Concept of the Foreign Policy of the Russian Federation, 2013*

The implementation section of Russia's 2014 published foreign policy document closes with a statement that a key element in the nation's foreign policy continues to be protection of Russian-speaking *compatriots* living outside Russia. The long-named organization responsible for carrying out this task is the Federal Agency for the Commonwealth of Independent States, Compatriots Living Abroad and International Humanitarian Cooperation. It participates in identifying proposals and implementing the foreign policy of the RF; assists in international development; provides international humanitarian cooperation, supporting Russian compatriots living abroad; actions to strengthen the position of the Russian language in the world; and helps in developing a world network of Russian scientific and cultural centers (MFA 2013).

4.4.3 Against All Enemies

Russia has a long list of *enemies* or rather, nations that its citizens perceive to be hostile to the state. Several are among the smallest nations in Europe: Estonia and Latvia. It should not be any surprise that a 2013 poll of Russian citizens named the United States as the most hostile to Russian security (Table 4.1). For the first

Table 4.1   Countries Russians Most Consider Enemies, 2005–2013 (% of Respondents)

Country	Year

Country	2005	2006	2007	2009	2010	2011	2012	2013
United States	23	37	35	45	26	33	35	38
Georgia	38	44	46	62	57	50	41	33
Latvia	46	46	36	35	36	35	26	31
Lithuania	32	42	32	35	35	34	25	17
Estonia	13	28	60	30	28	30	23	16
Ukraine	12	27	23	41	13	20	15	11
Afghanistan	3	12	11	7	14	15	8	10
United Kingdom	4	5	3	8	6	8	7	9
Poland	6	7	20	10	14	20	8	8
Iraq	10	4	3	3	3	9	6	7

Source: Mahaptra, L. Who are Russia's allies and enemies? Here's how Russians view other countries. International Business Times (September 21), 2013; Levada Center, Russian public opinion, 2005–2013, available at http://www.levada.ru/print/18-06-2013/vneshnepoliticheskie-vragi-i-druzya-rossii (retrieved June 3, 2014), 2013.

Note: 2008 data missing from source.

time in the eight years of the private polling, the United States is considered to be the country most antagonistic to Russia. The percentage naming the United States hostile to Russia increased to 38% from 23% in 2005. Russians rate Georgia and the three Baltic states above or close behind the United States as enemies of the RF. Until 2013, Georgia was seen as Russia's greatest enemy every year of the poll since 2005; at one time, it was so perceived by 62% of all respondents.

Events in Georgia, Estonia and Ukraine indicated that Russian foreign policy points to Russia's willingness to use hard power to achieve its will. Nye (2004) defined hard as the ability of a nation to achieve its political goals through the use of economic and military force to make other nations follow your policies. Putin has become a master at determining how far to go when applying hard power and when to shift to soft power approaches in his relations with its former republics and client states (Nye 2004; Wilson 2008; Grigas 2012).

Throughout the 1990s, Yeltsin had shown little interest in foreign policy. This state of affairs changed with Putin's rise to power in 2000. By the beginning of Putin's second term of office, it was clear that Russia's major foreign policy emphasis had evolved from the use of soft power to achieve its foreign policy aims to greater emphasis on the use of hard power.

Russia has used a variety of hard power weapons against its border states since Putin came to power. Hard power tactics have included invasions; advising and providing weapons and supplies to separatists; boycotts of imported products, including food items; cyber warfare; economic efforts to control the transportation infrastructure and transit business; and, most often, limiting access and charging very high prices for its exports energy sector. The Baltic states, for example, are 100% dependent upon Russia for natural gas and from 80% to 90% for fuel oil. Shutting off oil or gas pipelines in winter has been employed more than once; from 2000 to 2006, Russia cut off energy supplies to the Baltic states and the EU close to 40 times since 2000. Moreover, Russia makes the Baltic states pay full international market price for energy supplies, whereas more-friendly neighboring states are offered the same goods at deep discounts.

Russia's neighboring states are increasingly skeptical of the assertion in Point 21 of the policy document that an aim of Russia's foreign policy is to "consistently advocate" reducing the instance of the use of force in settling transborder relations in order to enhance both its strategic and regional stability. Of course, supporting a reasonably well-equipped army of more than 1 million men helps a little. It has generally been accepted that many of the cyber attacks aimed at the United States and its allies originate in Russia. However, it is not as well known that Russia's published foreign policy includes the intention to take all necessary measures to ensure information security, including threats to the nation's security that emerge in information space. Moreover, it will work to ensure that information and communication technologies are not used for military or political purposes.

4.5 Russia's Use of Soft Power

Soft power in foreign policy is the use of tactics that enable a nation to achieve desired political results without the use of intimidation by the threat or actual exercise of an armed incursion. Joseph Nye, who created the term in 2004, defined soft power as the ability of a nation to get what it wants from others through attraction or agreement rather than coercion or payment, thereby making it possible to influence others to help attain the outcome desired. The story in Box 4.1 illustrates how Russia is using soft power in Europe to influence public opinion.

Soft power in the West is generally carried out by actors in a pluralistic, vibrant civil society, through easy access to elements of a culture that encourages self-expression and personal freedom. In Russia, soft power is the exclusive tool of state-sponsored agencies supported by state-controlled media. The underlying message is promotion of a common faith in the superiority of approved behavioral standards and supremacy of conservative, orthodox cultural norms. Under Putin, the nascent civil society that emerged after the breakup of the Soviet Union was eliminated or severely curtailed under the resurgent strong-state government model. Internal

BOX 4.1   RUSSIA'S USE OF SOFT POWER IN EUROPE TO INFLUENCE PUBLIC OPINION

France has been identified as the probable primary target for a massive soft power campaign by the Russian Federation to sway public opinion. A *Radio Free Europe* story in June 2014 identified a long list of organizations in France that were promoting actions by the Russian Federation; many of the organizations were said to be receiving Russian state funding.

The Paris-based Russian think tank *Institute of Democracy and Cooperation* (IDC) was one of the organizations named. The focus of IDC's published study mission is on "East–West relations and the place of Russia in Europe." The IDC receives its funding from the Foundation for Historical Outlook based in Moscow; the foundation reportedly is funded by "anonymous donors." Both the IDC in Paris and the Foundation in Moscow are directed by Natalya Narochnitgskaya, a former Russian diplomat and member of the Russian state legislature, the duma. The IDC's director of studies is John Laughland, a British citizen whose views are said to "closely match the Kremlin's on a wide range of issues, including Ukrainian politics."

Russian media organizations with branches in France produce programs or print pro-Russian communications in French. The main media outlet defender of Russian policies was *ProrussianTV*, an online television channel that broadcast in French, but was forced off the air because of the problems of its owner, a Russian state–owned station. Before its closing, ProrussianTV broadcast programs that were described as "totally political and ultra-right-wing" (Kanevskaya 2014).

critics, nearly all of whom have been silenced in one way or another, are forced to accept the present model as a carbon copy of the old Soviet system (Baker and Glasser 2007). External critics shrug off the government's soft power messages, regarding them as indications of the return of typical Russian propaganda.

Soft power tactics employed by Russia since the 1990s have included low-interest loans to the governments of the breakaway states, foreign direct investment, cultural events, scholarships to local students for studies in the RF and providing support for Russian minorities, including funding pro-Russian political parties; radio and television broadcasting with stories putting Russia in the most favorable light possible and other economic, political and energy networks.

Moscow has enjoyed a number of advantages that improve the effectiveness of its soft power tactics in their neighboring, *special-interest* small states. A major advantage is the large numbers of ethnic Russians now residing in the bordering states. The state supported media broadcast and print-approved media in the Russian language, which in many states was no longer available. Until the decline in oil prices in 2014, there were nearly unlimited funds to support the many cultural programs promoting the message of a common history and pride in the scientific, military and economic achievements of the Soviet Empire. Moscow also provides scholarships for students for studying in Russian universities and has initiated a visa-free program for migrant workers for work in Russia, thereby benefiting substantially from migrant workers' remittances. The beginnings of an EU-like common market and customs union hold promise for further economic benefits, although in 2014, only Belarus and Kazakhstan had joined.

Under Gorbachev and Yeltsin, Russia appeared to be seeking a rapprochement with the West, particularly with the United States; under Putin, Russia decided to be mostly anti-Western. In this way, Russia could cooperate with the West when it was in their best interests to do so, as its agreement with the United States on anti-terrorist activity after 2001, but would not require it to be subject to Western dictates. Russia would do whatever it took to remain *Russian* while working to again be a global superpower. One way it would do was to establish and maintain strong links with its diaspora populations. This meant strengthening its ties with the thousands of Russians living in the former republics. The ties would be officially administered by the *Rossotrudnichestvo*—the Federal Agency for the Commonwealth of Independent States, Compatriots Living Abroad and International Humanitarian Cooperation (Lavrov 2012).

A defining objective of the *Rossotrudnichestvo* has been the promotion of Russian culture and language throughout the former Soviet territories and other nations. As King and McNabb described in 2014, the *Rossotrudnichestvo* was established by presidential decree in 2008 as an agency under the Russian Ministry of Foreign Affairs, with Konstantin Kosachev as the agency director. During an April 2012 visit to Paris, Kosachev announced plans to have agency cultural missions in more than 100 countries. He added that working with neighboring countries—where 20 million "compatriots living abroad" reside—was to be a top priority of the agency. By the word *compatriots* he meant all the ethnic Russians who were moved into or peaceably migrated to the neighboring territories during the 60 years of Soviet control.

Rossotrudnichestvo's program goals in the countries where it operates are the support of the Russian language and implementing cultural and educational programs that allow the *compatriots* to maintain their *spiritual ties* with the Russian homeland. The 20 million ethnic Russians living in former Soviet republics "still have many humanitarian, social, legal problems with the governments of the former Soviet territories where they now live, and that they are counting on support from Russia in dealing with those problems," said Kosachev (MIR 2013). The implication was that the *Rossotrudnichestvo* would be providing this support.

The *Rossotrudnichestvo* program has included establishment of cultural centers in former client states. One such center, the *House of Moscow*, is located in Riga, the capital city of Latvia. The center, funded by the Moscow city government, promotes Russian culture by sponsoring festivals and cultural events such as concerts and plays. Local businesses owned by ethnic Russians also provide financial support for these events. Programs such as the *Days of Russian Culture in Latvia* and the *Days of Latvian Culture in Russia* promote Russia's views of the benefits that both countries have gained by their close connection. Similar programs take place in Lithuania. One such event is sponsored by the Ukio Bank, which is owned by an ethnic Russian, who sponsors a cultural charity with Russian art each year. Russian and Soviet films and television programs in the Russian language are also shown where large-enough minority populations make it feasible. Finally, sporting teams and events sponsored and controlled by Russian owners have large followings.

Another valuable soft power weapon used by Russia is its citizenship policy (Grigas 2012). Russia considers all its ethnic Russians living in its borderlands as citizens of the RF, including providing these *compatriots* with Russian passports. Russia has used the stated policy of protecting the rights and well-being of these ethnic Russians as an excuse for going to war with Georgia and supporting the breakaway status of Georgia's provinces of South Ossetia and North Abkhazia. In 2014, Russia used this same excuse for annexing the Crimean Peninsula from Ukraine and arming and supporting ethnic Russian separatists in eastern and southern Ukraine. Clearly, Russia plans to assist the Ukraine's provinces with large Russian minorities in eventually declaring their independence and special status under the protection, if not outright annexation, of Russia.

4.5.1 Building Friendly Networks

The RF has a population of 141 million and a low or negative replacement rate. It needs allies—especially big, strong ones—if it is going to survive and prosper. It has two of the biggest now: China and India, both of which have nuclear weapons. Since 2005, the Russian public has increasingly viewed China and India as countries that support Russia and its foreign policy. The Russians' attitudes toward China as an ally have increased from 12% to 20%; perceptions of India as an ally, while still positive, declined from 16% to just 7%.

Other states that the Russians have considered allies are Iran, Iraq and Germany. Both of the Middle Eastern states have dropped from the friendlies list. Iraq, once a major trading partner and ally of Russia, has been on the list of Russia's enemies since its occupation by US forces. Belarus and Kazakhstan are consistently named as the countries friendliest to the goals and aims of the RF. The percentage of the Russian public perceiving China as an important ally has increased nearly every year, growing from just 12% in 2005 to 20% in 2013 (Table 4.2).

The 2013 poll was taken prior to the 2013 revolution in Ukraine, resulting in the odd result of Ukraine names both as a friend and an enemy to Russia. Germany, a member of the hated NATO, has been seen as an ally of Russia in every year since 2005. However, the Russian public's perception of Germany as an ally has declined each year from its highs of 24% in 2007 and again in 2009 to 17% in 2012 and 14% in 2013. During this entire period, Germany has become reliant on Russia for oil and

Table 4.2 Countries Russian Residents Consider Friends, 2005–2013 (% of Respondents)

Country	Year							
	2005	*2006*	*2007*	*2009*	*2010*	*2011*	*2012*	*2013*
Belarus	46	47	38	50	49	35	34	46
Kazakhstan	20	33	39	32	32	33	28	31
China	12	24	19	18	16	18	16	20
Ukraine	17	10	11	3	20	21	13	16
Germany	23	22	24	17	24	20	17	14
Armenia	9	14	15	15	15	11	11	12
Cuba	11	10	9	9	8	9	7	10
Bulgaria	n/a	n/a	8	11	10	13	8	9
Azerbaijan	5	7	5	10	8	6	9	8
India	16	15	14	12	14	16	9	7

Source: Mahaptra, L. Who are Russia's allies and enemies? Here's how Russians view other countries. *International Business Times* (September 21), 2013; Levada Center, Russian public opinion, 2005–2013, available at http://www.levada .ru/print/18-06-2013/vneshnepoliticheskie-vragi-i-druzya-rossii (retrieved June 3, 2014), 2013.

Note: 2008 data missing from source.

gas supplies, even going so far as to partner with Russia's Gazprom and several smaller German, Dutch and other firms in the construction and operation of a Baltic Sea gas twin pipeline. The construction of the more than 1 billion euro undersea project began in 2010 and was completed the next year. The route is shown in Map 4.1.

The power of this pipeline to influence bilateral relations between Russia and the EU cannot be overestimated. Extensions of this gas pipeline deliver Russian natural gas to the United Kingdom and other EU states. As the list of perceived enemies in Table 4.1 attests, Russia has never forgiven Estonia, Latvia or Lithuania—once important export routes and ports for Russian energy—for seceding from the USSR and then becoming members of NATO. The Russian–German pipeline was constructed to avoid transiting these states. The ice-free Latvian port of Ventspils on the Baltic Sea was a particularly important port for Russian exports. This strategically important port has long been the transshipment hub for oil products, liquid chemicals, potassium salt, coal, grain, general cargoes and other cargoes.

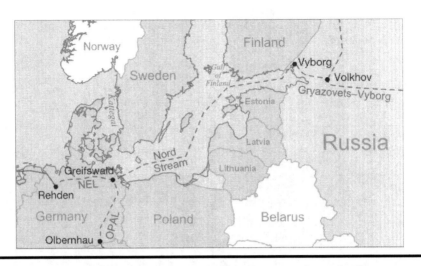

Map 4.1   Route of the Russian–German Baltic Sea natural gas pipeline.

4.6 Conclusion

While the aggressive foreign policy followed by Russia from the 2012 return to power of Vladimir Putin has been blunted somewhat by events beyond his control, the imperialistic threat he represents has not been eliminated. The Russian economy has undergone a series of internal and external crises, the price of Russia's major export commodity oil and natural gas is less than half what it was before Russia's theft of Crimea from Ukraine, and the West's sanctions against Russia continue to cause economic pain. Russia is in the early stages of a second sever recession; it cut its budget for 2015 by 10 percent and announced another five percent cut to take place in the 2016 budget. Cuts were made across the board—except for spending on its military. There is little likelihood in the near future of further aggression toward its former republics or annexation of additional neighboring territories. Yet, in the middle of 2015, Russia was still supporting breakaway forces in the eastern provinces of Ukraine and no Russian forces were departing the Crimea. Russia's annual military budget to 2015 was $145 billion, still below that of the United States with $577.1 billion but far greater than China's 60.4 billion (Globalfirepower.com 2015). Russia's continued spending on rearming and reforming its military remains a worry for its much smaller and weaker neighbors.

The 2012 conclusion of Kuchins and Zevelev that the danger of Putin adopting an "overtly anti-Western policy peaked with the Georgia war" was exploded with "Russia's invasion and annexation of the Crimea in 2013–14 and the West's tepid response" (p. 159). The gloves are off. Russia has warned its near-abroad Central Asian former satellites that their foreign policies from now on will have to jibe with Russia's. Moreover, the *significant factor* that Kuchins and Zevelev said would trigger a reversal in the warming trend extant in early Russia–US relations under President Obama has occurred. The relations are now colder than they have been since the US invasion of Iraq—a Russian ally—in 1991 under President George W. Bush.

Chapter 5

Building Defensive Barriers

5.1 Introduction

Russia has always included a strong defensive strategy along with its policies of aggressive expansion. Geography has been a major contributor to the expansionist policies of Russia since the arrival of the earliest Slavic people. Its vast empty stretches have also worked in its defenses. There were no natural borders on the west, whereas to the east was the seemingly endless treeless steppe that harbored only nomadic herders constantly on the move. To the north were first mixed forests, then marshes and the tundra in which only reindeer herders flourished. To the south were the early Persian and expanding Byzantine empires and a series of mountain ranges. Where natural barriers to invasion seemed insufficient, Russia erected barriers composed of buffer states and alliances. Once the buffer states were acquired, Russia instituted a policy of colonization of the territories, replacing indigenous people with Russians from the overpopulated western regions. Trustworthy ethnic Russians were then in a position to man the barriers against invasion if necessary. Near the end of the Romanov dynasty, this more or less benign policy of colonizing the east with Russians was augmented with an often-deadly policy of mass deportations of *problem* ethnic groups.

Russia's policy of building barriers was in force in both the western and eastern borderlands. In nearly all cases, the territory destined to become a barrier that invaders had to cross before reaching the Russian heartland was acquired by force. Russian armies conquered the existing residents of the region or won the region after victory in one of the wars against a distant overlord of the region. Examples of war-related territorial expansions include wars against Sweden, Poland and the Ottoman Empire in the west and south and Japan and China in the east.

5.2 Building Barriers in the West

Occupation by Soviet forces after World War II (WWII) gave it the power to establish sympathetic postwar communist governments in Eastern Europe. Stalin called these convenient socialist governments *people's democracies* (CIA 1965; Curtis 1992; Baev 2003). Those satellite governments depended on Soviet military power—and local basing of Red Army troops—to stay in power. In the early years after WWII, Russia signed a series of bilateral treaties with the occupied countries and aligned states. These treaties were expanded upon in January 1949 with the establishment of the Council of Mutual Economic Assistance (also known as CMEA and after 1971, Comecon).

The move toward a more formal military connection began with a secret summit conference held in Moscow in January 1951. That conference produced a Coordination Committee for the coordination and expansion of local military forces in the people's democracies, as well as a four-year plan for their rearmament. By the end of 1954, the Eastern European armies were fully aligned with the Soviet WWII military system, including training and combat control principles. Justification for the rearming was the perceived threat from rearming occurring in Western countries, including West Germany. In April 1955, Soviet Minister of Defense Marshal Zhukov was told to prepare a draft of a proposed joint military alliance. The draft treaty was presented to the representatives in a meeting in Warsaw on May 13, 1955. The Warsaw Treaty Organization (WTO), later to be referred to simply as the Warsaw Pact (WP), was formed. It was to be guided by a Political Consultative Committee representing the defense ministries of all seven states and the establishment of a Joint Armed Forces under a unified command. The organization had two objectives: secure the solidarity of the socialist countries and provide a defense against a North Atlantic Treaty Organization (NATO)–led invasion, which was perceived in Moscow as being inevitable.

Soviet Russia formalized and solidified its alliances with the occupied countries in May 1955 when it established the WP as a counterweight to the US-led NATO. Satellite member states included Bulgaria, Czechoslovakia, East Germany, Hungary, Poland and Romania. Socialist governments in Albania and Yugoslavia opted to stay out of the alliance. The WP did not have an independent organizational structure such as that in NATO but instead was controlled administratively and strategically by the Soviet Ministry of Defense. Soviet control remained a key factor all throughout the history of the alliance. As late as the 1980s, the WP was still under complete control of the Soviet Ministry of Defense. It did not have any independent command structure, logistics network, air defense system or operations command separate from the ministry (Map 5.1).

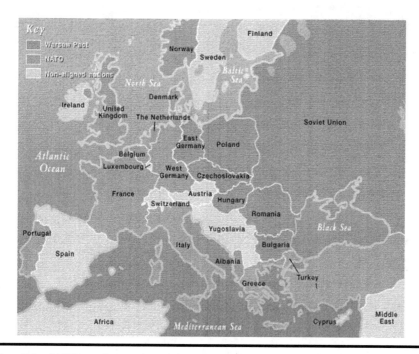

Map 5.1   NATO and Warsaw Pact countries in the Cold War.

Russia claimed that the pact's function was to be collective self-defense of the member states against aggression by an external military. It was conceived by Russia as a way of keeping its Eastern European allies under political and military control. Member nations Albania, Bulgaria, Czechoslovakia, Hungary, Poland, Romania and Russia signed the WP. East Germany was admitted in 1956. The East Germany occupation police force was made a fully-fledged army at the same time.

For most of the organization's existence, the Soviet Union used the WP military structure primarily as a reliable tool for ensuring that its allies remained in line with Moscow's military and political policy directives. Until the mid-1970s, all important decisions and military recommendations were taken by the Soviet Ministry of Armed Forces and the Soviet High Command (Baev 2003). When Albania, Hungary and Yugoslavia moved away from the Soviet alliance, the Soviets began to transform the pact into a weapon for preventing defections from other states. One part of this transformation was to place all pact nations under the absolute control of the Soviet military. Rebellions in Hungary and Czechoslovakia revealed the fragile nature of the member states' attachment to the Soviet system. The Red Army alone put down the 1956 Hungarian Revolution in a quick and bloody campaign. But in 1968, a force of 23 Soviet Army divisions invaded Czechoslovakia after Czech President Dubcek began implementing liberalization of the political system.

Hungarian, East German, Bulgarian and Polish contingents also took part in the Czech invasion, whereas the leaders of Albania and Romania refused to participate in the invasion.

According to Library of Congress analyst Glenn Curtis (1992, p. 12), the pact invasion of Czechoslovakia "showed the hollowness of the Soviet alliance system in Eastern Europe in both its political and its military aspects." Troops from four Soviet Bloc armies—Hungary, Poland, East Germany and Bulgaria—took part in the Soviet-led invasion, suggesting that considerable unity remained in the WP. However, the invasion also served to erode that which was left. The invasion of Czechoslovakia proved that joint defense against foreign invasion was less important than keeping orthodox Eastern European Communist Party regimes in power and others from breaking from that line; it was no longer possible to hide the fact that the WP was the tool for the Soviet Union's control of Eastern Europe.

5.2.1 The Brezhnev Doctrine

The 1968 crisis in Czechoslovakia resulted in the Czech Communist Party introducing a number of reforms, including ousting the conservative leader Antonin Novotny, abolition of censorship, economic reforms and open calls for further freedoms. Leaders in Moscow, remembering the 1956 uprising in Hungary, and mindful of possible similar actions in Ukraine, Lithuania, Latvia and Estonia, decided to end the Prague Spring and return government to Czechoslovakia. WP forces invaded on August 20. After finally establishing a stable government in April 1969, Dubcek was forced out of office.

In response to the Czechoslovakian revolt, the Soviet Union initiated policies designed to strengthen the pact by fighting any action by WP member states that is deemed to be *antisocialist* (Halsall 1997). The invasion of Czechoslovakia and the subsequent policy were justified in a November 1968 speech to Polish workers by Soviet leader Leonid Brezhnev. The policy called for the use of WP forces to intervene in any Soviet Bloc nation that was seen as compromising Soviet rule, either by trying to leave the Soviet sphere of influence or liberalizing its policies similar to what happened in Czechoslovakia. In what became known as the Brezhnev Doctrine, Brezhnev said,

> In connection with the events in Czechoslovakia the question of the correlation and interdependence of the national interests of the socialist countries and their international duties acquire particular topical and acute importance. The measures taken by the Soviet Union, jointly with other socialist countries, in defending the socialist gains of the Czechoslovak people are of greatest significance for strengthening the socialist community, which is the main achievement of the international working class....

This means that each Communist party is responsible not only to its own people, but also to all the socialist countries, to the entire Communist movement. Whoever forgets this, in stressing only the independence of the Communist party becomes onesided. He deviates from his international duty....Discharging their internationalist duty toward the fraternal peoples of Czechoslovakia and defending their own socialist gains, the USSR and the other socialist states had to act decisively and they did act against the antisocialist forces in Czechoslovakia.

P. Halsall
Modern History Sourcebook: The Brezhnev Doctrine, 1997

5.2.1.1 Changing Strategic Doctrines

From 1945, Soviet military planning was designed around defending against a massive land army invasion from the West led by the United States. However, when that invasion never materialized by the late 1950s, a major shift took place in the thinking of the Russian military. From what had been instructions to prepare for the possibility of a land war beginning with a selective nuclear strike with use of nuclear weapons, Moscow began warning its European allies that a major *rocket-nuclear war* with the West was no longer just possible—it was inevitable. When the war began, Russian allies would receive rocket-nuclear weapons to be used as they wished. Hence, training in their use would be provided to all WP members.

A second fundamental shift occurred in the 1960s. This time the idea of rocket-nuclear war had been replaced with acceptance of a US determination that small, local wars were more likely to occur than the major land wars fought in Europe. As a result, defense energy needed to focus on developing the arms and armies needed to fight those smaller wars as well as to be prepared to conduct and survive nuclear war. Meanwhile, the defense ministries of the smaller states were voicing dissatisfaction with the dominant planning and strategy role played by Russia. A secret CIA analysis of WP strategy distributed in June 1965 and cleared for public distribution in 2007 described the new strategy as calling for "highly integrated and coordinated series of Soviet–East European offensive and defensive operations." Eastern European forces were to act as fillers for battle-depleted Soviet units and as national units earmarked for special tasks but still under Soviet command.

The changes in mission and command and control structure were in place by 1969, although some were more cosmetic than real. WTO members were encouraged to join Russia in reducing the size of their military forces. By 1969, the more than 4 million-strong force of Russian and WP military forces in the 1950s was reduced to a combined total of a little more than 2.8 million. The relative sizes of forces and staff officer distribution are shown in Table 5.1.

Table 5.1 WP Armed Forces in 1969

Country	Army (000)	Divisions	Air Forces (000)	Aircraft	Naval Personnel (000)	Ships	Person Totals (000)	WP Staff
Hungary	95	6	7	140	–	–	102	6.0%
GDR	85	6	25	270	16	184	136	6.0%
Bulgaria	125	12	22	250	6	31	153	7.0%
Romania	150	9	15	240	6	63	173	10.0%
Czechoslovakia	175	14	50	600	–	–	225	13.0%
Poland	185	15	70	750	19	134	274	13.5%
USSR	2000	140	305	10,000	465	2000	2770	44.5%
TOTAL	2815	202	494	12,250	514	2412	3833	100%

Source: Baev, J., *The Organization and Doctrinal Evolution of the Warsaw Pact (1955–1969)*, paper presented at an international conference at Spitzbergen Island, Norway and published in Bulgaria, 2003.

5.2.1.2 Russia's European Alliances 1970–1989

The 1970s saw a relaxation and stabilization in US–Soviet relations, allowing East European WP members the opportunity to exercise greater independence from Soviet domination. The US Secretary of State's official historian wrote that this was when non-Soviet WP countries began to push back against tight Moscow control over their militaries. Romania was the first to successfully exercise a more independent role. Russia, on the other hand, insisted on greater military integration as the price to pay for giving member states a greater role in pact decisions. Senior Russian officers meet more regularly to *consult* with member armed forces while using the meetings to identify and monitor their loyalty and stress greater coordination.

The key development of the 1970s decade was the *Final Act* signed by 35 nations at the closing of the Helsinki Conference on Security and Cooperation in Europe—also called the Helsinki Accords. The accords were an effort to reduce the Cold War tension that existed between the USSR and the West by having all parties agree to the *status quo* of borders and areas of interest as established after WWII. The conference resulted in recognizing the Soviet's presence in the Warsaw bloc of satellite nations. Talks were held on four topics: questions of European security; cooperation in economics, science and technology and the environment; humanitarian and cultural cooperation; and plans for a follow-up to the conference. In effect, the final accord served as an official end to WWII by recognizing all European national frontiers, including the division of Germany into two countries. The United States maintains a full-time organization, the Commission on Security and Cooperation in Europe (the US Helsinki Commission), to monitor and maintain continued international cooperation. The Organization for Security and Cooperation in Europe (OSCE) sets standards in such areas as military security, economic and environmental cooperation and human rights and humanitarian concerns. Member states of the OSCE also develop preventive diplomacy initiatives to prevent, manage and resolve conflict within and among the participating nations (CSCE 2014).

5.3 Building Barriers in the East

Writing in 2008, the Russian director of the Security Institute Ivan Safranchuk identified two distinct schools of thought influencing the current foreign policy in Russia. One was a remnant of an early post-Soviet belief that the Russian Federation was too weak to openly defend its national interests or even to clearly formulate them. Although the approach was never openly expressed, it was reflected in the foreign policy followed in the last half of the 1990s by Foreign Minister Primakov. Based on this belief, the idea was to wait until Russia was again strong before becoming politically assertive, instead couching its arguments against NATO expansion into the former Soviet republics and military actions in the former Yugoslavia in terms of internal law.

The position of the second approach—the *liberal empire concept*—was that Russia had no alternative than to expand its economic and political influence in the European and Asian states on its borders, i.e., the states where it retained a *special interest*. This approach was considered particularly important in Central Asia, where to promote its interests, it formed four organizations with the region's now independent states and with other nations with similar interests: the Commonwealth of Independent States (CIS), formed shortly after the collapse of the Soviet Union; the Collective Security Treaty Organization (CSTO); the Shanghai Cooperation Organizations (SCO); and the Eurasian Economic Community. Russia's plan was to use the organizations to coordinate and promote collective decisions, implement its policies and maintain positions of leadership and influence in its former territories. The governing board of each organization included the heads of states of each country.

Three of the organizations had regional security responsibilities: the CIS, CSTO and SCO (Map 5.2). The responsibilities of the CIS included participation in Central Asian peacekeeping, the common Air Defense System and the Antiterrorist Center. Because of the loosely formed nature of the CIS, Moscow arranged for duplicate systems in the other organizations: a uniform air defense system in the CSTO and an antiterrorist facility in the SCO.

The CSTO was formed in 2003 after ratification of the Collective Security Treaty in 2000. Member states included Armenia, Belarus, Kazakhstan, Kyrgyzstan, Russia, Tajikistan and Uzbekistan. The CSTO's primary responsibility was coordination of a number of existing bilateral and multilateral security treaty organizations including the East European Allied Forces (Russia and Belarus 1999);

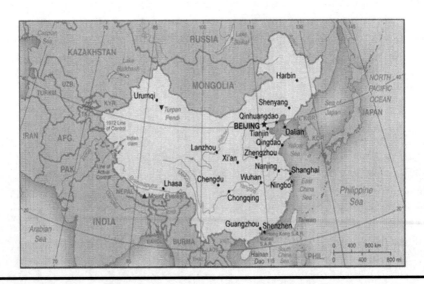

Map 5.2   East Asia with countries of geopolitical interest to Russia.

Caucasus Allied Forces (Russia and Armenia 1996); Collective Rapid Deployment Force for Central Asia (2001); and special forces in planning and regional allied forces determined by special agreement and treaties (Map 5.3). The structure was formalized in the Protocol on the Formation and Functioning of the Forces and Facilities of the Collective Security System of Collective Security Treaty Signatory Countries signed in 2001.

The Shanghai Cooperation Organization was established in 2001 with Uzbekistan's joining of a group of five Central Asian countries that had agreed on common borders in 1996. Beginning in 1992, China, long concerned with security issues on its western borders, negotiated a series of bilateral security agreements with Russia and the newly independent Central Asian states. Enhancements to those treaties were negotiated during conferences in Shanghai and Moscow in 1995 and 1996. The *Shanghai Five*—China, Russia, Kazakhstan, Kyrgyzstan and Tajikistan—were joined by Uzbekistan in 2001 to formally establish the Shanghai Cooperation Organization for controlling terrorism, separatism and extremism. Their 2002 charter led to a series of joint military exercises and force basing. According to China scholar David Schneider (2008), the military doctrine of the SCO has two aims: (1), building confidence among the states and the efficacy of the organization itself, counterterrorism and border security within the SCO but not toward events outside of the collective region; and (2), military activities are multilateral and guided by individual states. However, the practical outcome is that China has been able to insert itself in regions of Asia that have been Russian since the nineteenth century.

Map 5.3   Map of the Caucasus and Central Asia.

5.3.1 Strategic Aims in Central Asia

Russia views Central Asia as a zone of its exclusive interest despite the incursion of the United States and China in the region. Maintaining a strong position in the region is considered an indispensable building block in creating the multipolar, strong state world. Russia's policies toward Central Asia are, therefore, designed to achieve the following strategic aims (Muzalevsky 2009):

- Reforming the Central Asian states as a buffer zone against encirclement and foreign invasion of the Greater Russia by traditional enemies
- Reestablishing and reinforcing Russian influence as a great power in Central Asia and the greater international brotherhood of nations
- Regain influence—or, where possible, control—over the region's markets and resources, particularly the expanding energy and strategic materials exploitation and exports, including road, rail and pipeline transportation
- Improve internal and external security in Central Asia and the Russian Federation through joint combating of smuggling, narcotics trafficking, organized crime and ethnic terrorism

5.3.2 Alliances in East, South and Southeast Asia

Russia has maintained alliances with a number of states in East Asia, South Asia and Southeast Asia. The major countries and their population estimates are included in Table 5.2. Among the most important to Russia in the East are China, India, Japan, South Korea and Vietnam. Russia also maintains important trade relations with Japan, Indonesia and Taiwan. In a move toward increasing its influence in Asia, Russia became a member of the newly formed East Asia Summit in 2011. China is Russia's largest trading partner, with an annual export value of close

Table 5.2 East, South and Southeast Asian Countries and 2013 Population Estimates

Region	Countries	Total Population
East Asia	China, Japan, North Korea, South Korea, Mongolia, Taiwan	1.5 billion
South Asia	Afghanistan, Bangladesh, Bhutan, India, Maldives, Nepal, Pakistan, Sri Lanka	1.671 billion
Southeast Asia	Brunei, Cambodia, Indonesia, Laos, Malaysia, Myanmar (Burma), Philippines, Singapore, Thailand, Vietnam	625.9 million

to US$90 billion. Together, Japan and South Korea add another US$60 billion in annual Russian purchases from Russia.

China, with the longest border with Russia, is increasingly becoming a major political and military partner as well as the largest energy supplier to much of the region. In 2012, China was described as the *core country* and the Russian–Chinese strategic partnership as the *axis* in Russia's East Asian foreign policy (Kireeva 2012, p. 58; Tsygankov 2013). India and Russia have been close allies for many years, although since the collapse of the Soviet Union, India has moved somewhat closer to the United States, although officially, India remains nonaligned. In 2014, India, with the other BRICS (Brazil, Russia, India, China and South Africa) countries, endorsed Putin's aggressive policies in Ukraine (Pillalamarri 2014).

5.3.3 Maintaining Russia's East Asian Policy

UK University Asian scholar Sergey Radchenko (2014) and others see Russia taking a distinct foreign policy shift from its traditional focus on Europe to instead building stronger relations with the East. Putin is particularly interested in forging an alliance with China, the largest and fastest-growing Asian power, as a counterweight to US influence in Asia. This Asian policy is being shaped by a triad of forces: (1) favorable bilateral and regional relations based on strong economic ties, (2) building alliances based on achieving common strategic goals and (3) leveraging military capabilities for territorial defense and antiterrorist security (Figure 5.1).

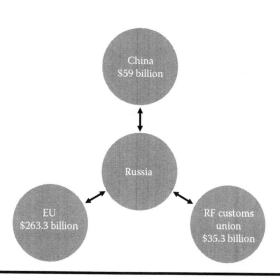

Figure 5.1 **First-half 2014 trade values for Russia's major trading partners.**

5.3.3.1 Economic Strengths

As long as oil prices remain high, demand continues strong and supplies remain economically attainable, Russia is in an enviable position of economic strength. The opposite is true when oil and gas prices drop. Russia's primary exports to resource-poor Asian markets are oil and liquefied natural gas. These energy products are in high demand in China, Japan and South Korea. In addition, China, Japan and South Korea, while unlikely to take up arms to help Russia repel an armed invader, have similar reasons for maintaining good relations with China. In addition to energy products, they all import minerals, timber and seafoods from Russia, commodities that do not compete with their own exports.

Economic ties between Russia and China, while not perfect, continue to improve. One reason is that they have few strong friends to call on for support of their interventionist adventures; Russia can count on eight formal allies; China has one: North Korea (Ikenberry 2014). Hence, they appear to be depending upon each other more and more for defensive alliances. The main security arrangements between China and Russia are incorporated in treaties that formed the Collective Security Treaty Organization (CSTO) and the Shanghai Cooperation Organization (SCO). Membership in these organizations also includes most but not all of the former Soviet Central Asian states. A joint agreement on strengthening security in the Asia-Pacific region was reached in 2005. In 2010, a branch line of the East Siberia–Pacific Ocean was constructed from Russia to the northeastern Chinese city of Daqing, the location of China's most important oil production center, with the result of stabilizing trade and security agreements between China and Russia.

In 2014, Russia and China signed agreements on two large energy supply contracts. A 30-year agreement announced in May, estimated to be valued at US$400 billion, called for delivery of gas to western China. This agreement makes it possible for China to shift some coal-fired generating plants to cleaner natural gas. A second agreement, announced in November, was a contract worth more than US$284 billion to supply Russian gas from Siberia to eastern China. Russia is thus able to reduce dependence on sales to European markets and to continue to use energy exports to Asia to maintain its favorable balance of trade well into the second quarter of the twenty-first century. However, competition may reduce the efficacy of this factor in shaping its foreign policy into the second half of the century and beyond. China asserted its intention to drill for oil in the South China Sea. The potential for regionally produced fractured supplies of natural gas and trade sanctions resulting from its incursions into Ukraine and annexation of Crimea are real concerns.

5.3.3.2 Strategic Alliances

For centuries, Russia's defense strategy in Asia involved territorial acquisitions and establishment of bases in the acquired territories and in countries it considered to be necessary for defense; that expansion was never designed to open markets for Russian exports. Modern examples in Asia include establishing bases in non-Soviet locations such as Mongolia in 1968, Vietnam in 1979 and its invasion of Afghanistan in 1979. When a strong Japan and an increasingly strong and assertive China made expansion into Asia no longer possible, Russia turned to forging defensive alliances. Gorbachev's idea of establishing an *Iron Triangle* alliance consisting of China, India and Russia to counter Western influences in Asia failed, however. India and China continue to have border disagreements that periodically result in military actions. That concept continues to surface periodically, although not always with the same partners.

China's President Xi Jinping called for creation of a new Asian security alliance of China and Russia during the May 2014 conference of 24 member states of the Conference on Interaction and Confidence-Building Measures in Asia (CICA) in Shanghai. The group could serve as a counteralliance to the United States and NATO. CICA is a foreign minister organization for talks on enhancing cooperation in promoting peace, security and stability in Asia. It is based on the concept that peace, security and stability in Asia and in the rest of the world are related. The organization avows that member states feel that peace and security in Asia and the rest of the world can be achieved through talks and cooperation that lead to a common understanding. CICA was first proposed by Kazakhstan in 1992 and formed in 1992. The Chinese president proposed an expanded role for CICA, with it functioning as a security response center and conference body of Asian country–only members. Japan is only an observer, possibly because of its close ties with the United States (Clackson 2014).

In 2014, China and Russia were both involved in external conflicts. China and Japan, together with other Southeast Asian countries, were disputing mineral rights in the South China Sea, whereas China and Vietnam were disputing China's movement of an oil rig in the South China Sea some 150 miles off the coast of Vietnam. Meanwhile, Russia is covering all its bases: in 2009, Russia sold Vietnam six diesel submarines. Deliveries began in 2014.

5.3.3.3 Military Forces

A strong, modern military and defense industry to support it is the third element necessary for achieving world power status even for nations with a large nuclear arsenal such as Russia. As will be discussed in Chapter 6, Russia's armed forces were experiencing rapid decline as early as the 1980s. That decline accelerated after the collapse of the Soviet Union. It could no longer maintain its multimillion-man army and the bases it established along its militarized border with China after the collapse of the Sino–Soviet alliance in 1969. Hostilities with

China continued through the 1970s, only improving in the 1980s under the guidance of Mikhail Gorbachev.

Despite his inability to secure agreement among senior officers during his first two terms as president of the Russian Federation, Putin has continued to work toward achieving the badly needed changes in the armed forces of Russia. Recent exercises and Russia's incursions in Ukraine suggest that some reform goals have been achieved. More importantly, joint maneuvers with the Chinese army and navy have shown that considerable progress in reform has been achieved. Russian and chinese naval forces began joint military exercises in the East China Sea in what is considered by the United States and Japan to be a show of strength following Japan's announced remilitarization.

5.4 Colonization and Deportation in the Conquered Territories

Colonization and deportation were two of the most effective policies employed for solidifying empire-building territorial gains and for curtailing unrest among conquered people during both the third and fourth Russian empires. Many, but by no means all, of Russia's colonization activities resulted in the slow fading of indigenous societies as ethnic Slavic people came to outnumber earlier populations. The greatest movement of persons under the colonial policy activity occurred during the last 30 years of the Romanov Empire in what has been described as a massive peasant migration (see Box 5.1). Millions of peasant settlers migrated from European Russia to the eastern borderlands (Sunderland 2000). Colonization usually accompanied pacification and integration of the indigenous population into a Russified social structure and universal use of the Russian language.

Deportation rather than colonization was practiced extensively over a 34-year period, beginning after the revolution in 1918 and only ending in the early 1950s. All told, the Soviet government exiled 11,890,000 people during this nearly 35-year period (Statiev 2009). Millions of those deported died, some during transportation, but most due to poor planning for the millions moved by the Soviet government. Most of those deported were members of ethnic groups who Soviets felt were a risk to the stability and growth of the socialist system. Access to information after the collapse of the Soviet system suggests that the mass movement was less a planned policy to exterminate the deported ethnic groups that they were a consequence of the do-it-now and no-questions-asked Soviet political system, poor planning, periodic shortages of food, particularly war-caused shortages, and the speed at which the movements were conducted.

BOX 5.1   THE COMBINATION OF DEPORTATION AND COLLECTIVIZATION: AN ESTONIAN EXAMPLE

Stalin's policy of collectivization of farms in Russia, Belarus and Ukraine began in the late 1920s but had to wait until after the allied victory over Nazi Germany in 1945 to begin doing so in the Baltic states. The experience in Estonia was typical of the way deportations and collectivization occurred in the Soviet Union.

Estonia, Latvia and Lithuania took advantage of the turmoil occurring in Russia during the 1920 revolution to secede and declare their independence. They remained independent until after the start of WWII. The Soviets first occupied the Baltic states in 1940 and 1941 and again after their forcing out Germans in 1944. With the ultimate goal of complete annexation, the Soviets immediately began to enforce the same domestic policies in the Baltic states that were common in the rest of the Soviet Union. Among those was collectivization of private farmlands. But, before collectivization could begin, thousands of Estonians, Latvians and Lithuanians had to be forcibly removed from their homes and deported to the East. Deportations of Baltic state intellectuals, military officers and local residents suspected of opposition began during the Soviet's first occupation.

After 1945, mass deportations of large numbers of Estonian farm families and anyone suspected of collaboration with the Germans were either deported to Siberia or Kazakhstan, killed or shipped to Siberian labor camps. By the time mass deportations ended in 1951, the number of Estonian citizens deported has been estimated to be as high as 80,000 or from 7% to 13% of the Estonian farm population. Collectivization of Estonia farms began in 1949 and, like the deportations, continued until it was considered complete in 1951 (Taagepera 1980).

5.4.1 Colonization in Muscovite Russia

Colonization during the Muscovite era was an opportunity for serfs and landlords to move to more productive farmlands, a way of staffing military garrisons in the borderlands and a way to establish and ensure boyars' (nobles) loyalty to the tsar (Kollmann 2009). Estates were either held heredity or assigned to military or government officers during their period of service. Beginning in the fifteenth century, settlers were moved from the core lands of the Muscovite empire to staff estates in newly conquered lands. The practice of colonizing newly awarded estates also became a way of revitalizing the economies of conquered regions devastated by warfare.

5.4.2 Colonization in the Romanov Empire

Colonization continued to be a tool of the Russian Empire's economic development and security policies. Turning millions of acres of steppe grasslands into more valuable fields of grain, livestock and orchards added to the wealth of the empire as well as provided a way for peasants to become greater contributors to the business of nation-building in conquered lands. Serfdom had been the law of the land in Russia since 1649 (Lynch 2003). Serfs were not slaves but were controlled by the landlords of the land on which they lived and labored. Landlords were given the right to forbid serfs from moving from the land, making their lives much the same as that of slaves if not in name.

Serfs were found mostly on the large fiefdoms in the grain-growing west of the empire, where they constituted approximately one-third of the population. Serfs were free to move where they wished only after serfdom was abolished in 1861. By this time, the empire had begun to provide some aid to families moving from overcrowded farms in the West to the new virgin lands in the East. The majority of these settlers were poor, land-hungry peasants. They brought their religion, culture and the Russian language with them: in a word, they became the agents of *Russification*.

It is important to remember that, despite the importance of colonization to the growth of the Russian Empire, the colonization practices common in the eighteenth and nineteenth centuries were not by any means restricted to Russia. Wars over these policies have been common for thousands of years. A major force behind colonization has long been the gaining, growth or maintaining of empires. Moreover, the acquisition of territory for colonization has long been the rationale for going to war. For example, Mueller (2009) found that 199 of the 244 wars fought between 1789 and 1917 were wars of colonization or decolonization; at least 149 colonial and imperial wars were waged between 1816 and 1992.

5.4.2.1 Colonization for Economic Growth

Colonization of acquired territory and deportation of indigenous populations have been used for economic development as well as for maintaining control of conquered territories. Initially, colonization of the conquered territories of the Russian Empire was entirely voluntary and was open to members of all ethnic groups in settled Russian lands. It was encouraged because it meant increased food production and resulted in improved economic development. Russian and non-Russian peasants alike were considered resources that were needed to raise agricultural production after years of peasant misuse of the increasingly crowded heartland. In the fifteenth and sixteenth centuries, colonization was done for imperial-building purposes. By the eighteenth and nineteenth centuries, it was equated with *progress* and *modernization*.

Colonization became an official state-funded policy in 1896 when a state-sponsored Resettlement Administration (RA) was set up in the Ministry of the Interior: by 1905, it had become an official agricultural policy of the state with the

Colonization Administration's transfer to the Ministry of Agriculture. The purpose of the program was "to amass a huge amount of land in order to develop Russian agriculture, in what [administrators] determined was the most economically rational and socially desirable manner" (Holquist 2010, p. 154).

Colonization at this time had come to mean more than *resettlement*. At the time, Tsar Nicholas II was building the Trans-Siberian Railroad. To secure future trade opportunities in the unsettled north and east, settlers had to be brought into the lands to build the agriculture, mining and forestry industries possible in these regions. Officials in the RA looked upon colonization as a program sponsored by the state in order to gain the greatest value from the human and productive resources of the empire. At the same time, however, military and political administrators considered the security benefits from moving ethnic Russians into the regions as the more important reason for colonization.

5.4.2.2 Colonization for Security

The use of colonization and deportation for the security of the Russian heartland had long been a goal of the Russian tsars, particularly after the experience of invasions by European armies such as those of Sweden, Poland and France and the memories of earlier invasions of Mongol hordes. Colonization was thus to be employed as a defensive weapon against the native populations in the southern regions of the empire. In this sense, colonization policies called for colonizing the peripheries of the empire with only ethnic Russians.

Russian colonization in the west and northwest, and particularly as implemented in the Baltic states of Estonia, Latvia and Lithuania, took place during two separate empire-building periods of Russian history. The first was introduced in the Russian Empire's nineteenth-century period of expansion. The second time was when the Soviet Union annexed the Baltic region during the WWII. The underlying motive for colonization was different in each of these eras. Industrialization was a driving force for moving factory workers into the Baltics to supplement the regions' agrarian populations. Total Russification became the motive for expanding the movement of ethnic Russians into the region after 1945.

5.4.2.2.1 Soviet-Era Deportations

Russia has had to cope with centuries of aggression by invaders from the East and from the West. Mongol invasions occurred in the thirteenth century; armies of Charles XII of Sweden occurred in the early eighteenth century; and Napoleon took his French army as far as Moscow in the nineteenth century. Acquiring territory that could serve as a barrier to these invasions helped in the growth of a multi-ethnic empire. Simple acquisition of territory did not ensure the docility of the regions conquered. Over time, Russia elected to simply deport the more troublesome populations while colonizing the conquered lands with ethnic Russians.

While the forced movement of people who the Russian Empire felt were potential or real dangers to the states was a common occurrence, in the Stalin era of
Soviet history saw the policy carried to its extreme. Entire territories were erased
from the map, and millions were deprived of their citizenship or forced to change
their *traditional* means of making a livelihood. The large number of *punished
people*—the ethnic groups forcibly deported during the Stalin era, has been called
ethnocide (Tishkov 1991, p. 607). By the time the policies fell into disfavor in the
decade after the end of WWII, the numbers deported had reached more than
2.7 million, among which were 1.2 million ethnic Germans, 316,000 Chechens,
165,000 Crimean Tatars, 100,000 Lithuanians, 81,000 Kalmyks, 63,000 Karachai
and 52,000 Greeks, along with a dozen or more other groups.

5.5 Conclusion

A unifying theme of Russian history since at least the early days of the Muscovite
Empire has been territorial expansion. Analysts have suggested many different reasons for this. One is the huge, open Eurasian landmass that spreads some 8000
miles from the Baltic to the Pacific, most of that distance without any major barriers or powerful enemies competing for the same territories. That same central
position of the Muscovite Empire within this landmass has been offered as a reason
for Russia's expansion westward to the Baltic Sea, eastward to the Pacific Ocean
and southward to the Black Sea. The nature of the Russian autocratic political
system has also been given as a reason for the empire's outward expansion—there
were no strong forces within the empire to contest the expansionist actions of the
tsars. Additional territories were needed to reward loyal followers (Kissinger 1994;
Donaldson and Nogee 2005).

Russia in the twenty-first century is a country playing catch-up. It has lost its
empire and the ability to exercise significant influence in many if not all of the
post-Soviet states in Europe. China, on the other hand, is a nation in ascendancy.
Both Russia and China are flexing their military muscle to gain greater regional
influence in Asia. Russia has had two wars with its separatists in Chechnya; fought
a brief way in Georgia; conducted a quick annexation of Ukrainian Crimea; continues to threaten Estonia, Latvia and Moldova; and continues to maintain military bases in Central Asian former republics. Russia's only reasonably dependable
ally in the West is Belarus; in the East, it is Kazakhstan. It appears to have lost any
chance of regaining any friendship it ever had with Ukraine, particularly in light
of continuing support to ethnic Russians in eastern Ukraine. Still, Putin continues
to be driven by dreams of reclaiming Russia's dominance in its *near abroad*, as he
continues to modernize the Russian armed forces and sell ships and combat aircraft
to China.

With the WP now a fading memory along with any favorable influence he
might have had in Ukraine, Putin has paced greater emphasis on the East. All

of Central Asia was long open only to Russian influence. In East Asia, his only competitor for the hearts and minds of locals was a weak China, and a Japan after WWII sworn to peaceful coexistence with the world. However, his efforts to cement relations with China, India and Iran along with the five Central Asian states clearly indicated that his interest in Asia has been revitalized. Russia's oil and gas income has given Putin the wherewithal to carry out his actions to reestablish a Central and Eastern Asian buffer zone.

The end of the Cold War may have put an end to the use of colonization and mass deportation as a path for colonizing conquered lands or for creating or expanding an empire. Mass murder such as has occurred in parts of Africa, in Serbia and in Cambodia appears to have replaced colonization and deportation. They, too, occur but on a much smaller scale than was more or less common practice in the last half of the twentieth century. However, traces of all three of these policies remain. Empire building by annexation, colonization or deportation has long been "one of the great epoch-defining constants in history" (Mueller 2009, p. 306). As events in the first decades of the twenty-first century reveal, there is no assurance that empire building is a thing of the past.

RUSSIA'S FOREIGN POLICY WEAPONS

Chapter 6

Reforming and Rearming Russia's Military

6.1 Introduction

Reform of the Russian military became a pressing need with dissolution of the Soviet Union. With a standing army of between 3 and 4 million troops disbursed in all of the former republics and Warsaw Pact European allies, the Soviet Army was kept under arms as an artifact of Soviet generals' penchant for mass armies prepared to fight an invasion like that of the Nazis in 1941. In 2014, the three armed forces of the Russian Federation were reported to consist of something in the neighborhood of 700,000 men, although planned for a force closer to 1 million.

6.2 The Need for Reforms

One of the largest problems facing the Russian military has been its inability to follow through with announced needed structural reforms. Generals were all trained in the tradition of a large army battle with massed tanks against an invasion by Western forces led by the North Atlantic Treaty Organization (NATO). They refused to make the changes needed to deal with modern problems against terrorists and armed insurgents and to protect ethnic Russians living in the borderlands. What was needed was a smaller, more professional force trained for quick reaction in relatively small battles. To meet the threat they had long planned for, the generals have depended upon large armies of conscripts. Twenty-five years after collapse of the Soviet Union, these plans continue to influence Russia's strategic thinking—this despite the existence of an even greater concern: Russia has no young men to draft.

The Soviet military's visions of armies of 3 million or more men are no longer achievable. Today's thinking calls for a force of 1 million men, consisting of 150,000 to 200,000 officers, 150,000 to 170,000 *contract* soldiers (volunteers) and the rest draftees serving their one-year military commitment. In 2011, this meant drafting some 300,000 young men each year. However, with the existing system of deferments, declining demographics and medical excuses, only something like 134,000 men could be drafted in that year. The shortfall in eligible draft-age men continues to exist; understaffing in military units reached from 40% to 60% that year, according to the new defense minister. Only the Southern military district, which includes forces stationed along the border with Ukraine, was manned at close to 95% of designated staffing levels.

6.2.1 Military Budgets

The total world defense spending was US$1.538 trillion in 2013 and projected to increase to US$1.547 trillion in 2014. The increased defense spending of Russia made the country surpass the spending of Britain, making it the third-largest spender after the United States and China. Still engaged in wars in Iraq and Afghanistan, the United States continued to spend far more than all other countries on defense spending. The US defense budget of $600.4 billion in 2013 was 2.7 times greater than that of China (US$112.2 billion) and Russia (US$68.2 billion) combined and nearly 11% more than 17 other nations combined. Russia continues to spend heavily for rebuilding its armed forces. In 2013, its nearly US$150 billion defense budget was the world's third highest, surpassed only by the United States and China (Young 2014). Comparing the military budget amounts in Figure 6.1 of the 20 nations with the largest 2013 defense budgets will illustrate the disparity in armaments between Russia and her close neighbors; only China spends more than Russia.

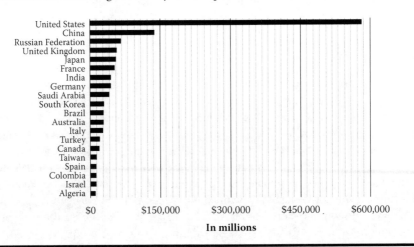

Figure 6.1   Top 20 defense budgets in 2013.

Despite financial problems, President Putin was insisting on going ahead with a ten-year, $770 billion defense rearmament program that was scheduled to begin in 2015, with the largest amount going for upgrading the Russian nuclear arsenal—now the chief defensive weapon against a feared invasion by a US-led NATO force (Young 2014). The Russian Federation now has the world's third largest defense budget after only the United States and China (Figure 6.1).

6.3 2000–2008 Military Reforms

In addition to many other sources, this section depends largely upon descriptions, translated reports and analyses of several versions of Putin-era reforms and reorganizations of the Russian armed forces. Important sources included a 2011 monograph by UK professor Rod Thornton for the US Army's Strategic Studies Institute (SSI) and a 2014 report by Major Kaspars Mazitans of the Latvian National Armed Forces, published in the *Baltic Security and Defense Review*, a publication the Baltic Defense College in Tartu, Estonia.

6.3.1 Objections to Proposed Reform

By 2002, it was clear that after the breakup of the Soviet Empire it was never going to be reborn. However, among many senior officers, the justification for maintaining a large army for defense against another invasion by the West remained as important as ever. The consensus was that the announced expansion eastward of NATO and the 1999 NATO war against Russia's long-time ally Serbia were clear indications that Mother Russia was again encircled by its enemies—this time without a security cordon of captive states in place (Jackson 2002).

6.3.2 Effects of the Chechnya Insurgencies

Most analysts generally agree that the reforms currently underway in the armed forces of the Russian Federation have been under discussion almost since the 1991 dissolution of the Soviet Union, but the need for the changes is considered critical as a result of modern wars with Russian Chechnya in 1994 to 1996 and 1999 to 2000 and the Chechnya insurgency phase from 2000 to 2009. However, the problems of the army were brought excruciatingly home during the 2008 war with Georgia. The main problem with the Army was that it was a 4-million-man army designed to fight a land war like the Nazi invasion of the Second World War. Not only was it far larger than could be maintained; in many ways, it was also still armed with Second World War technology.

The long series of reform attempts actually began as early as the presidency of Mikhail Gorbachev who started the reforms that facilitated the end of the Cold War. His first success was bringing strength down from 5 to 4 million. When Boris

Yeltsin replaced Gorbachev, he continued to push for cutbacks, including the end of the conscript and large reserve force practice and a change to an all-volunteer military. A Yeltsin edict in 1996 required the armed forces to begin *professionalization* and do away with the draft. Senior officers successfully fought the plan, however, and continued as before. Yeltsin was able to incur further cuts in staffing, from the army's 4 million men in 203 divisions at the end of the Soviet Union to 2.8 million by 1992; most of the decline was the result of the deferments and decline in the size of the pool of men available, not to any definitive action by the military.

The army had declined to just 1.4 million men when Putin succeeded Yeltsin in 2000; Putin continued to push for armed forces reform. The military in force in 2000 was large on paper but in reality was "a largely ineffectual fighting force and certainly not capable of deploying, with any appreciable size, on any expeditionary operation. Putin lamented that 'The army ... has 1.4 million men, but there is no one to wage war'" (Thornton 2011).

Putin succeeded in the 2003 enactment of the first major reform plan of his presidency, the federal targeted program for the Conversion of the Military to Contract Service. The plan called for the number of contract personnel (i.e., volunteers) to increase from 22,000 in 2003 to 148,000 by 2008 despite the senior officers' resistance to any personnel reduction (Arbatov 2004). The term of conscript service was dropped from two years to 18 months, and then in 2007 to one year. The General Staff's foot-dragging and downright obstruction resulted in a cut in the target number of professionals from 148,000 to 133,000, and then to 125,000.

By 2009, the program was announced as a success, and the 100,000-strong force target was achieved. However, in February 2010, the general staff of General Makarov admitted that the transition to an all-volunteer army was a failure. Many high-ranking officers urged cancelling the program entirely. Funds in the budget for the 2004–2007 period for its implementation had been siphoned off for such purposes as procuring weapons and raising salaries; a large number of volunteers were discharged in 2010, leaving only a little more than 100,000 still in the service. Despite the lack of support for the idea, President Medvedev approved increasing the number of contract personnel to 425,000 by 2017 (Nichol 2011). Budgets for reform were consistently redirected maintaining over-large forces and new equipment; the needed maintenance was ignored, resulting in degrading of the army's technological and warfighting capabilities.

Recognizing the need for help in achieving desired reform, in February 2007, Putin appointed Anatoliy Serdyukov as the new defense minister. Serdyukov began with a housecleaning of officers suspected of corruption. Meanwhile, the size of the army continued to drop; in his first year of office, the military was 1.3 million strong, with Serdyukov planning to cut another 200,000. In 2008, there were 355,300 officers and 140,000 warrant officers on duty. Cuts were to bring the numbers down by 2012 to just 150,000 officers; the warrant rank was to be discontinued and all warrant officers either discharged or appointed to other ranks, which were to be increased from 623,500 to 850,000—180,000 of which were to be volunteers.

6.3.3 Impact of the War with Georgia

The war with Georgia brought the proposed changes to a halt and revealed the sorry state of the Russian Army and Air Force. Russian tanks were obsolete and did not change much beyond what was available at the end of Second World War. The troops lacked arms, equipment and leadership; electronic equipment either failed to work or broke down under battlefield conditions. Russian satellites—many had simply dropped out of the sky years earlier—were unable to provide global positioning data to warring troops. Despite these and other difficulties, Russia won the little war and Georgia lost South Ossetia and Abkhazia, territories under Georgian sovereignty with large ethnic Russian populations. Senior Russian officers still fighting the reforms were forced to accept a significant retreat in their efforts to maintain a large army capable of beating an invasion by NATO forces. However, that reform required several iterations.

Defense Minister Serdyukov and the Chief of the General Staff Nikoilai Makarov cooperated in implementing core elements of the 2008 reforms until Serdyukov's replacement in November 2012. Agitation by members of the reduced officer corps and arms industry representatives is thought to have forced curtailment of the reforms and Serdyukov's replacement by Sergei Shoigu (Klein and Pester 2014). A military outsider, Shoigu brought to the post years of administrative and political infighting experience. An economist by training, he had served as Minister for Emergency Situations, a Moscow district governor and head of the Russian tax service. His style is to work with generals on reforms rather than by forcing his will upon the military establishment.

The 2013–2014 confrontation and threatened military action in Ukraine have slowed the pace of reforms but have not curtailed them. An analysts' consensus opinion is that the reforms have improved Russia's military but remain limited in scope (Weitz and Zimmerman 2014). The Russian military force in July 2014 consisted of approximately 845,000 military personnel with another 2 million with recent military experience and ready for a potential mobilization. Military pay has roughly tripled since 2012; the number of contract personnel continues to grow; some housing improvements have occurred and veteran's benefits improved.

6.4 2008–2015 Military Reforms and Reorganizations

The Russian army's poor performance in the 2008 war with Georgia reinforced the critical need for reforming and reorganizing all branches of the Russian military. Several problems that surfaced during the war were particularly disturbing. The first was the lack of a coordinated command-and-control system (C2). During the war, commands—often conflicting—were received from three different command levels: the General Staff, the Military district headquarters and the 58th Army headquarters. Infantry and airborne regiments were independent and under their own command structure. Headquarters were overstaffed: there were 52,000 officers in the different levels of command, whereas there were only 100,000 combat troops involved.

The second issue was the inappropriate organization; fully half of the force consisted of officers and warrant officers. In addition, the army included too many senior grade officers and far too few lieutenants and captains. Mazitans (2014) described the force as being *egg shaped* rather than pyramid shaped. The third issue was the low combat readiness of the force. In 2008, only 13% of the total Russian military was combat ready; the land army was only 17% combat ready, the air force 7% and the navy 70%. At the time, only the strategic missile and airborne forces were considered combat ready. The fourth issue was the poor quality of the equipment with which soldiers were armed. Essentially no large-scale military armament or equipment purchases were made from the collapse of the Soviet Union in 1991 to 2008. The troops were armed with old weapons systems and equipment, much of which were not only obsolete—some did not work at all. More than half of the air force equipment was faulty.

6.4.1 Objectives of the Reforms

As a result of the sorry state of the army and air force revealed in the war with Georgia, when appointed in 2012, Defense Minister Sergei Shoigu would have a number of very important reforms to implement. Objects underlying the reforms included the following:

1. Increase combat readiness and capabilities
2. Continue reducing personnel numbers
3. Reorganize the structure and limit the number of officers
4. Build a professional noncommissioned officer (NCO) system
5. Reorganize and centralize military education
6. Reorganize the military district system
7. Transform land forces from a division base to a brigade base
8. Reduce the number of units and bases
9. Begin outsourcing logistic support
10. Improve military housing and social services

6.4.1.1 Reorganizing the Russian Army

The reorganization of the Russian army that began in 2008 has had some definite successes and some disappointing setbacks. Many of the successes are too new to determine their long-term effectiveness. The chief successes may be the shift from a regimental structure to a brigade system, overall reduction in the overall size of the military, cuts in the number of officers, the reform of the complicated and inefficient C2, small gains in the number of professional NCOs and volunteers, improved pay and benefits for serving personnel and their families and some acquisition of new equipment. Possibly the most important of failure in the reformation has been the slow transition to a volunteer army and the continued reliance upon a highly unpopular draft. Maintenance and repair of equipment remain less than satisfactory. Finally, large-scale corruption in the defense industry production and procurement system remains a problem.

6.4.1.2 Command-and-Control and Organizational Changes

One of the more pressing changes needed was reforming the C2. Changes at the top include revising the military administrative division system. Until 2010, the country was divided into six military districts: Moscow, Leningrad, Volga-Urals, North Caucasus, Siberian and Far Eastern. These were reorganized in 2012 to just four new Operational Strategic Commands (OSCs; see Figure 6.2): Western (West OSC), Central (Center OSC), Southern (South OSC) and Eastern (East OSC). The West OSC is responsible for defense issues in the Moscow and Leningrad districts and the Baltic and Northern fleets. In peacetime, these four districts are referred to as military districts; in times of war, their titles were to be changed to OSCs.

All OSCs are joint commands, with joint control over Army, Air Force and Naval Force in their districts—with exceptions. Airborne Forces are an independent branch under direct control of the Chief of Defense. Also, separate commands are for air assault brigades under central control. Strategic Missile Forces and the Aerospace Defense Forces are also independent branches. The old system for four levels in the C2 has been changed to a three-level system: OSC, Army headquarters and brigade.

Figure 6.2 **Regional distribution of Russian military districts after reorganization.**

6.4.1.3 Land Forces Reorganization

The reorganization of land forces from the division structure to brigade structure was included in the major reforms. Russian World War II divisions consisted of 50,000 men; an average regiment size was 2500; the average Russian brigade consists of 4000 to 4500 men. The Russian Land Forces in 2010 were reorganized into 39 infantry brigades, 21 artillery and rocket launcher brigades, 7 air defense brigades, 12 communications brigades, 2 electronic warfare brigades and 4 air assault brigades. A typical infantry brigade includes brigade headquarters; three motorized rifle battalions; one tank battalion; two self-propelled howitzer battalions; and one battalion each of anti-tank, surface-to-air missile, air defense, rocket artillery, engineer, repair and maintenance, communication, logistics, reconnaissance, command and artillery battery, nuclear, biological and chemical company and one radio-electronic warfare company.

In 2014, the Russian Ground Forces remained heavily mechanized with 15,500 tanks, 27,607 armored personnel carriers (now armored fighting vehicles or AFVs), 5990 self-propelled guns, 3781 multiple-launch rocket systems and 4625 towed artillery pieces (Global Fire Power 2014).

6.4.1.3.1 Reorganizing the Russian Air Force

The Air Force is the second largest military arm in Russia. Few reforms were included early in the overhaul of the Russian military. Possibly the most significant early change was the transfer of all of the army's aviation personnel and equipment to the Air Force in 2003. In 2008, Russia's newest aircraft and air defense systems were from 15 to 20 years old. Command-and-control reforms began in December 2009. In 2014, the Air Force had a total of 3082 aircraft of all types. Of these, 736 were fighters/interceptors, and 1289 were fixed-wing attack aircraft. The others 730 transports, 303 trainers, 973 helicopters, and 114 attack helicopters (Global Fire Power 2014).

The planned new organization established independent commands: Air Force Command, Air Defense Command, Long-Range Aviation Command and Military Transport Aviation Command. All commands have their own air bases, defense and logistic units. The Long-Range Command controls all long-range bombers, refueling tankers and Navy missile–carrying aircraft. The Military Transport command transports troops as needed, delivers airborne forces and transports personnel and equipment. Territorial commands were created to match the army's four-regional-district structure. In 2010, the reorganization focused on reducing and consolidating the number of active air bases. The Air Force has planned to replace 80% of the air fleet by 2020.

This reorganization plan was superseded by the decision to merge all air force aviation and army aviation, antiaircraft defense forces, missile defense forces and space forces into what would be known as the Russian Aerospace Forces. A December 18, 2014 announcement in the Russian news agency reported that the consolidation was expected to be completed by the summer of 2015. No ground forces units were to be included in consolidated Aerospace Forces.

6.4.1.3.2 Reorganizing the Russian Navy

The Russian Navy, while in many ways in better shape than the ground forces, was in dire need of the same reform processes as well as all but a few special units. The 1990s were hard on the navy. Chronic shortages of funding for repairs and maintenance and of personnel with an oversupply of officers had resulted in the loss of 40% of the number of ships it possessed. By 2007, that loss included 85% of its active warships and 60% of its naval personnel (Box 6.1).

Among the common objects for the reform included in the reform process that begun in 2008 were the reorganization of the navy's C2 and discontinuation of many special command headquarters and units; personnel reductions, including the numbers of officers and warrant officers; reorganization of coastal defense and marine forces to bring them to combat readiness; transfer of naval aviation and air bases to Air Force control; and integration of submarine command and fleets into the new military district (OSC) command structure (Global Security 2014; Mazitans 2014).

BOX 6.1 RUSSIAN MILITARY REFORMS INCLUDE MORE MISSILES AND NUCLEAR SUBMARINES

In January 2015, Julian Borger, diplomatic editor of *The Guardian* newspaper, warned that the US and NATO reaction to Russia's deployment and external marketing of a new cruise missile and building of new nuclear missile submarines threatens to return the world to an era of nuclear rivalry and Cold War threats of mutual mass destruction. Russia is building a new generation of ballistic missile submarines and attack submarines that are equal to or superior to US vessels in "performance and stealth." Russian submarines with missiles capable of carrying nuclear warheads that regularly approach the US coast on training exercises and to observe US aircraft carrier battle groups have been reported.

Russia has announced that it is also reintroducing nuclear missile railroad trains that are continuously moving to make them harder to hit in an attack, increasing the number of nuclear warheads for missiles launched by submarines, testing a new medium-range missile and marketing a new missile that, complete with its launcher, can be hidden inside a shipping container until it is fired. The United States has warned that it may reintroduce cruise missiles into Europe, and a number of US legislators are pushing for "a more robust American response to the Russian [cruise] missile" (Borger 2015).

6.4.1.3.2.1 Fleet Reorganization

By 2012, reform and reorganization of the navy has resulted in closure of 240 naval units, a decline of active naval bases to 123 and discontinuance of all naval reserve units. Attaching all fleets to three of the new military districts (none for the Central district) was achieved. Naval command and control was downsized and placed under military district command; fleet headquarters were reduced from their position as a separate force like the Army and Air Force to that of a coordinator under district headquarters command. The Naval Central Command Post was abolished in 2011, with the headquarters staff reduced from 850 officers to just 90.

In 2003, Russian naval strength consisted of 300 ships of all types and 400 aircraft and helicopters. By 2014, the number of ships had increased to 352, the types and numbers of which included a single aircraft carrier, 4 frigates, 13 destroyers, 74 corvettes, 63 submarines (which include nuclear and diesel-powered types), 65 coastal defense craft and 34 minelayers and minesweeper vessels. All naval aircraft were assigned to the Air Force (Global Fire Power 2014; Global Security 2014).

6.5 All-Forces Personnel Reductions

A goal of Russian military reform advocates since the 1980s was reduction in the number of officers and men in all branches of service. That goal was to be nearly fully complete by 2012. The key step was cutting the total authorized ground forces personnel from 1.34 million to 1 million while also changing the shape of the military from an egg shape to a pyramid structure. In the egg shape, the largest number of officers was the combined number of colonels, lieutenant colonels and majors. In the pyramid structure, the lowest three ranks make up the largest group (Table 6.1). The warrant officer was to be abolished, with the 160,000 warrant

Table 6.1 Changes in the Numbers of Army Officer Positions from 2008 to 2012

Military Rank	Positions in 2008	Positions in 2012	Change Percent
General	1106	866	−22%
Colonel	15,365	3141	−80%
Lieutenant colonel	19,300	7500	−61%
Major	99,550	30,000	−70%
Captain	90,000	40,000	−56%
First lieutenant	30,000	35,000	+17%
Second lieutenant	20,000	26,000	+30%

Source: Mazitans, K., *Baltic Security & Defense Review*, 16(1), 20, 2014.

officers in service in 2008 to either be discharged or changed to NCO ranks. As of 2011, the Russian army was reported to consist of 200,000 officers, 184,000 NCOs and approximately 600,000 conscripts.

6.6 Rearming the Russian Military

Reform of the Russian military not only included restructuring and downsizing but also rearming all branches. As noted earlier, little or no replacement or modernization occurred during the 1990s under Yeltsin. Buoyed by very high prices for its oil and gas exports, plans were announced for extensive spending for military equipment and repair along with renewed spending on research and development. Failure to get all interested parties on board and Yeltsin's interest only in cutting costs killed several early military reform proposals. Under Presidents Putin and Medvedev, the first of two new approaches began in 2006 with implementation of the State Armament Plans (SAPs): 2007–2017 (SAP 2015). This was followed by yet another effort in 2011: 2011–2020 (SAP 2020).

6.6.1 The 2007–2015 Rearmament Plan

The first substantial Putin-era reform plan (SAP 2015) ran into problems early, as the weakened defense industry was unable to comply with procurement and delivery requirements. In a 2008 speech, Putin's handpicked successor President Dmitry Medvedev called for the rearming program to occur at a rate of 9%–11% per year for the following decade, with a goal of modernizing 70% of the Russian military by 2010. At the time, the defense industry was only able to achieve rearming goals at a rate of just 2% per year (Gorenburg 2010).

6.6.2 The 2011–2020 Plan

When the problems of the defense industry were seen to be insurmountable, Medvedev and his military advisors decided to revise the SAP 2015 plan with more achievable targets: SAP 2020. By 2011, the restructuring of the military called for in SAP 2015 had been completed; the need for rearming was becoming critical. When completed as planned, the rearmament is projected to cost 19.5 trillion roubles (approximately US$616 billion), with the distribution of funds to be allocated according to Table 6.2.

With 26% of the more than 19 trillion roubles allocated for long-term reform, reorganization and rearming of Russia's military forces, the Russian Navy will receive the largest percentage of the SAP 2020 military reform budget. The Aerospace Forces' 21% share is the second largest amount (Table 6.3). Prior to the 2014 steep drop in income from oil and gas exports, Russia had planned to

Table 6.2   Spending Distribution of SAP 2010 Budget Allocation

Category	Total Share	Russian Roubles	US Dollars
Allocation amount	100%	19.5 trillion	616 billion
Weapons and equipment	70%	13.65 trillion	431 billion
Repairs and upgrades	14%	2.73 trillion	86 billion
Research and development	16%	3.12 trillion	98.6 billion

Source: Mazitans, K., *Baltic Security & Defense Review*, 16(1): 5–45, 2014; Odia, R., Russian rearming program, Ukraine crisis just tip of the iceberg. *Prophecy News Watch* (March 4). Available at http://www.prophecynewswatch.com /7014/March04/042.html (retrieved October 29), 2014.

Table 6.3   Force Share of SAP 2020 Rearming Plan with Equipment Examples

Branch	% of Total	Est. Amount (in Trillion Roubles)	Sample Types of Equipment
Navy, including naval nuclear force	14.4	2.6	12 submarines (nuclear or diesel); 51 ships including 15 frigates and up to 25 corvettes
Air Force	27.8	5.0	600 aircraft and 1000 helicopters
Aerospace defense	22.2	4.0	92 batteries of various SAM missile systems; integrated C2; 100 spacecraft
Army and airborne troops	14.4	2.6	2300 mail battle tanks, 2000 artillery systems, more than 30,000 vehicles
Strategic Missile Force	5.6	1.0	280 ICBMs, development of new missiles
Misc., others	15.6	2.8	New C2 and communication and reconnaissance systems; new infantry equipment
Totals[a]	100	18–19	

Source: Fedorov, Y., State armament program 2020: Current state and outlook. *Trialogue Club International*. Available at http://www.pircenter.org/media /content/files/11/13781899761.pdf, 2013 (accessed October 29, 2014), from open source material.

[a] Total as estimates due to rounding.

spend US$22 billion for new weapons and for modernizing the force. Space projects planned included development of advanced rocket technology, modernization of the space center and development of new space launch vehicles.

6.7 Conclusion

One of the difficulties in determining the actual force makeup and procurement results of the Russian military is the lack of transparency in budget planning and disbursement. In the past, funds allocated for new armaments and training had to be spent on basic food and other personnel expenses. It was not unknown for facilities commanders to farm out troops for local labor to augment insufficient operating funds. Moreover, the military budget also includes funding for a large number of internal security organizations that do not publicize their activities. Also included are a number of nontraditional and special forces controlled by different branches of the government. These include units of the Ministry of Internal Affairs and other armed organizations not controlled by the defense ministry. These include internal security forces, border patrol troops and other leftover units from the Soviet Union days. In theory, military reform applies to these groups as well as the traditional and special-purpose branches of the military (Arbatov 2004).

Efforts to reform the Russian military have never been easy. Doing so became even more difficult with the decisions by Gorbachev and Yeltsin to permit, and in many cases encourage, military officers to seek election to the national parliament, where military reform bills often face difficulty getting out of committee. In addition, when Putin became president, he appointed many of his former colleagues in the FSB that replaced the KGB to positions of authority in the government where they are able to influence reform decisions. Yet, despite these and additional difficulties, there have been a number of important changes and upgrading in all branches of the Russian military. One change that has not yet occurred is replacement of the current conscript system with a professional, all-voluntary force.

Chapter 7

Russia's Undeclared Cyber Wars

7.1 Introduction

Post-Soviet Russia continues to exercise a *get-tough* attitude toward its former possessions. With each successful foray, its treatment toward the newly independent states that were once part of the Russian Empire becomes more and more assertive if not more aggressive. Neither US sanctions nor North Atlantic Treaty Organization's (NATO's) tepid verbal reprimands seem to have had much effect in controlling Russia's aggressive foreign policy. This chapter examines some of the cyber warfare tactics Russia is suspected of supporting or actually using against its smaller neighbors and *enemies*. These cyber attacks have also taken place in association with armed incursions (Table 7.1).

Marine Corps General James Cartwright, former vice chairman of the US Joint Chiefs of Staff, defined cyber war as "the deployment of cyber capabilities where the primary purpose is to achieve military objectives or effects in or through cyberspace" (Cartwright 2013, p. 8). A detailed dictionary of US cyberspace concepts and accepted terms and definitions is included in Appendix I. Russia's use of these weapons goes back at least to the Yeltsin years, albeit this time, they were used in Chechnya as political weapons against Russia (Tikk et al. 2008). Chechen separatists used the Internet for delivering pro-Chechen and anti-Russian propaganda. During the second Chechen war in 1999–2000, Russians were accused of hacking into Chechen websites. US and NATO computers were attacked from an unidentified source during the 1999 Kosovo campaign, although Russia had been an ally of Serbia and strongly objected to the war. The allegedly Russian state-sponsored hacker group APT28 was identified in an October 2014 newspaper article as the hackers behind

Table 7.1 Comparison of Cyber Warfare in Post-Soviet States

	Estonia 2007	*Georgia 2008*	*Lithuania 2008*
Triggering event	Political events: relocating a Soviet memorial	Surprise attack by Georgia against South Ossetian forces resulted in Russian incursion; cyber and military attacks	Political events: Lithuanian law banning display of Soviet era symbols and playing of Soviet national anthem
Duration	April 27–May 18, 2007	July 19–August 27, 2008	June 28–June 30, 2008
Cyber targets	Political, services (banking, internet service providers (ISPs), online media, personal and random)	Political: president, parliament, bank, government sites, online services, ISPs	Political and public sites (all hosted on the same ISP)
Damage	Unestimated	Unestimated	Unestimated
Attack types	DoS, DDoS, defacement, email and content spam; some target hacks using SQL injections	DoS, DDoS, defacement, TCP SYN, TCP RST floods, higher intensity attacks than Estonia 2007	Defacement, DoS
Attackers	Unknown. Attacks globally sourced using paid botnets and random internet users; instructions widely available on the internet	Unknown. Attacks globally sourced using paid botnets and random internet users; instructions widely available on the internet	Attacks via proxy servers; confusing info on server location; some originate from servers outside of Lithuania, others to servers in eastern Lithuania
Defensive and organizational actions	CERT-EE and network of specialists and international cooperation; technical countermeasures; political, media and law enforcement	Georgian University CERT, CERT-EE, CERT-PL, CERT-FR cooperation; political and media coverage; technical countermeasures	CERT-LT, academic and research network CERT cooperation; political and media coverage; technical countermeasures; police action

Source: NATO Cooperative Cyber Defense Centre of Exellence (CCDCOE) 2008.

the attacks to the governments of Georgia, the Caucasus and Eastern Europe and conducting cyber espionage with attacks on NATO and defense contractors in Western Europe (Fox-Brewster 2014).

7.2 Cyber Tactics

In 2007 and 2008, Russia conducted a series of soft and hard attacks against several of its former satellites; the first was a bloodless cyber war; the second was also a cyber war, but this one occurred along with a shooting war. The first substantial attack began on April 26, 2007 against Estonia. The second began on August 7, 2008 against Georgia. The next documented occurrence took place in 2009 when Lithuania was hit by cyber attacks; in a case of IP spoofing, Russian flags were placed onto more than 300 Lithuanian websites, and anti-Lithuania songs were played. The last cyber attack occurred in Ukraine. Another 2009 attack that occurred began on January 28 when Kyrgyzstan's two main servers were hit with DoS attacks, essentially stopping all of its email service. Lithuania cyberspace was hit again in 2003. A new target was struck in 2014 when hackers reported to be from Russia struck again, this time against Ukraine; as had occurred in Georgia, hackers attacked in concert with more bloodletting: at a small cost to Russia, it ended with the addition of more than 18,000 square miles of Crimea to the rebuilding Russian Empire.

The attack against Estonia employed cyber weapons exclusively. It was more of an application of cyberterrorism than warfare; no shots were fired; no lives were lost on either side. The cyber attacks against Georgia were followed a day after they began with an armored invasion of Georgian territory. By any definition, Russia's invasion of South Ossetia, an integral part of the Georgian state despite its independent administration, was an act of war.

Regardless of the rationale behind the attacks or the details of the tactics used, these and the subsequent aggressive actions signaled the willingness of Russia to use whatever weapon or weapons it believed appropriate to intimidate the small sovereign states that until 1990 were components of first the Russian and later the Soviet Empires. In 2014, Russia began the next step in its plan to reassemble its former empire. This time, the victim was Ukraine.

The row of former Soviet territories in North and Central Europe for which it still holds a *special interest* includes Finland, Estonia, Latvia, Lithuania, Kaliningrad, Belarus, Moldova and Ukraine (Map 7.1). Putin has never hesitated to inform the West that these, together with similar newly independent states to Russia's south and east, constitute regions of special interests, and Russia will go to extreme ends to protect those interests.

The excuse given by Putin for intimidating states like Estonia, Latvia, Lithuania and Ukraine is Russia's sacred commitment to protect ethnic Russians living in those states. The relatively good minority relations between Russia and Belarus are

Map 7.1 Ukraine, including the Crimean Peninsula.

the model that Putin would like to see expanded to other former Soviet republics, although some analysts suggest that Russia's aggression in Ukraine and annexation of Crimea have moved Belarus to question whether to continue with Kazakhstan to join Russia in formation of the Eurasian Union (Wilson 2014). The trade union between Russia and its closest neighbors is scheduled to commence in 2015. The announced institutional model for the Russian Union is the European Union (EU). One of the causes for the Maidan riots and demonstrations in Kiev was the Ukrainian president's decision to reject a trade agreement substituting a plan to join the Russian Union instead.

7.3 2007: Cyber War with Estonia

Estonia, the northernmost and smallest former Soviet Union republic on the Baltic Sea, shares a long border along with Russia. Quoting unnamed sources, Richard Clarke (Clarke and Knake 2010, p. 30) noted that some analysts were calling the cyber attacks on Estonia WWI for Web War One. The weapons used in this war are listed in Box 7.1.

This proximity and strategic importance location on the Gulf of Finland justified Soviet colonization after regaining Estonia during World War II. As a consequence of the Soviet-era occupation, in 2014, more than 25% of the population of Estonia consisted of ethnic Russians. The map of Estonia shows its long eastern border with Russia and its northern border the Gulf of Finland, which provides maritime access to Russia's old capitol St. Petersburg (Map 7.2). To the south, it shares a border with Latvia, the Baltic nation with an even larger Russian minority. Estonia's two northeastern provinces and the capital city of Tallinn house Estonia's largest concentrations of ethnic Russians. These regions are also the location of the

BOX 7.1 WEAPONS IN THE CYBER WAR ARSENAL

For as long as there has been Internet, cyber warriors have been drawn to ways to prove their skills by sabotaging or simply annoying other software users. As their skills have improved, so have the number of weapons they use and the potential impact of their actions. In the realm of cyber warfare, these weapons—and others—are known to be used (Pool 2013):

- Denial-of-service (DoS) programs that introduce a digital assault on a network, resulting in an avalanche of access requests that, in turn, cuts networking to a crawl or freezes it altogether.
- Distributed denial-of-service (DDoS) programs, more concentrated versions of the DoS attacks, that use multiple *zombie* computers—often by the thousands—in a massive attack on a single network. The collection of massed computers are referred to as a *botnet*.
- Permanent denial-of-service (PDoS) programs that cause enough damage to a network that it is permanently shut down; new hardware is needed before the network is again operational.
- Malicious programming, often in the form of a *virus*, disrupts the normal computer functions or allows a perpetrator to gain control of the computer. An upgraded version is the *worm* that acts like a virus but uses information transfer to spread from computer to computer—even as far as allowing external control of the device. An even more malicious version is *polymorphic malicious programming*, a software program that changes its computer code each time it replicates itself. Because than can occur millions of times, it makes the software extremely difficult to detect. A fourth version of malicious programming is known as a *logic bomb*. This *bomb* can remain dormant for long periods, lulling the program user into thinking that it performs an important function but, when activated, allows remote control of the computer, allowing it to become a *zombie* unit in a botnet.
- IP spoofing is a software program that lets a hacker create a web page identical to a trusted online web page, such as that of a financial institution. The false web page tricks the user into inserting personal information such as credit card numbers and social security numbers.
- SQL injection. SQL international coding is the language for database management and web page development. Hackers use the language to gain access to databases, thereby obtaining usernames and passwords in the database to conduct cyber espionage or to launch other malicious cyber attacks such as logic bombs.

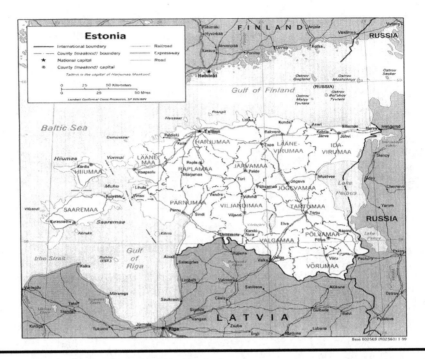

Map 7.2 Estonia and bordering states.

Estonian shale oil and gas deposits; this important resource extends across northern Estonia and into Russia. These deposits make up most of Estonia's energy needs; only 15% of its energy comes from imported Russian natural gas.

Estonian cyberspace was invaded on April 27, 2007, shortly after the Estonian government went ahead with plans to move a memorial—the Bronze Soldier—commemorating the Red Army's liberation of Estonia from the Nazis. To the Russians, moving the memorial was seen as additional "marginalization of their ethnic identity," whereas native Estonians considered the Bronze Soldier a reminder of Soviet oppression (Herzog 2011, p. 51). The memorial was to be moved from its location in central Tallinn to a less prominent nearby military cemetery. The announcement resulted in riots among ethnic Russians living in Estonia, followed by a dangerous and expensive cyberterrorism attack against Estonia's economic and government institutions. Although the perpetrators of the attack were never identified to everyone's satisfaction, subsequent investigations point to *Nashi*—a Russian group founded by Vladimir Putin and funded by the Russian Business Network. Security analysts agree that Russian officials encouraged the hackers' actions by accusing Estonia of "altering history, perpetrating human rights violations, and encouraging fascism" (Herzog 2011, p. 55). The DoS attack targeted Estonia's largest banks, cut online access to its largest newspapers, severely restricted web traffic and shut down telephone lines used by emergency services (Shackelford 2010; Pool 2013).

Estonia has long been Europe's *most wired country*, relying heavily on the Internet for much of its communications infrastructure. Government functions, parliament's email, electric power grids, safety and security services and water supplies are Internet dependent; 97% of bank transactions, income tax filing and utility payments occurred online—it gave Estonia the right to claim the title of *paperless government*. In March 2007, Estonia allowed Internet voting for parliamentary elections, becoming the first country to do so.

As for the cyberterrorism attack on Estonia, while severe and costly—one bank alone announced losses of more than US$1 million—the consequences could have been even more damaging; the odds are high that future cyberterrorism attacks will be more damaging. One analyst predicts that

> In future assaults, hackers may target a state's traffic lights, water supply, power grids, air traffic controls, or even its military weapon systems. As the Estonian crisis indicates, the Internet has become a powerful asymmetric tool for transnational groups who view themselves as disenfranchised and seek to intimidate the nation-states and other actors presumably responsible for their grievances. This is an issue of national sovereignty, as the digital networks and critical infrastructure targeted by the hackers are the property of—or on the territory of—nation-states.
>
> **S. Herzog**
> *Journal of Strategic Security, 2011*

Both the perpetrators and defenders in the Estonian cyber crisis have learned what to do next time to both improve the efficacy of their incursions and to protect against similar incursions in the future. China, which has an unenviable record of committing cyber crime against commercial and military targets, particularly in the United States, has likely joined Russia in analyzing Estonia's weaknesses and the West's responses to improve their cyber warfare capabilities. Russia has been linked to cyber attacks on Georgia in 2008 and Poland in 2009. Four organizations have some responsibility for information security or offensive applications: the Russian Security Council, the Federal Agency for Government Communications and Information, the State Technical Commission and the Russian Armed Forces. Despite the shock value of the cyberwar assault on Estonia and immediate disruption to that nation's government and banking, the consensus among military analysts is that Estonia suffered very little long-term damage from the attack (Singer and Friedman 2014).

Meanwhile, the EU, NATO and the US military have taken steps to better defend against future cyberterrorism while also developing countermeasures. In April 2008, NATO adopted a uniform policy on cyber defense and formed the Cyber Defense Management Authority to coordinate and centralize cyber defenses in all member states. In August of the same year, NATO's cyber security headquarters, the

Cooperative Cyber Defense Center of Excellence, was established in Tallinn. In 2010, the EU included cyber warfare defense elements in its Internal Security Strategy.

7.4 2008: Cyber War with Lithuania

Lithuania was the target of hacker attacks in July 2008, three days after it passed a law outlawing the use of Soviet and communist symbols. More than 300 websites were attacked, some by DoS attacks and others vandalized with the Soviet hammer and sickle. A map of Lithuania and adjoining states is shown in Map 7.3. The Kaliningrad Oblast possession of Russia is seen at the lower-west corner. A treaty signed between Lithuania and Russia guarantees Russian land access to the enclave (prior to 1945, this area was East Prussia).

According to Ashmore (2007), before the attacks and the passage of the law, ties between Russia and Lithuania were never strong since Lithuania declared its renewed independence from the Soviet Union in 1991 and became even more fragile when Russia refused to compensate Lithuanian victims of Soviet labor camps. Lithuania also resented Russia's usage of its energy resources for political gain. Lithuania, an EU member state only since 2004, blocked talks of a Russian–EU partnership. This and other acrimony led later analysts to conclude that the attacks

Map 7.3 Lithuania and adjacent states.

came from hackers within Russia, with or without official sanction. Moreover, the underlying rationale for the cyber attacks against Lithuania followed the pattern of cyber attacks against Estonia; both attacks followed government action that was unpopular to Russians.

7.5 2009: Kyrgyzstan under Cyber Attack

The next country to suffer a DoS cyber attack from computers in Russia was Kyrgyzstan. Kyrgyzstan's two main Internet servers came under DoS attacks on January 18, 2009, shutting down websites and email within the country. The attacks occurred on the same day that the Russian government was pressuring Kyrgyzstan to stop US access to the airbase at Bishkek.

The cyber attacks in Kyrgyzstan were more of a nuisance than a successful curtailment of government, social or economic services. The United States continued to use the base from its opening in 2001 until June 2014 when its closure began—although at a much higher rental rate. The base was the main logistic center supporting US war and NATO efforts in Afghanistan. As seen in Map 7.4, Bishkek is located in the north central center of the country near to the border with Kazakhstan.

The DDoS attacks appeared to be directed at any oppositional organization or group that did not support the closure of the airbase. While it is again impossible to prove whether the Russian government was behind the attacks, the implication is that

Map 7.4　Kyrgyzstan and bordering states.

cyber attacks will be used against any opposition to the Russian government (Ashmore 2009). Personnel and cargo airlift missions have now been moved to the Forward Operating Site Mihail Kogalniceanu near the Black Sea port of Constanta in Romania.

7.6 2009: Cyber and Shooting War with Georgia

Georgia was the next state target for cyber attacks. On August 7, 2008, soldiers from Georgia's small army began a surprise attack against local separatist irregular forces in South Ossetia. NATO's Cooperative Cyber Defense Centre of Excellence (CCDCOE) issued a comprehensive unclassified record of the cyber attacks against Georgia three months (November 2008) after the small war concluded (Tikk et al. 2008). Elements of that report are included in here (Map 7.5).

The South Ossetia province had gained *de facto* independence from Georgia at the 1991 collapse from the Soviet Union. The international community failed to recognize the independence, leaving Ossetia under Georgian administration. An ineffective peace-keeping force from Georgia, South Ossetia and Russia was formed in 1992 to be led by Russian officers. Tensions between Georgia and Russian-backed Ossetian separatists grew, leading eventually to Georgia's decision to invade.

The next day, August 8, Russian forces that had been conveniently stationed close to the Russian–Georgian border invaded Ossetia. Their stated rational was ostensibly to protect ethnic Russians in the internecine fight between Georgians and ethnic Russians residing in South Ossetia. Georgia considered Russia's armed aggression an act of war. Actually, the intervention began a day earlier, almost in concert with Georgian troops' entry into Ossetia. Cyber attacks had been launched against a large number of Georgian government websites on August 7. These included

Map 7.5   Georgia with South Ossetia and Abkhazia.

DoS and defacement of official websites. On August 9, 2008, Georgia's president Mikheil Saakashvili announced that a state of war existed between Georgia and Russia. Subsequent cyber attacks hit Georgian domestic media outlets.

The first hint of more intense attacks to follow took place on July 19, 2008 with the website of the Georgian president becoming unavailable for more than 24 hours as a result of a three-sourced DDoS attack. In defense, the site was moved to a server in the United States. Once this attack was successfully corrected, no other DoSs occurred until August 8, when the DDoS attacks and defacements of selected websites began in earnest. Defacements of the website included tacking the face of Adolf Hitler over that of the Georgian president and a montage of faces of multiple dictators on other websites. DoSs occurred against the Georgian Ministry of Defense, Ministry of Foreign Affairs, Georgian police, courts including the Supreme Court and many others. On August 9, the largest commercial bank in Georgia came under cyber attack; banking services were shut down for ten days. By August 10, attack sites had increased to include parliament, domestic and international news organizations, other banks and commercial institutions. The last large cyber attack on Georgian websites occurred on August 27. Ultimately, 54 websites in Georgia in communications, finance and the government were attacked by elements in Russia (Hollis 2011). After August 28, most of the attacker sites had been successfully blocked.

The cyber attacks directed at Estonia and Georgia are considered by many reports on the scope of cyberwarfare to have been the beginning salvoes in the changing nature of war in the twenty-first century. The CCDCOE 2008 comparison of the cyber attacks in Estonia, Georgia and Lithuania is shown in Table 7.1 (e.g., Tikk et al. 2008; Ashmore 2009; Goel 2011; Stapleton-Gray and Woodcock 2011).

7.7 Cyber Wars with Ukraine

The onset of Russia's aggression against Ukraine can be said to have begun on August 14, 2003 when Russia began a trade war by stopping all Ukrainian exports to Russia in a clumsy, but successful, effort to stop Ukraine from signing a trade agreement with the EU. Four months later, a group of pro-Russian Ukrainian hackers directed an attack on several NATO websites, claiming that the attacks took place because NATO officers were present in Ukraine (Box 7.2).

The cyber war in Ukraine took on a new intensity in 2014, beginning with an attack by a group of anti-Russian hackers in Ukraine who claimed responsibility for shutting down the websites of Russian language newspapers and electronic media websites. This was followed by a similar attack against the Moscow-based Russian language online news source, Lenta.ru.

A series of cyber attacks were carried out in 2013 and 2014 by the Russian Military Intelligence on the government and Armed Forces of Ukraine. In an attempt to instill confusion among government offices in December 2013, pro-Russian hackers in Ukraine attacked all Ukrainian government websites, posted personal information

BOX 7.2   HACKERS HIT US BUSINESSES OVER UKRAINE STANDOFF

In an October 14, 2014 news report, *New York Times* reporter Mark Scott wrote that Russian-sponsored hackers "used a bug in Microsoft Windows to spy on several Western governments, NATO and the Ukrainian government." The report was released by iSIGHT Partners, a computer security firm in Dallas.

The targets included a September 2014 NATO conference in Wales, the Ukrainian government, at least one American organization, European energy and telecommunications companies and at least one US university. The report did not say what information the hackers retrieved, only that the information was often related to the Ukraine, Russia and US confrontation. The *hacking activities* started as early as 2009 and used a variety of techniques to gain access to confidential information.

In a *New York Times* article, Scott (2014) wrote,

> The discovery of [this] hacking is the latest in a series of world-wide attacks that have affected individuals, government agencies and companies. Many of these attacks have originated in Russia and other Eastern European countries, though the purpose of the hackers' efforts has often varied.

In October 2014, JP Morgan Chase revealed that it had been the victim of a cyberattack, "which experts believe originated in Russia, had compromised the banking accounts of roughly 76 million households and seven million small businesses."

about Ukraine's senior government officials and published stolen information. All important communications systems were hit, along with government websites and social networks. The communications systems of Ukrainian forces in Crimea were almost completely shut down as nontraditional forces took control of strategic sites prior to the eventual annexation of Crimea by Russia. A series of DoS attacks were launched in March 2014 against government and commercial websites.

7.8 Conclusion

The impact of Russia's real and suspected harassing of its former possessions has been minimal. However, the fear of more effective attacks in the future, such as shutting down electric grids and other utilities, interfering with land and air transportation systems, stripping assets of financial institutions and a barrage of misleading propaganda, has resulted in billions being spent on developing more effective defenses and countermeasures.

Today, warfare is no longer limited to shooting wars, destruction of property or the killing of civilians of both sides. The Internet, once the weapon of the future, has become the weapon of the now. Friends and enemies alike are openly employing cyber espionage, cyber crime and cyberterrorism in their wargaming exercises. Because of the difficulty of identifying the source of the attack, friends conduct these attacks on their friends as well as their real and potential enemies. The great benefit of this approach to warfare is that the actions are relatively inexpensive. Cyber attacks provide results that are disproportionately high for the investment required. Moreover, they take place without fear of attacking force casualties. They have been and are likely to continue to be carried out by unidentified men and women sitting in comfortable rooms in front of computer screens—all without fear of retaliation.

Estonia, together with the other two Baltic states, Latvia and Lithuania, became a member of NATO in 2004; Georgia's application was derailed by its brief 2008 war with Russia but continues to move toward acceptance into the European security organization.

In 2014, Georgia was the largest non-NATO troop contributor to the International Security Assistance Force (ISAF) in Afghanistan while also serving as a transit country for ISAF supplies. Georgia also supports NATO's counterterrorist maritime surveillance operation in the Mediterranean and has offered to participate in the NATO Response Force, the 14,000-personnel-strong quick response force formed in 2013.

A consensus among military planners reveals a real concern over the potential effects of cyber war in the future. What has taken place so far has been more in the way of what has been termed *cyber skirmishing*. The effects of cyber attacks in the former Soviet republics were minimal although remarkable when the very low cost is considered. The general thinking 15 or more years ago was that wars are won or lost on the battle field. Today, however, advanced technology is recognized as playing an ever large part in the outcomes. There is, of course, some truth to that belief. However, as advanced countries continue to create newer and better cyber countermeasures and establish stronger and stronger defensive links among them as was seen in the way other countries came to the aid of Estonia, Georgia and Lithuania, it is also clear that gaining cyber superiority is getting harder and harder to achieve. Small nations such as the newly independent former Soviet republics are paying heed to the caveat of Stapleton-Gray and Woodcock (2001, p. 54): "Ensuring the Internet security of a small nation-state entails investment in four areas: ensuring physical network robustness; securing the interconnection of participating networks through exchange points; securing the data and services required to keep the Internet running; and developing an effective response community." In the meantime, Russian-sponsored hacking into US, NATO and allies' computer systems continues. Another Ukraine-related attack was discovered in October 2014.

Chapter 8

The Energy Weapon in Russia's Foreign Policy

8.1 Introduction

According to the US Energy Information Administration, Russia was the world's third-largest producer of petroleum in 2013 behind only Saudi Arabia and the United States. In the same year, Russia was also the world's second-largest producer of natural gas, behind only the United States. In 2012, Russia's oil production was 10.4 million barrels per day, whereas domestic consumption was just 3.2 million barrels per day. Only 19% of Russia's energy needs are supplied by petroleum products, with natural gas accounting for just 14%. Russia's post-Chernobyl plan to phase out all nuclear-generating facilities has been quietly forgotten. Not only are they to stay in production, but also construction of ten new nuclear generating plants has been announced. This chapter looks at Russia's willingness to use these energy assets as weapons to punish and coerce errant former republics and satellites.

A result of this vast supply of energy resources now and for decades to come is that President Putin has not felt constrained enough by threats of sanctions by Russia's captive European Union (EU) markets to exercise any restraint in using energy as a geopolitical weapon. He has curtailed exports affecting Europe at least three major times and used the threat of supply restrictions or price increases any number of times in his efforts to bring the former Soviet-era satellites back in line. Russia first cut off gas deliveries in 2006, then again in 2009 and again in June of 2014. Except for Norway, Europeans continue to be dependent upon external sources for their energy supplies. Table 8.1 shows that for 12 of the member states with largest economies, dependence upon imports for all energy supplies in 2012 ranged from 30.7% for the Netherlands to 84.8% for Italy.

Table 8.1 Russia's 2014 Oil Production by Region (Thousand Barrels per Day)

Region	Average Production in Thousand Barrels per Day
Major Fields	
Western Siberia	6422
Urals-Volga	2312
Minor Fields	
Krasnoyarsk	368
Sakhalin	283
Komi Republic	259
Arkhangelsk	249
Irkutsk	201
Yakutiya	133
North Caucasus	64
Kaliningrad	28
Total	10,317

Source: US Energy Information Administration (USEIA). 2014 (updated March 12). Overview of Russia's 2013 Oil Production by Region. Available at http://www.eia.gov/countries/cab.cfm?fips=rs (retrieved April 15, 2015).

How has Russia been able to get away with its energy banditry for so long? It has been successful in its use of energy as a weapon because it possesses all of the elements necessary for the energy weapon to be effective (Stegen 2011). These include (1) state control over resources in demand by energy-deficient markets; (2) state control over major transit routes and transit modes; (3) the means for implementing such tactics as threats, arbitrary price increases and actual disruptions of supply without fear of meaningful retribution; and (4) the existence of a compliant leadership in key markets allowing itself to be held hostage for fear of the use of the energy weapon. Each of these elements is discussed in greater detail in this chapter.

8.2 State Control of Energy Resources

Unlike the United States where property owners typically have ownership of mineral rights on private property, the Russian state is the sole owner of all such rights throughout the federation. It increasingly assigns the rights to developing these resources to organizations in which it either owns outright or has a controlling interest. It uses the state taxing power to encourage resource development, but always for limited periods, after which the agreement may not be renewed. In this way, it has enticed major global energy corporations to open new fields in such difficult regions as the Arctic Ocean.

8.2.1 Decentralized Production

One of the advantages—and disadvantages—of the energy resources of the Russian Federation is the wide diversification of its energy sources. Fuels are found from the Caspian Sea to the Arctic Ocean and from the White Sea to the Pacific Ocean. A strategic advantage is that they are located reasonably close to politically stable energy-dependent major markets. A disadvantage is that their wide distribution often makes it difficult to get the finished products where and when they are needed. As a result of these opposing factors, Russia has become extremely proficient at the construction of pipelines in geographic conditions that range from permafrost to deserts.

8.2.1.1 Oil Production Areas

Most of Russia's oil is produced from two fields in Western Siberia and from several fields in the older Urals-Volga region, including the Caspian Basin. Production in the West Siberian region is greater than 6.4 million barrels per day; production in the Urals-Volga region exceeds 2.3 million barrels per day. Both of these regions are in the mature stage of production and can be expected to decline somewhat in the near future, although new technology is likely to renew production in older wells. In addition, the new fields coming into production more or less regularly can be expected to make up for any short-term loss in the older production regions (Table 8.2).

8.2.1.2 Gas Production Areas

Hydrocarbon reserves in Eastern Siberia, the Arctic, North Caspian Sea and Sakhalin Island hold great promise for long-term, stable production of oil and for both dry and wet gas (natural gas consists of methane, ethane, butane and pentane; *dry gas* has a higher methane concentration; gases containing higher amounts of ethane, butane, pentane or natural gasoline are referred to as natural gas liquids, condensates or *wet gas*). West Siberia remains Russia's main source of natural gas production, producing close to two-thirds of Russia's 2014 gas production.

Table 8.2   One-Day High and Low Spot Prices for European Brent Crude, November 2013–October 2014

	Prices per Barrel in Current US Dollars	
Year and Month	Highest	Lowest
2013		
November	112.04	103.08
December	113.06	108.91
2014		
January	109.69	106.44
February	110.18	106.55
March	111.26	103.37
April	109.79	105.73
May	111.32	108.17
June	113.74	108.43
July	110.84	104.73
August	104.94	99.37
September	101.21	95.08
October	94.57	84.02

Source: US Energy Information Administration (USEIA). 2014 (updated March 12). Overview of Russia's 2013 Oil Production by Region. Available at http://www.eia.gov /countries/cab.cfm?fips=rs (retrieved April 15, 2015).

8.3 Control of Transit Routes and Modes

To achieve its aims and maintain its ability to shape favorable political policies in the governments of its oil and gas customers, Russia continues to work to achieve and maintain monopoly over resource production, transmission and distribution. In the Baltic states, for example, the state-owned gas monopoly *Gazprom* not only delivers gas from its own wells in central and northern Russia but has also acquired near-controlling interests in all three Baltic state national gas companies: Eesti Gaas in Estonia, Latvijas Gaze in Latvia and Lietuvos Dujos in Lithuania. Gazprom has also established a network of local gas retail distribution companies, including Itera in Estonia and Latvia and Dujotekana, Stella Vitae and Vikonds in Lithuania. Although small, the Baltic state markets for Gazprom are very profitable; the Baltic states must all buy gas at the international price as opposed to the long-term discounted prices paid by Germany and other EU countries (Grigas 2012). Gazprom also profits from its state in the national and local distribution companies, as well as from its controlling interests in the large gas storage facility in Latvia.

Despite the profits the Russian state-owned gas company earns from sales in the Baltic states, Putin has not hesitated to punish the Baltics by cutting off their supplies of oil and gas more than once. In 2007, for example, deliveries were withheld to Estonia in retaliation for that country's decision to move a Russian soldier war memorial from its location in the center of the capital city Tallinn to a military cemetery. Stating that track repairs were needed on the Russian-owned railway, all rail deliveries of Russian crude oil, gasoline and other resources were halted and remained so for several months.

8.3.1 Alternative Sources of Supply

As early as the mid-1990s, energy-rich former Soviet republics concluded that they were not benefiting as much as they should have from Russian control of their energy production, sale and distribution. Moreover, European customers were beginning to recognize the peril of depending nearly exclusively upon Russia for oil and natural gas. The use of energy as a weapon was threatened or had already been used against former Soviet states. Some European customer countries determined that by going into partnership with Russian energy producers, their supplies would be less likely to suffer disruption. The Nord Stream pipeline, which is 51% owned by Russia's Gazprom, is divided among four European minority partners. Germany's Wintershall owns 15.5%; E-ON, also a German company, has another 15.5%; Gasunie of the Netherlands owns 9%; and GDF Suez owns 9%. The Nord Stream pipeline route is shown in Map 8.1.

The Nord Stream pipeline runs under the Baltic Sea from the Russian port of Vyborg, Russia to Greifswald, Germany. Construction of the Nord Steam double pipeline system began in 2010 and was completed in 2011. The decision to build the line was supported by Russia and its European customers as a way of guaranteeing reliable supplies of natural gas from Western Siberia. Previously, gas was transshipped across the Baltic states. Economic and political disagreements thus resulted in stoppage of shipments by Russia. Similar issues have resulted in halting shipments of oil through pipelines to Latvia and to Lithuania. Both of these Baltic nations had received substantial income from transshipment fees. Russia also stopped supplies of oil to a Lithuanian refinery when the Lithuanian government declined to sell an interest in the refinery to the Russian pipeline organization.

8.3.2 Southern Pipeline Proposals

Former southern republics with large gas reserves are eager to be able to supply the European market with gas in competition with Gazprom. Negotiations and planning for pipelines that do not pass through any Russian territory have been discussed since the breakup of the Soviet Union. Among the pipelines under discussion or planned for what is referred to as the Southern Gas Corridor include the Trans-Caspian pipeline, the Trans-Anatolia pipeline, the Trans-Adriatic pipeline, the Turkey–Greece–Italy interconnector, the Nabucco–West (or Turkey–Austria) pipeline and the South Stream pipeline sponsored by Gazprom to compete with the Nabucco–West pipeline. Interest in the Trans-Caspian pipeline, which had been off the table for some time, was renewed after Russia's invasion of Crimea and support of Russian separatists in eastern Ukraine in 2014.

8.3.2.1 The South Stream Pipeline

To counter competition from former republics in the Caspian Sea region, in 2007, Russia announced plans to construct its own pipeline through the Southern Gas Corridor. Called the *South Stream*, the route of the 63 billion cubic meter per year capacity pipeline would take it across the Black Sea directly to Bulgaria and then through Serbia to Hungary and Austria, thereby eliminating problems of transit through Ukraine (*Stratfor* 2014b). Construction of the South Stream pipeline began in 2012. First deliveries of gas were to occur in 2015 with final completion of the project in 2018. The estimated cost of the project had increased to nearly $30 billion.

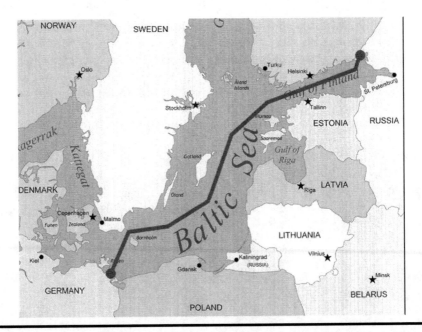

Map 8.1   Route of the Nord Stream natural gas pipeline from Russia to Germany.

However, Russia's aggression in Ukraine and the West's economic sanctions against Russia changed the schedule. Russia announced that it was abandoning construction of the line through Southeastern and Central Europe; instead Russia and Turkey agreed on extending the line to the latter. The agreement with Turkey included increasing Turkey's current 6% discount for Russian gas to 15% as payment as a transit state. The importance of energy pipelines to Turkey is described in Box 8.1.

8.3.2.2 The Trans-Caspian Pipeline

When built, the Trans-Caspian Pipeline (TCP) would move Turkmenistan natural gas from its port of Turkmenbashi under the Caspian Sea to Baku, Azerbaijan, then to Tbilisi in southern Georgia and Erzurum in Turkey via the Baku–Tbilisi–Erzurum pipeline. From Turkey, Turkmenistan and Azerbaijan gas was to be routed to Southern Europe via the planned Trans-Anatolian Pipeline route across the Bosporus and southern Greece, then onto Central and Eastern Europe via a tie-in with the Nabucco–West pipeline (Map 9.2). Supply from this source is expected to be long term and highly reliable: Turkmenistan is said to have the world's fourth-largest gas reserves. Clearly, the EU considers this project to be an excellent opportunity to reduce its alliance upon Russia as the sole supplier of natural gas. However, there is still a big question as to whether the TCP will ever be built (Wallwork 2014).

Turkey had considered the Trans-Caspian pipeline to be vital to its future energy demands—the demand for natural gas by Turkey is projected to increase by 77% over the next 15 years. In 2014, all Turkey's needs for gas were supplied by either Russia or Iran, both of which have opposed the pipeline across the Caspian. After first having been discussed in 1996, it was not until 2012 that Turkey, Azerbaijan, Turkmenistan, and the EU met to negotiate an agreement for its route and eventual construction. The route is shown in Map 8.2. Commencing construction of the TCP in the near future is not assured, however. Putin has expressed deep concern over the idea and the movement of Turkmenistan and Azerbaijan closer to the West.

8.3.2.3 The Turkmenistan–China Pipeline

As China continues to diversify its sources of natural gas, Russia is using its vast resources to undercut competitors from its former Central Asian republics. The last deal was an agreement with China on a $400 billion deal for the delivery of natural gas to China beginning in 2018 from a newly opened field in Northeast Siberia. The decision was the latest in a series of competitive deals negotiated by China. The contest began in 2009, when Turkmenistan gas began flowing through a Chinese-built pipeline that runs from Turkmenistan, through Uzbekistan and Kazakhstan, to China's northwest region (Map 8.3). The event essentially ended the Russian near monopoly over Central Asian exports of natural gas (Pannier 2009).

BOX 8.1   2014 EUROPEAN ENERGY SECURITY STRATEGY

In May 2014, the EC published an updated *EU Energy Security Strategy* that described EU concern over the Russian action in Ukraine and results of an in-depth study of member states' energy dependence. Elements of the published strategy document as edited include (USEIA 2014)

- *Short term*: The Commission will conduct energy security stress tests to simulate a disruption in the gas supply for the coming winter. The aims are to check how the EU energy system can cope with supply risks and to develop emergency plans and backup mechanisms, which may include
    - Increasing gas stocks
    - Developing emergency infrastructure such as reverse flows
    - Reducing short-term energy demand
    - Switching to alternative fuels
- *Medium to long term*: Responses to medium- and long-term security of supply challenges are planned in five key areas:
    - Increasing energy efficiency and reaching the proposed 2030 energy and climate goals, with a focus on buildings and industry, which use 40% and 25% of total EU energy, respectively, and to help consumers lower their energy consumption.
    - Increasing energy production in the EU and diversifying supplier countries and routes. This includes further use of renewables, sustainable production of fossil fuels, safe nuclear where the option is chosen and negotiation with current major energy partners such as Russia, Norway or Saudi Arabia, as well as new partners such as countries in the Caspian Basin region.
    - Completing the internal energy market and missing infrastructure links to quickly respond to supply disruptions and redirect energy across the EU as needed.
    - Speaking with one voice in external energy policy, including having members inform the commission early on with regard to planned agreements with third-party countries, which may affect the EU's security of supply.
    - Strengthening emergency and solidarity mechanisms and protecting critical infrastructure, including more coordination between members to use existing storage facilities, develop reverse flows, conduct risk assessments and put in place security of supply plans at the regional and EU level.

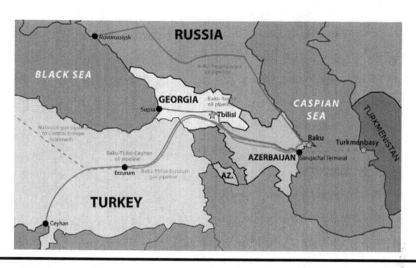

Map 8.2   Route of the Trans-Caspian gas pipeline and connection to Azerbaijan and Turkey.

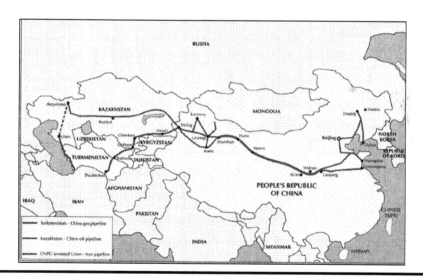

Map 8.3   Route of Turkmenistan to China and other Asian gas pipelines to China.

Russia was contracted to purchase between 50 and 65 billion cubic meters (bcm) of natural gas from Turkmenistan, but no deliveries were made following another unexplained explosion of a connector line in 2009.

The Turkmen–China pipeline is capable of delivering from 30 to 40 bcm per year. This is only one of several lines to be constructed along the same route.

A third line (line C) began shipping Turkmenistan gas in June 2014. On May 8, 2014, the president of Turkmenistan announced an agreement to add a fourth pipeline through Uzbekistan, Tajikistan and Kyrgyzstan (line D) to the route, adding another 8.7 bcm of gas to be shipped to China. The deal also included China's intent to construct an additional $600 million facility for collecting and processing the gas for shipment. However, that break in the Russian dominance of the Central Chinese gas market was not to last long.

In June 2014, after ten years of negotiations, Russia and China signed a 30-year, US$400 billion agreement for the delivery of some 38 bcm of eastern Siberia gas per year to China. The deal was finalized during President Putin's two-day visit to Beijing in May 2014. Deliveries of gas to China are to begin after completion of a pipeline in 2018. The gas will come from a new field in eastern Siberia via a new 2500-mile pipeline that is estimated to cost Russia $55 billion and China $20 billion to construct across the tundra. Russia has admitted that it will lose money for several years on all gas sold in this deal, but it expects to make up for that loss over the life of the contract.

The price to China is in the range of $350 per thousand cubic meters of gas—significantly lower than the average of $380.50 per cubic meter charge paid for by Europeans. The EU, which defines energy security as the "stable, uninterrupted [supply] at affordable prices," depends on Russia for 40 % of its natural gas supplies and for 30 % of its oil (Metais 2013; Boersma et al. 2014). They now see the Eastern shift as a distinct threat to their energy security. Russia's periodic punishment of its former satellites during price and transit fee negotiations has taught Europe to be wary of depending too heavily on Russia for supplies of natural gas, regardless of the long-term contracts and preferable prices.

In 2014, James Surowiecki saw Russia's willingness to quickly cut off energy supplies to its European customers as a strategy that promises more pain than gain. When the same tactics were employed in 2006 and 2009, Europe reacted quickly to reduce its vulnerability to Russian economic warfare by first increasing imports from Norway and Qatar, then constructing port facilities for liquefied natural gas (LNG) imports at several locations. Between 2008 and 2013, Qatar quadrupled the amount of gas it provides to Europe. It also improved domestic pipelines to make connectivity easier, upgraded gas and oil storage facilities and increased the use of coal for generating electricity. A major offshore port facility for receiving large quantities of LNG was planned for early construction.

8.4 Means for Implementing the Energy Weapon

The availability of the means for Russia's implementation of energy as a weapon differs by product form. Russia's market power is weakest in coal, moderate in electricity, limited in oil and strong in its diverse markets for natural gas. Coal is used mostly for domestic production of electricity, although it is purchased in relatively small quantities. The problem is transportation: coal is transported mostly via rail, and until recently, rail connections between the Ural supply sources and Chinese markets have been limited.

Many of the former Soviet republics remain tied into the Russian power grid, although thus far curtailing power supplies or steep price increases either has seldom been used or has not received much media notice. Estonia is the one Eastern European former republic that is able to generate its own power using supplies of oil shale; it has also connected to the Finnish grid. Where possible, EU encouragement in the form of grants and other assistance has resulted in a minor but growing use of renewable energy resources. Oil and gas remain Russia's major energy sources.

8.4.1 Problems and Pitfalls

Production of oil and gas is only valuable when there is a market or use for it. Because oil is produced around the globe, Russia is not a price setter of its oil but instead must sell its oil at the prices that buyers are willing to pay. About half of Russia's annual budget revenue comes from oil and gas sales. On a Wednesday in the middle of October 2014, Russia's weakness of depending upon oil and gas as a geopolitical weapon became clear: at the close of markets a day earlier, the price of Brent crude oil (North Sea, the price base for Russian oil) closed at close at about $81 a barrel—and Russia lost a little more than $150 million it would have received for its oil exports a month or two earlier. By the first week in December, the price for Brent crude was $66.30 per barrel and was continuing to decline; the price for West Texas crude was even lower at $63.01 per barrel (Figures 8.1 and 8.2). By the end of the second week in December, the price for West Texas crude was $59.95 per barrel and close to $60 for Brent crude. Analysts predict a continued drop in crude oil prices with no bottom foreseen.

In September, Russia Today (RT) America, the US arm of RT, the Russian communications system, reported that the sanctions against Russia in response to its accession of Ukraine's Crimea would probably result in a cut in Russia's 2014 gross domestic product by as much as 2% per year. At $111 per barrel per day and assuming roughly 70% for export use, of the roughly 10.5-barrels-per-day production, Russia would have earned approximately $808 million per day from oil sales. At $81 per barrel, with the same production and export rates, income would have dropped to $590 million per day; at $60 per barrel, income would be $437 million per day. The result would be a $371-million decline in income with each day's production.

The RT report also quoted Maksim Oreshkin, director of Russia's Finance Ministry's strategic planning department, who said that he believed that the price would stabilize in the area of $90 per barrel, well below the price of $105 per barrel used when preparing the 2014 national budget, as well as the $100-per-barrel price predicted for 2015. When prepared, the Russian budget for 2014 was established to balance when oil was priced at between $110 and $117 per barrel (*Economist* 2014).

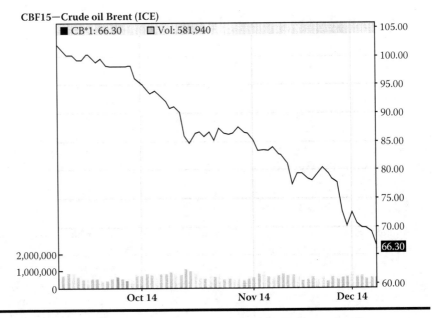

Figure 8.1 December 2014 spot prices for Brent (Europe) crude oil.

Figure 8.2 December 2014 spot prices for West Texas (US) crude oil.

The folly of basing an economy on a single commodity when the supplies are controlled by a large mix of other nations and the ability to influence demand that is squandered on geopolitical goals of a revanchist-oriented government were emphasized by this steep drop in the price of oil. It is important to look at this drop in the price of oil because sales of oil and gas make up the single largest income source for the Russian government: combined oil and gas sales make up 52% of total federal revenues and 70% of the value of annual exports. The decline in oil and gas prices is shown in Table 8.3.

As prices continue to drop, Russia's substantial hard currency reserves will be needed to fund the vital functions of the government, with little if any left for announced reforming of the country's armed forces. A 10-year multi-million dollar military forces modernization, upgrading and reform was included in earlier budgets. However, the drop in oil prices may defer completion of the full upgrade for some time. Moreover, the willingness to use energy as a geopolitical weapon has resulted in Russia's biggest market for oil and gas, the EU, beginning serious actions to line up alternative sources of supply.

8.4.2 Employing the Energy Weapon

While Russia is a price taker for its oil, its vast resources, efficient distribution system and the close proximity of energy-deficient customers make it a price maker in gas. As a result, Russia has been able to use price discounts and long-term delivery contracts as incentives for moving other nations closer to its position on political issues. At the same time, these same advantages have made it possible for Russia to use energy supplies as a weapon in coercing recalcitrant governments to withhold their disagreements over Russian foreign policies.

Russia is perceived now as, and will continue to be considered, an unreliable supplier, ready and willing to use its energy exports for political purposes as they did in 2006 and again in 2009 and 2014. Despite their fears, there appears to be little that European markets have been willing to do to climb out from under their heavy dependence upon Russian energy. Thus, for the foreseeable future, Russia's dominant position in the European energy market will have to remain *business as usual* (Boersma et al. 2014, p. 27). Recent uses of the energy weapon are clear indications that Russia under Putin is willing and able to achieve its foreign policy aims through coercive and aggressive diplomacy.

8.4.2.1 The 2006 Gas Crisis

Europe's fears that Russia would use its energy exports as a foreign policy and economic weapon materialized in January 2006, when Gazprom announced that from then on, the price to Ukraine for natural gas was to be increased from US$50 per thousand cubic meters (tcm) to $250 tcm (Light 2006). Ukraine refused to sign a long-term contract so Gazprom shut off gas flowing through the trans-Ukrainian pipeline that

Table 8.3 Average World Prices for Oil and US Price for Natural Gas, 2012–2015

Product	2012	2013	2014 (January–September)	2014 (December Prices)	2015 (October Estimate)	2015 (December Estimate)
West Texas Intermediate (dollars per barrel[a])	94.12	97.91	97.72	63.05	94.58	77.75
North Sea Brent (dollars per barrel[a])	111.65	108.64	104.42	66.30	101.67	83.42
Natural gas (dollars per thousand cubic feet[b])	10.65	10.30	11.05	11.06	11.13	11.06

Source: Energy Information Administration (EIA). 2015. Today in energy: Crude oil prices down sharply in fourth quarter of 2014. Available at http://www.eia.gov/todayinenergy/detail.cfm?id=19451 (retrieved April 15, 2015).

[a] Oil prices on December 8, 2014.
[b] Gas prices are US residential averages.

also delivered gas to Southern Europe. As the halt in supplies to Ukraine was taking place, three unexplained pipeline explosions occurred in Georgia. And, in December of that year, supplies of Russian oil to Belarus were halted in a move to emphasize an increase in price. Shortages then followed in Central and Eastern Europe (Walker 2007). The events were televised on New Year's Day. Luckily for gas customers, Russia and Ukraine reached an agreement just three days later; gas again flowed throughout Southern Europe. The dependence on imported gas by the EU's states with the strongest economies is illustrated by the gas import amounts shown in Table 8.4.

8.4.2.2 The 2009 Gas Crisis

In January 2009, another major gas supply crisis in Europe was brought on by Russia's supply disruption of the trans-Ukraine pipeline to Europe. As in 2006, it was brought on by pricing and political problems between Russia and Ukraine, although back then, the repercussions in Europe were more severe than they had been in 2006. Thousands of European customers were left without heat. Gazprom, the Russian gas monopoly, shut down the pipeline carrying gas across Ukraine to Europe just as a major snowstorm hit Europe driving temperatures below freezing point in much of the continent. This pipeline carried 40% of the gas imported by Europe. Mark Scott (2009), *Business Week Online* writer, described the EU's response at the time as loud and vicious accusations without much substance, the point being that while they were angry about the cutoff, they were unable or unwilling to do anything about it (Figure 8.3).

Causes for Gazprom's price increases were both economic and political. The economic factor was the higher prices for fuels. From 2003 to 2008, the price of

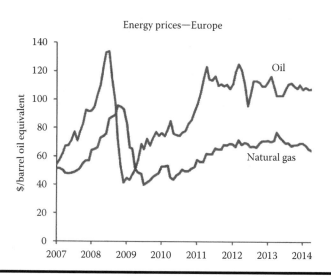

Figure 8.3 **Eight-year price averages for oil and gas for Europe, all sources of supply. Note: All quantities converted to US$ and billion-barrels-per-day equivalents.**

Table 8.4 Dependence upon Imported Energy for EU and Selected Nations, 2004–2012 (%)

	2002	2004	2006	2008	2010	2012
Total EU (28 countries)	47.4	50.1	53.6	54.7	52.7	53.4
Euro area (18 countries)	64.0	64.1	65.5	64.9	62.1	61.0
Austria	67.9	70.7	72.3	68.7	62.2	63.6
Belgium	77.5	79.7	79.5	81.1	78.2	74.0
France	51.1	50.8	51.5	50.8	49.1	48.1
Germany	60.1	60.9	60.8	60.8	60.0	61.1
Greece	71.5	72.7	71.9	73.3	69.1	66.6
Ireland	89.0	90.4	91.0	90.6	86.5	84.8
Italy	86.0	84.8	87.1	85.7	84.3	80.8
Netherlands	33.4	30.1	36.8	34.3	30.4	30.7
Norway	−802.8	−739.9	−665.2	−616.8	−514.2	−562.8
Portugal	84.1	83.9	84.0	83.4	75.1	79.5
Turkey	67.8	70.4	72.6	72.2	69.3	75.3
United Kingdom	−12.5	4.5	21.2	26.2	28.3	42.2

Source: Eurostat. 2014. Energy dependence of EU member states, 2001–2012. Available at http://www.eia.gov/countries/cab.cfm?fips=rs (retrieved October 16, 2014).

oil rose by some 370%, world prices for gas rose by 170%, and the price for coal rose by 460%. These increases were driven by rapid growth in the developed and emerging economies of the world (Rühl 2010). The growth came to a sudden halt late in 2008 with a global recession brought on by collapse of a real-estate bubble and the subsequent drop in demand for energy products. By the end of 2008, the price for oil had fallen by 75%, the price for gas declined by 58%, and the price for coal had declined by 62%. To stop the decline, the Organization of Oil Exporting Countries cut production enough so that by July 2008, the price of oil had increased to $147 per barrel—its highest price ever.

It was this price increase that brought Russia to regain lost income for energy sales by raising the form that is easiest to change: the price of gas to customers for whom little or no alternative source of supply was available. In 2009, Gazprom again cut off supply to Ukraine when that country balked at the price increase. This was the same pipeline that carried gas to Southern Europe. In 2010, Russia reduced gas supplied to Belarus for political purposes, and in 2013, it threatened to cut gas to Moldova if that former satellite did not drop its plans to sign a free-trade agreement with the EU (Surowiecki 2014).

8.4.3 2014 Cutoffs in Ukraine

Ratcheting up the conflict between Russia and Ukraine over steeply increased gas prices, Gazprom stopped all deliveries of natural gas to Ukraine and Southern Europe in June 2014. Gazprom claimed that Ukraine was in arrears in payments for gas to the tune of more than $4 billion; Ukraine countered that the price increase was unlawful and that the amount it owned was closer to $2 billion. However, Ukraine was not the only buyer to suffer from the drop; 20%–40% of the gas directed through the pipeline through Ukraine is supposed to be supplied to European customers.

The problem with implementing the energy weapon against transit countries such as Russia found in Latvia and Lithuania and in 2014 in Ukraine actions is that the products in the pipelines to Europe pass through countries that Russia wants to punish. Cutting off supplies to the transit countries also cuts off supplies to European markets. All of the cuts caused supply problems in parts of Europe, which receives some 15% of its supplies through the pipelines that pass through Ukraine and for which Ukraine charges a transit fee. On September 1, 2014, Russia cut gas deliveries to Slovakia by 50% in retaliation for Slovakia's strong support for sanctions for Russia's actions in Ukraine. The energy weapon was employed again in early October when Russia cut supplies of gas to Poland, which was back-shipping gas to Ukraine to help ease Russia's May 2014 cutoff of all gas to Ukraine over unpaid past purchases.

8.5 Acquiescence of Target Countries

In the final element, the unwillingness to retaliate in response to exercise of the energy weapon must exist for the weapon to be worth its political and economic costs. The EU's responses have been weak at best. Russia's permanent cutoff of all oil deliveries to Latvia in retaliation for that country's refusal to sell a stake in the port of Ventspils can only be looked upon as a failure of the energy weapon. The permanent refusal to sell the Lithuanian oil refinery Russian crude as punishment for selling a stake in the refinery to a Polish firm rather than a Russian firm must also be considered a failure. In both cases, Russian pressure was successfully blocked by these small former Soviet republics. Although still not proved, the pipeline explosions in Georgia have been conceived as a pressure tactic for influencing sale of pipeline assets to Russia. Georgia did not acquiesce; it still owns the facilities. However, that failure was likely instrumental in Russia's rapid reaction in providing assistance to separatist groups in South Ossetia and Abkhazia.

European reaction to disruptions in gas supplies has not been as effective. The 2014 crisis in Ukraine resulted in a call for a common EU agreement on energy policy with a common stance for future energy supply agreements with Russia. That has not been achieved. In a 2013 EU policy paper on a proposed market-based approach to dealing with Russia, Metais (2013) described the current inability to come to a common policy agreement as the result of a "state-driven approach rather than a market-driven one and demonstrates a structural change from a buyers' to a sellers' market." Individual EU members have negotiated highly favorable price agreements that they have been unwilling to jeopardize. The inability to agree upon a collective external energy policy continues because of the lack of the political will to stand up to Russia's bullying and the lack of an organizational structure to administer such an agreement. As a result, nothing has come from that call, although Russia's invasion and annexation of Crimea have generated renewed interest in a common policy.

The EU reacted to the deepening crisis in Ukraine by accelerating its search for an affordable substitute for Russian oil and gas by taking steps to improve its ability to withstand another depth of winter cutoff of its supplies of natural gas. Abbreviated details of the EU's 2014 energy security policy are included in Box 8.2.

Through the curtailments of its supply of gas as a hard power weapon and the willingness of European customers that are eager to negotiate long-term supply contracts with associated price discounts as a soft power weapon, Russia has put

BOX 8.2 TURKEY'S ROLE IN THE RUSSIA–EU GAS WARS

On December 1, 2014, Russian president Vladimir Putin and the CEO of the huge state-owned natural gas giant Gazprom, Alexei Miller, announced that they were halting construction of the South Steam pipeline directly to central Europe and instead had reached an agreement with Turkey to construct a line across the Black Sea directly to Turkey. The agreement was welcomed in Turkey. It increases supplies of energy and lowers its costs. Turkey's benefits from the agreement may have placed the plans for construction of the TCP from Turkmenistan and Azerbaijan in jeopardy. However, Turkey has emphasized its intent to serve as a partner of multiple energy suppliers.

Turkey, one of Russia's largest gas customers, is considered a key player in Eurasian energy politics. In addition to expanding its role as transshipper of Russian gas to Europe, it already transships Azerbaijani oil to Europe. The new pipeline agreement promises to improve the reliability of Turkey's energy supplies while also improving relations and avoiding confrontation with its large neighbor. Turkey, a member of NATO, is considered one of the West's major strategic partners in dealings with Russia (*Stratfor* [2014b] and Natural Gas Europe [2014]).

together the best kind of system for its future profits from the retail sale of its gas to Europe and China. However, Russia's willingness to cut off supplies to Europe for political purposes and to exercise threats of military action to enforce competitors away from the market has made Europe wary of continuing to depend so heavily on Russia for their energy supplies.

8.6 Conclusion

If, as a few analysts still agree, Russia is not engaged in a plan for rebuilding the empire it controlled from 1917 to 1989, it is making a good imitation of imperialistic behavior by employing what Mankoff (2014) calls *coercive diplomacy* but what is in truth more like the aggressive diplomacy described throughout this book. Under Putin, Russia's actions corral its former republics into what have been described as a "Eurasian bloc into cultural and geopolitical alternative to the West" under the guidance of the Moscow central core (Mankoff 2014, p. 66). To achieve that objective, Russia must exercise power within and without the revitalized empire. It has used a variety of weapons in this endless war. For targets within the former empire, it has fostered corruption and used bribes to influence political decisions, the promise of favorable trade ties, periodic episodes of cyber warfare and support for separatist movements that weaken any recalcitrant government that shows even the slightest inclination toward closer ties with the West. Russia's annexation of Crimea is a sign that Putin is willing to ratchet up its actions against its former territories. While Russia is increasingly adopting Western media technology for influencing ethnic Russians living outside of the Russian Federation and nearby external enemies, its greatest weapon has been the power to cut off their supplies of Russian energy, particularly natural gas. Over all external competitors for global influence stands Russia's huge arsenal of atomic weapons and the technology to deliver them to any foreign capital in the world.

Despite the 2014 fear of Russia's retaliation in the form of higher prices or reductions in supplies of natural gas, the EU has finally taken a stand by imposing economic sanctions against Russia for its actions in Ukraine. That and the steep cuts in the price of oil and gas on the world market have signaled to Russia that its monopoly power over energy supplies to Europe is not as unassailable as earlier assumed. Azerbaijan, Turkmenistan, Georgia, Moldova and Ukraine have moved closer to Europe and farther from their earlier dependence upon Russia. More importantly, they have sought and attained Western help for building gas and oil pipelines across South-Central Asia directly to Europe—completely avoiding all Russian territory. They are also selling more of their energy supplies to China, transshipped through trans-Asian pipelines that avoid Russian lands. More importantly as energy prices decline, and more other sources become available to European countries, Russia's ability to shape geopolitical planning becomes less and less sanguine.

RUSSIA'S FOREIGN POLICY IN ACTION

Chapter 9

Russian Aggression in Ukraine: Empire Revival

9.1 Introduction

The years 1991 and 2014 were seminal in the post-Soviet history of Ukraine. On August 24, 1991, the Supreme Soviet of the Ukraine declared the country an independent state. This was the sixth try to unite the several lands and culturally different people of this region of Eastern Europe into a single free nation-state; however, it was not to be the end of territorial dismemberment. On March 18, 2014, Russia's president Vladimir Putin signed legislation legalizing his annexation of Crimea. Crimea was occupied by pro-Russian forces during the 2013–2014 revolt that demanded the reversal of the decision by Ukraine's president regarding the country's movement toward closer ties with the West and instead sign a trade agreement with Moscow.

Ukraine shares a long border with the Russian Federation and Russian ally Belarus, with Moldavia and the European Union (EU) member states of Poland, Slovakia, Hungary and Romania (Map 9.1). For years, the three Slavic states, Ukraine, Russia and Belarus, the *Slavic Core*, were thought to be inseparable parts of the Russian and Soviet empires, but since 2005, Belarus is the only Eastern European republic that is an ally of Russia (Beauvois 1999).

9.2 History of Russian–Ukraine Relations

Russian possession of Crimea is not something new. Russia's armies of serfs under Catherine the Great added Crimea to the Russian Empire in 1783. Crimea was long

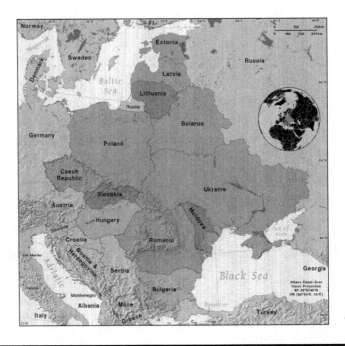

Map 9.1   Russia's *Special-Interest* States in North and Central Europe.

an outpost of Mongol invaders who first came to the peninsula in the early thirteenth century. During the fourteenth century, Crimea developed into the home of Tatar *Golden Horde*. In the mid-fifteenth century, it became a semi-autonomous Khanate (principality) of the Tatars and a protectorate of the Ottoman Empire. During Catherine the Great's wars with the Ottoman Empire in the eighteenth century, Crimea was taken over and annexed by the Russian Empire. The peninsula was the scene of a hard-fought battle between Russia and the Ottoman Empire and a group of its allies that included France, Great Britain and Sardinia.

In the nineteenth century, the far Western regions (i.e., the Right Bank of the Dnieper River) of Ukraine were controlled by the Austro-Hungarian Empire, whereas the Russian Empire controlled the Left Bank regions. Control of Ukraine changed again in the twentieth century. When the Russian and Austrian empires collapsed after World War I, Ukraine and Crimea declared their independence. That freedom was short lived, however. In 1919, western Ukraine was invaded by Poland, while the Red Army was pushing the small Ukraine National Army out of the Eastern lands. Soon afterward, Ukraine would be officially annexed by the Soviet Union in 1921 with Crimea following in 1922. During the revolution, Crimea became a base for the White Army. For a short period, White Russian troops occupied Kiev and attempted unsuccessfully to rule the country. After the Bolshevik victory, Crimea became the autonomous Soviet Socialist Republic in 1921, remaining so until the Russian Army retook it from the Germans in 1944. Germany had occupied Ukraine and Crimea in 1941. After Russian troops retook Crimea, Stalin deported all the Crimean Tatars and large numbers of Greeks and Armenians to Central Asia for what was their alleged collaboration with the Nazi invaders. The Tatar population was not allowed to return to Crimea until after 1991.

9.2.1 The Orange Revolution

In 2004–2005, the mass protests lasting for two months, in what became known as the Orange Revolution, helped bring to power pro-Western President Viktor Yushchenko, who defeated his rival Viktor Yanukovych in a 2004 runoff election. Yanukovych, who had been strongly endorsed by President Putin, had served as the prime minister from 2002 to 2004 and would again hold that post from 2006 to 2007. Yushchenko was running on an anticorruption platform. In September 2004, Yushchenko became ill. Tests revealed that he had been poisoned by dioxin—allegedly by the Ukrainian state police. He survived but suffered a disfigurement Box 9.1.

In the first election, Yanukovych and Yushchenko received about the same number of votes. Yanukovych was declared the winner in the runoff election. His victory set off a wave of protests against what was perceived as massive voter fraud. In December 2004, the Ukraine Supreme Court ruled that the election was fraudulent and therefore null and void. Yushchenko won the court-ordered third runoff election and was inaugurated on January 23, 2005 (Karatnycky 2005). Yanukovych was victorious in his second run for the office of the president in 2010. That election was not contested, and he fled the country during the Maidan sit-ins.

9.2.2 Ukrainians Protest Russian Language Law

In July 2012, hundreds of Ukrainians took to the streets of the nation's capital of Kiev to protest the approval by the parliament with very little debate of a law permitting Russian to be the official language in selected regions, including the Crimean peninsula and areas near the border with Russia. Police had to use tear gas to disburse the protests. Not long afterward, Russia reacted by boycotting imports of chocolates from one of Ukraine's largest candy makers. The act was apparently a warning to Ukraine to stop its long-term efforts to get closer to the EU and let the government continue its actions to strengthen ties with Russia.

In November 2013, the thousands of protesters of 2012 had become tens of thousands. Entire families took to the street in central Kiev's Maidan Square to protest the government's decision to abandon an earlier decision to sign an official association agreement with the EU. Protesters blamed the government for giving in to Russian pressure while continuing to permit rampant corruption within both the government and the private sector. The mass demonstrations—the

BOX 9.1 UKRAINE'S ORANGE REVOLUTION OF 2004

On the evening of November 22, 2004, more than 100,000 Ukrainians gathered in the Maidan, Kiev's Independence Square, to join the ruling party's attempt to hijack the country's presidential election. It was the opening salvo in what came to be known as Ukraine's Orange Revolution, which only ended in January 2005. The triggering event was the blatant attempt by Prime Minister Viktor Yanukovych's supporters to turn what appeared to be a loss in the November 21 runoff election into a victory. In exit polls, nonpartisan poll watchers were reporting a clear victory by the challenger Viktor Yushchenko. However, a reported last-minute surge in election results from districts with a large pro-Russian majority resulted in change in the voter count from the Russian-speaking average of 78%–80% to an overnight phenomenal count of 96.2%, with Yanukovych receiving from 92% to 97% of the votes cast in those same districts. Yanukovych was declared the victor by a margin of close to 800,000 votes.

Millions of Ukrainians staged a protest against the results, which became known as the Orange Revolution. The country's presidential election had been stolen by its corrupt rulers. According to Karatnycky (2005)

> By the time victory was announced—in the form of opposition leader Viktor Yushchenko's electoral triumph—the Orange Revolution had set a major new landmark in the post-communist history of eastern Europe, a seismic shift Westward in the geopolitics of the region. Ukraine's revolution was just the latest in a series of victories for 'people power' in Poland, Hungary and Czechoslovakia in the late 1980s and, more recently, in Serbia and Georgia.

biggest since the Orange Revolution—were triggered by Yanukovych's decision not to sign a wide-ranging trade agreement with stronger political ties with Russia instead of the agreement with the EU that had been negotiated by the earlier administration.

Russia, quickly moving to alleviate the fears and calm the increasingly destructive demonstrations, arranged a meeting in Moscow between Ukraine's President Viktor Yanukovych and President Vladimir Putin. At the same time, Putin announced that Russia would provide Ukraine the badly needed financial aid in the form of an 11-billion-euro (US$15 billion) loan. Shortly after the meeting, Putin announced a reduction in the price of gas sold to Ukraine—long an issue of concern to Ukrainians. Russia had ceased supplying gas to Ukraine twice before—in 2006 and 2009—over the arbitrary pricing practices of Gazprom.

9.2.2.1 The Maidan Protests

The slow movement of Ukraine to get closer to Europe was derailed in November 2013 when, bowing to pressure from Moscow, President Yanukovych replaced a planned agreement for closer political and economic ties between the EU and Ukraine with a similar agreement with Russia. Protesters gathered into Kiev's Maidan Square in what became the largest demonstrations since the Orange Revolution of 2004–2005. Maidan Square eventually came to be known as the *Euromaidan* because of the protesters' demands for ties with Europe. The demonstrations calling for Yanukovych's resignation continued into December, with protesters at one time occupying Kiev's city hall. The protests grew when Putin announced an agreement to reduce the price of natural gas and purchase US$15 billion in Ukrainian bonds. By the end of December, the protest had grown to include hundreds of thousands. Several days earlier, the journalist Tetyana Chornovol, who had accused Yanukovych of corruption, was driven off the road and beaten to death by men who were believed to be agents of the government (Diuk 2014; Shuster 2014; Yerofeyev 2014; Zasenko 2014).

In an effort to put a stop to the demonstrations, Yanukovych signed a series of laws in January 2014 restricting the people's right to protest. Bloody rioting followed, with dozens of protesters and police injured. Two protesters were killed on January 22 in battles with security forces. Protesters occupied the justice ministry in Kiev, and the parliament hastily repealed the antiprotest measures. In early February, hundreds of protesters were released from jail as part of a negotiation; in turn, the demonstrators evacuated government buildings. However, on February 18, protesters demanding more reforms again surrounded the parliament building and government buildings in several other cities in Western Ukraine. In Kiev, security forces beat back the protesters; stormed the barricades erected to defend the demonstrators' camp in Maidan Square; and used water cannon, tear gas, clubs and other weapons in an effort to clear the roughly ten square-block camp in central Kiev. By the end of the day, twenty protesters and seven police were dead. During the night, police continued their fight for the Maidan; the protesters fought back with rocks and Molotov cocktails. Although police had successfully destroyed a first line of barricades, others held. The protesters still held their ground.

An EU-brokered agreement brought the violence to an end three days later. President Yanukovych agreed to early elections and formed an interim government. The parliament approved restoration of the constitution approved after the Orange Revolution in 2004. The parliament then approved a measure granting full amnesty to protesters, fired Internal Affairs Minister Vitaliy Zakharchenko for his role in ordering the crackdown on demonstrators and decriminalized elements of the legal code. On February 24, the interim government charged Yanukovych with mass murder in the deaths of the Maidan protesters and issued a warrant for his arrest. Yanukovych disappeared before the warrant of his arrest could be implemented. He resurfaced in Russia on February 28, at which time he made a speech in Russian proclaiming he was still the rightful president of Ukraine. He did not return.

By February 2014, no compromise had been reached with the thousands of pro-Western demonstrators. In the most deadly week of the demonstrations, Ukrainian police fired on the crowds, killing more than 75 protesters. The EU imposed selected sanctions, and protesters in Ukraine seized government buildings in Kiev. President Yanukovych conceded his loss in early presidential elections. Shortly afterward, he fled to Russia. The parliament then elected Olexander Turchyhnov as interim president. Elections, which were supposed to be held in March, occurred instead on May 25, 2014. Businessman and former cabinet minister and bank president Petro Poroshenko was elected to a five-year term, having received 54.7% of the votes cast.

9.3 Putin's Revenge

In March 2014, armed pro-Russian separatists stormed important government buildings in the Crimean capital, while uniformed and masked soldiers took up positions at entrances to major airports and Ukrainian military bases in Crimea. The Russian parliament approved Putin's request for the use of Russian Armed Forces in Ukraine. After their appearance in Ukraine, Putin denied that the soldiers were Russians, insisting instead that they and the armed men who took over the government buildings were local self-defense forces.

Crimea has officially been a part of Ukraine only since 1954. In a move to placate ill feelings and armed resistance to Russian rule in Ukraine, Soviet leader Nikita Khrushchev turned Crimea over to Ukraine as a *gift*. Ukraine was, of course, at the time a member in reasonably good standing of the Union of Soviet Socialist Republics (USSR). However, by the time of Vladimir Putin's early twenty-first century drive to reconnect the former parts of the Russian/Soviet Empire, the generosity of Khrushchev no longer mattered. Putin believed that Ukraine, beginning with the Crimean Peninsula, should again be a part of the Russian Empire and be ruled from Moscow. If Ukraine could not actually become a physical part of Russia without an armed invasion, it would have at least to be strongly encouraged to remain a firm, friendly supporter of the Russian Federation. The loss of Crimea, it was believed, would make this point abundantly clear to the people of Ukraine. After all, taking control of Crimea by Russia could be justified by ethnicity alone: ethnic Russians comprised more than 60% of the population.

The autonomous Crimean government kicked off the campaign on March 6, 2014 by authorizing a referendum to establish whether the citizens wanted Crimea to secede from Ukraine and become a part of the Russian Federation or if they wanted to accept a position of greater autonomy while remaining within Ukraine. The vote occurred on March 16. A large majority of voters approved becoming a part of Russia. An even greater majority voted the same way in the City of Sevastopol. The Ukraine government, the EU and the United States all considered the election to be illegal to no effect. When Putin went ahead with the annexation, both the EU and the United States applied several bouts of sanctions against Russia. As 2014 was coming to a close, those sanctions and the planned drop in energy prices were reported to have driven the Russian economy into another recession in 2015.

President Putin signed a Russian parliament bill authorizing Russia's annexation of Crimea on March 21, 2014. Putin's annexation of the Crimea may indeed have been a strategically important move for Russia: the majority of Russia's Black Sea fleet has long been stationed at the Crimean naval base near Sebastopol. However, the ousting of its pro-Russia president by Ukraine sent a signal that Putin could not ignore. For Putin, the revolution in Ukraine had revealed a strategic weakness that had to be addressed: the southern wing of Russia's resurgent naval force was under threat. Annexing the Crimea would not only preserve the fleet and its base but would also serve as a warning to other former republics that Russia was not afraid to exercise armed aggression when and when its interests were threatened. However, annexation of Crimea meant loss of the large pro-Russian buffer zone that Russia depended on economically and politically.

9.3.1 The Importance of Crimea

Ukraine and Crimea have long been important to Russia. Ukraine is important because it sits as a buffer zone between the Russian heartland and Europe and the West. Additionally, its rich farmlands made it the breadbasket first of the Tsarist Russian Empire and then of the Soviet Union. Crimea is important for several reasons, not the least of which is its position as the home of the Black Sea Fleet. The Crimean city of Sevastopol has been home of the Black Sea Fleet since it was established by Catherine the Great. From Sevastopol, the fleet has access west to the Mediterranean and greater world's oceans and beyond.

The Black Sea Fleet of warships and supply vessels is projected to be completely modernized by 2020, according to Defense Minister Sergei Shoigu. In 2014, new air defense units and marine formations were formed providing protection for fleet actions. Shoigu announced that new submarines and surface warships were scheduled to be delivered to the Black Sea Fleet in 2014. Furthermore, 86 billion roubles (1.8 billion euros or $2.52 billion [2012 US dollars]) will be spent on adding some 30 vessels to the fleet by 2020 (Lally 2014).

The fleet is badly in need of modernization. According to New York University Professor Mark Galeotti

> Against a modern Western navy the Black Sea Fleet could easily be defeated, and, as a warfighting force, the Fleet was not impressive. The fleet's major ships were 'basically built to fight other ships and so is only useful in fighting a naval war. It's got the *Moskva*, an aging guided-missile cruiser; a large anti-submarine warfare cruiser—very dated; a destroyer and two frigates, which are more versatile; landing ships; and a diesel attack submarine. It's not a particularly powerful force. The Italian navy alone could

easily destroy it....It is moderately competent. It's not at the level of the American or British or German military, but it's better than in the 1990s. The [Russian] military is good at bullying small neighbors, but it would not be effective against NATO. It would not be able to defeat China.

K. Lally
Russian forces in Ukraine:
What does the Black Sea Fleet in Crimea look like?, 2014

A Ukraine friendly with the West had become an enemy. Putin had to salvage something from this loss. He found a relatively cheap means to accomplish this: He would support separatist unrest in the districts of Ukraine with large ethnic Russian minorities. This would not only disrupt Ukraine's political stability but also be a drain on that country's already-depressed economy. The German international news agency *Deutsche Welle* refers to Putin's aggression in Ukraine and take-over of Crimea as *Russia's slow invasion of Ukraine* (Goncharenko 2014). This was clearly a changed tactical approach, different from the outright warfare with lines of tanks, artillery, aircraft and armed personnel carriers that characterized Russia's incursions in Chechnya and its 2008 war with Georgia.

The separatists' rebellion remains unresolved at the time of this book's publication. A 2014 United Nations newspaper report revealed that the death toll in the eastern Ukraine districts since the conflict began in April 2014 had reached 4707, with more than 10,022 wounded. More than 25% of the deaths had occurred after a cease-fire that was agreed to by Russia and Ukraine (Heilprin 2014).

Russia's financial cost for the 2014 war in Ukraine and annexation of Ukraine's Crimea peninsula was almost as cheap as its ongoing verbal wars against Estonia, Latvia and Lithuania. Pro-Russian separatist residents of Crimea, led or advised by a few Russian Special Forces troops, did all the dirty work. They occupied all Ukrainian military bases and strategic locations. The spoils of victory for Russia in that "small war that never was" was annexation of the some 18,000-square-mile Crimean Peninsula. The real cost was something Putin could easily deal with: even greater distrust by the West.

In 2013, the Crimean peninsula had been a semi-autonomous region with its own capitol and parliament, Simferopol. However, it was officially ruled from Kiev. Of the greatest importance to Russia, Crimea was also the location of Sevastopol, the home base for Russia's Black Sea Fleet and the small Ukrainian fleet (Newman 2014).

Putin's signing of the bill authorized the use of Russian Armed Forces in Ukraine's sovereign territory to "protect ethnic Russians." The well-planned occupation of Crimea and Russian forces–led ongoing separatist campaign followed a revolutionary regime change in the Ukrainian capital. The results of a popularity poll in Russia indicated that Russians strongly supported Putin for his actions in Crimea. This gave him the backing necessary to continue with his aggressive diplomacy toward former Soviet republics and signaled continuation of the reconstruction of the Russian Empire. However, while Putin may indeed have reacquired Crimea relatively cheaply, many Western analysts believe that he has lost the larger and infinitely more important Ukraine permanently (Mankoff 2014; Strauss 2014).

9.3.2 The Continuing War

Russia's 2014 *little war* with Ukraine after annexation of Crimea did not erode into a full-scale shooting war. Instead, separatists supported, armed and led by the Russian military occupied key government offices and military bases in major cities and military posts in Crimea and the eastern Ukraine that bordered on Russia. These actions occurred in most cases with the support of local citizens and without firing a shot. However, this quiet takeover did not stop there; in just weeks, the world saw Russia's *de facto* and subsequent—as far as Russia was concerned—*de jure* annexation of Crimea. At the time of this writing, Russia was continuing to arm ethnic Russian separatists' forces along Ukraine's eastern border with Russia. The implication is that Putin will follow the same plan as he did in Georgia: Russia will help the Eastern Ukraine regions secede, after which time they will be absorbed into the ever-growing revitalized empire.

In 2014, reports of the number of Russian troops stationed along the border with Ukraine ranged from 20,000 to 50,000. On April 6, 2014, masked, well-equipped armed men occupied Ukrainian government buildings in the eastern Ukraine provinces of Donetsk and Kharkiv, along with security service buildings in Luhansk. The conflict escalated on April 12 with the police and security buildings across the districts were seized.

Armed men in combat uniform wearing black ski masks came across the porous Ukraine–Russian border in small numbers, and kept coming. They brought *humanitarian aid* with them—Putin's term for small arms and as of June 14, 2014, tanks and heavy weapons. They were Russian Special Forces, determined to stir up much conflict between pro-Russian separatists and Ukrainian Defense Forces in Ukraine's eastern districts. Local observers reported that small convoys of army trucks, loaded with armed men and tons of firearms, continue to enter Ukraine daily through its unprotected border with Russia.

Events in Russia's *slow invasion* and annexation of the Crimean Peninsula heated up when civilian protests in Kiev resulted in removal of the elected pro-Russian president of Ukraine Victor Yanukovych on February 22, 2014. On February 23, armed individuals without any visible military identification began to take control of strategic locations and facilities in Ukraine's Crimean Peninsula. At the time, Russia's president Vladimir Putin insisted that they were not Russian military personnel but rather local self-defense forces that were there to protect ethnic Russians from potential violence—the démarche theme that Russia has both a right and a moral responsibility to protect Russian speakers outside its borders (Evans 2014). Control of the Crimea, the location of Russia's major Black Sea port, would assure Russia access to what had been theirs on a long-term lease.

9.3.2.1 *The Takeover of Crimea*

As the antigovernment protests were coming to a shaky climax in Western Ukraine, events in Crimea and eastern Ukraine were becoming more unsettled (Makuch 2014). Crimea has long been a semi-autonomous district with its own parliament and elected officials, although its laws were all in keeping with legal and political systems in Ukraine. This would change quickly, when in early March 2014, masked gunmen wearing uniforms without identification occupied the Crimean parliament building, raised a Russian flag, dismissed the existing government and installed the leader of the Russian Unity Party as independent Crimea's prime minister. Communications between Crimea and Ukraine were cut and Russian troops openly moved into Crimea. Later, Putin explained that this was only done to protect Russian citizens and military assets in Crimea (Map 9.2).

The Crimean parliament then voted to secede from Ukraine and join the Russian Federation. A public vote on the question was scheduled for March 16, 2014. Election results were overwhelming in favor of joining Russia. On March 18, Putin signed a treaty incorporating Crimea into the Russian Federation. Within hours of the treaty's signing, a Ukrainian soldier was killed when masked gunmen stormed a Ukrainian military base outside Simferopol. No longer hiding their identity, Russian troops occupied bases throughout Crimea, including Ukrainian naval headquarters in Sevastopol. To avoid an armed confrontation, Ukraine began evacuation of some 25,000 military personnel and their families from Crimea. On

Map 9.2   Russian map of Crimea.

March 21, after the ratification of the annexation treaty by the Russian parliament, Putin signed a law formally integrating Crimea into Russia.

With the annexation of Crimea completed without any meaningful reaction, Ukrainian forces were unable to counter the occupation of Crimea by pro-Russian informal armed forces already underway (see Map 8.1). The Russian parliament's bill also authorized the use of armed force in Ukraine's sovereign territory if it was deemed necessary to protect ethnic Russians. The well-planned occupation, accompanied by the start of an ongoing separatist campaign in Ukraine's eastern districts and the revolutionary regime change in the Ukrainian capital, drastically changed Russia's relations with the West, while it was also solidifying Putin's reputation among Russian citizens.

After a massive demonstration of Russian might and power at the opening ceremonies of the Olympic Games in Sochi increased popular support for Putin's actions in Ukraine, he was ready to take another step in the reconstruction of the Russian Empire. Russia acquired Crimea cheaply, indeed (Mankoff 2014; Strauss 2014).

Russia's armed forces, while a far cry from their peak in 1990, are still a force to be reckoned with, particularly so by its much smaller neighboring former republics. Table 9.1 is an estimate of Russia's army, navy and air force, together with numbers in the same categories for the armed forces of Ukraine. Considering the much larger geographical area to defend and the continuing need to keep troops stationed in Chechnya, near the Chinese border and the Pacific, it follows that Ukraine is at less of a disadvantage that simple numbers might appear. However, any advantage gained by proximity is countered by the obsolete state of much of Ukraine's

Table 9.1   Russian and Ukrainian Military Comparisons in 2013

Element	Russia	Ukraine
World rank by military strength	2	21
Active military personnel	845,000	129,950
Reserves	2,000,000	1,000,000
Number of tanks	2750+	1150
Number of tanks retained in storage	18,000	1435
Combat aircraft	1571	231
Combat helicopters	392	139
Combat ships	82	10
Artillery	8969+	1952

Source: Russia Today (RT). Sanctions and weaker oil prices could cost Russia 4% of GDP—official. Available from http://rt.com/business/19628-sanctions-gdp-russia-oil-price/ (retrieved October 14, 2014).

military arsenal—all of which has been handed down from Soviet stocks. With the collapse of the Soviet Union, Russian nuclear stocks in Ukraine were at risk of a takeover by Ukrainian forces. However, Russia was successful in moving all its nuclear weapons into areas controlled by the Russian Federation after the dissolution of the USSR. Still, it is unlikely that Russia would employ tactical nuclear devices in any war with its smaller or weaker neighbors.

Wall Street Journal reporters Adam Entous and Julian Barnes reported on March 28, 2014 that Russian troops in place near the Ukrainian border exceeded 50,000, ostensibly participating in or preparing for an *exercise*. The report also said that the Russian forces were concealing their positions and building supply lines that could be used in a *prolonged deployment*. The character of the buildup suggests that Russia was preparing for another incursion into Ukraine and not the training exercise it was purported to be.

Putin has continually denied any Russian assistance for the separatists in Ukraine. However, in November, leaders of the eastern Ukraine separatist movement were flown to Moscow to meet with Russian government and military advisors, reportedly to plot strategy for closer relations with Moscow (Williams 2014). The separatists claimed the results of the early November plebiscite in the eastern districts, which were overwhelming in favor of becoming a part of Russia.

9.4 What Happens Next?

When asked whether Putin can be expected to continue his policy of reviving the Russian Empire and getting tough with the West, and whether the Russian people support his actions, Russian sociologist and behind-the-scenes Russian political activist Olga Kryshanovskaya was quoted in the report of the interview:

> I believe that if Putin went beyond the cases of Abkhazia, South Ossetia, and Crimea, it would mean self-destruction for him from a political point of view. I believe rather that he will continue to transform Russia into an empire inside its current borders.... The demand for imperial resurgence revealed itself during the Crimean crisis. For the first time in my career as a researcher, I can confirm that the people and the powers that be are united. For Russia, this is a unique situation because on antagonism between society and those in charge is the norm for our country.

I. Victorov
Baltic Worlds, 2014

Kryshanovskaya went on to cite Putin's understanding and agreement with large numbers of the Russian public. They have forgotten shortages and lack of personal freedom but remember what it was like to live in the powerful and feared Soviet

Union. They hold near-sacred memories of the victories of the Red Army over Nazi Germany. When the USSR collapsed, the Russian people had to live with the loss of everything that held the Soviet Empire together; they lost the values that gave their sacrifices justification along with their sense of self-respect. For many Russians, Putin's aggression against former satellites, annexation of Crimea and thumbing his nose at the United States, EU and North Atlantic Treaty Organization (NATO) have provided them with a new sense of national pride. The annexation of Crimea was welcomed by the people, the military and security agencies, and it has given Putin strength to continue on his dangerous path of empire building.

BOX 9.2   NATO'S REACTION TO RUSSIAN AGGRESSION IN UKRAINE

The following elements of the official statement issued after a September 2014 conference in Wales highlight the great seriousness that NATO and the United States attach to Russia's aggressive actions in Ukraine and Crimea:

> We, the heads of State and government of the member countries of the North Atlantic Alliance, have gathered in Wales at a pivotal moment in euro-Atlantic security. Russia's aggressive actions against Ukraine have fundamentally challenged our vision of a Europe whole, free and at peace...
>
> We condemn in the strongest terms Russia's escalating and illegal military intervention in Ukraine and demand that Russia stop and withdraw its forces from inside Ukraine and along the Ukrainian border. This violation of Ukraine's sovereignty and territorial integrity is a serious breach of international law and a major challenge to Euro-Atlantic security. We do not and will not recognize Russia's illegal and illegitimate 'annexation' of Crimea. We demand that Russia comply with international law and its international obligations and responsibilities; end its illegitimate occupation of Crimea; refrain from aggressive actions against Ukraine; withdraw its troops; halt the flow of weapons, equipment, people and money across the border to the separatists; and stop fomenting tension along and across the Ukrainian border. Russia must use its influence with the separatists to de-escalate the situation and take concrete steps to allow for a political and diplomatic solution which respects Ukraine' sovereignty, territorial integrity and internationally recognized borders.

NATO
Wales Summit Declaration, 2014

NATO reacted quickly to Russia's intervention in Ukraine and annexation of Crimea. Heads of State and government representatives participating in September 2014 in Wales issued a statement connecting events in Ukraine and official NATO policy. The first 2 of 123 items in the report are included in Box 9.2. NATO's demands did not include *or else*. It does not appear that they have generated much fear in Moscow; Russia still holds Crimea and continues to arm and support separatists in the Ukrainian territories that border Russia.

9.4.1 Economic Warfare

Putin's strategy for driving Ukraine away from the West and back under the *protective* umbrella of Russia also includes economic weapons. The most obvious one is increasing the price of oil and gas imports despite the global drop in prices for energy. However, the need for an increase in defense spending, high fuel costs and loss of exports to Russia have resulted in a projected decline in gross domestic product by more than 4% and an increase in inflation by 13%.

9.5 Conclusion

The Ukrainian Crisis of 2013 and 2014 has resulted in a distinct cooling of relations among the United States, EU and Vladimir Putin's Russia. This severity of reaction was missing in the aftermath of Russia's earlier incursions with the smaller former Soviet republics on the Russian borderlands, such as Estonia, Lithuania, Georgia and Azerbaijan. What made Russia's intervention in Ukraine different was what NATO's ministers have called the "illegal and illegitimate annexation of Crimea." As of December 2014, more than 4000 lives have been lost in the separatist regions, and Russian support continues unabated. Meanwhile, Ukraine continues on its path to closer ties with the West, including the desire for NATO and EU membership.

Ukraine continues to proceed on its path toward establishing long and permanent ties with Europe. However, Russia is also committed to either curtailing or reversing the loss of dominant influence over Ukraine. In addition to its arming and financial support for separatists in Ukraine's eastern districts, Putin has also begun squeezing the Ukrainian economy. Ukraine pays high prices for Russian gas. In addition, Russia has passed a law that would forbid remittances by the many Ukrainians working in Russia—a projected loss of $11 to $13 billion if the ban is put into effect.

The majority of Ukrainians have rejected what they felt were the *foreign* culture emanating from Moscow and reflected in the underlying Eurasian characteristics that they have been forced to live with during the 350 years of Russian Empire domination. The whole Russia continues to expand its connections to the Far East; Ukrainians are continuing the long-drawn-out negotiations for becoming a member of the EU and of NATO.

Chapter 10

Russian Intimidation in the Baltic and Nordic States

10.1 Introduction

Russia's annexation of Crimea and support of separatists in Ukraine's eastern regions have forced the many small nations on the Baltic and North Seas to again look at Russia's actions as a signal that they, too, could ultimately face similar attacks. As a consequence, the Nordic and Baltic states are rethinking their security policies and preparations. Russia's aggression and provocations in Northern Europe are certainly not new; rather, they are now occurring more regularly and at a higher provocation scale than at any time since the end of the Cold War. The Nordic–Baltic region has experienced an increasing number of threatening moves by Russian forces. Moreover, since 2008, Russia's threatening activity aimed toward the Baltic Sea and Nordic countries has increased significantly (Gotkowska 2014; Järvenpää 2014). Their hostile actions have become even more threatening since Russia's annexation of Crimea and the West's retaliation in response to that annexation. In addition to the former Soviet republics of Estonia, Latvia and Lithuania, Sweden, Finland, Norway and Poland are now targets of Russian provocation. As seen in Map 10.1, most of Europe's small states are within close proximity to the Russian border.

Among the newest members of the North Atlantic Treaty Organization (NATO), the three Baltic states are targeted by Russian intimidation in order to undercut their faith in the ability and willingness of NATO to respond to an armed incursion by Russian forces. Finland and Sweden are threatened in order to keep them out of NATO and convinced that they are better off by reaching a compromise with Russia's empire-building intentions. The statement in Box 10.1 is indicative of the way Nordic and Baltic countries view the importance of Russia's annexation of Crimea to regional security.

EUROPE

Map 10.1 Europe with all countries bordering on the Baltic Sea.

BOX 10.1 NORDIC–BALTIC SECURITY COOPERATION

The Nordic–Baltic region holds a special place when it comes to the resilience of free and democratic societies. Today, more than ever in the last 25 years, the integrity of the "West" is at stake. Nordic–Baltic–US security cooperation is at the heart of the future of the region. Sharing values and norms and a commitment to pragmatic cooperation and as net contributors to economic growth, foreign policy management, development assistance and security, the Nordic–Baltic countries remain strong partners for the United States. The region shows that market democracy works, human rights and the rule of law are respected; a positive outward vision of the world is still possible; and that there is still important work ahead for transatlantic cooperation. When Cold War tensions faded, the countries of the region turned from being security importers to being security exporters. For over a decade, these countries proved their ability to deploy and conduct operations a long way from Europe, in Afghanistan. Now, a whole new set of challenges to a Europe whole and free has emerged. Northern European insecurities have returned, sparked in particular by Russia's illegal annexation of the Crimean region of Ukraine; its active support for Ukrainian separatists; deployment of thousands of troops into Ukraine and on the Russian–Ukrainian border; cyber attacks in Estonia; provocative military activities toward the Baltic states, Finland and Sweden; and efforts to intimidate Baltic and other European energy consumers. Greater uncertainties also beset the High North, with its shared borders and special neighborhood, due to the rapid rate of climate change, the pace of natural resource development, the nature and rate of public and private investments, changing transportation patterns and potential security challenges [in] Arctic and non-Arctic states alike (Hamilton et al. 2014).

The increase in severity began in 2009, when Russia conducted simulated military attacks against the Baltic states and Poland. The Polish attack climaxed with a simulated nuclear missile attack against Warsaw. In early 2013, Russian bombers, escorted by jet fighters, conducted an exercise toward Sweden that included a fake nuclear missile attack on Stockholm. Other major military exercises followed in September 2013, when forces from Russia, Belarus and Kaliningrad carried out a hypothetical amphibious attack on the Baltic Sea coasts. Russians announced the exercise (Järvenpää 2014), which only involved a little more than 20,000 troops. However, if support and backup forces are included, the true number was estimated to be closer to 90,000 men. In 2-14m an estimated 150,000 Russian troops took part in a Western military zone mobilization exercise at the same time that Russia was involved in Ukraine.

The consistent and recently expanded level of Russian aggressive posturing toward the Baltic and Nordic countries became greatly amplified in 2013 and 2014 following the West's reactions to Russia's involvement in the Ukrainian Crisis. NATO fighter jets newly based in Poland intercepted Russian spy planes approaching Latvia and Lithuania in a threatening manner several times in November 2014. During 2014, NATO jets intercepted more than 100 Russian fighters testing the North and Central Europe borderlands. This was three times the number of interceptions in 2013. Russian forces violated the airspace of Great Britain, Estonia, the Netherlands and Sweden during the year, harassed Canadian naval vessels in international waters, practiced missile and bomber attacks against the United States and conducted large-scale mock amphibious attacks in the Baltic Sea. Hostile underwater testing of Swedish coastal defenses by units believed to be Russians began again in 2014. The purpose of these and similar hostile actions has been to intimidate the former Soviet territories and as a warning to NATO's upgrading of forces based in the Baltic and Nordic regions. Both Sweden and Finland, not members of NATO, continue to cooperate with and conduct joint exercises with NATO forces.

10.1.1 NATO and Baltic/Nordic Defense

Norway, Poland, Denmark and Germany are among the 28 nations that are members of NATO; Sweden and Finland are officially nonaligned nations and therefore not members of NATO, although they maintain a close working relationship with the organization. Estonia, Latvia and Lithuania joined NATO's Partnership for Peace program in 1993, and became members of the European Union (EU) and NATO in 2004. In 2011, Estonia became a member of the Eurozone, with Latvia planning to join later and Lithuania planning to do so even thereafter. However, after more than 20 years of independence and phenomenal social, economic and political achievements, Baltic state citizens appear more than ever unwilling to trust their leaders to protect them from a return to subjection at the feet of powerful neighbors at best or anarchy at worst. Distrust of government, their neighbors and society in general, lack of involvement in political and social activities and large-scale outward migration of the young and educated for economic opportunity remain worrisome problems (Box 10.2).

The citizens of these three small countries still remember what it was like to live under a manifestly corrupt and inefficient government, when the only avenue open for civic engagement was through Communist Party–approved organizations. Widespread theft of resources during the early years of privatization, strong-arm tactics of organized crime and deeply entrenched corruption of public officials were characteristics of their societies during and immediately after their separation from the Soviet Union and reinforced their distrust of government (Lieven 1994).

In September 2014, masked and armed men set off smoke grenades at an Estonia and Russia border crossing, cut off all of the station's radio and telephone communications and dragged an Estonia counterintelligence officer into Russia. The abduction

**BOX 10.2   RUSSIA'S AGGRESSIVE MILITARY EXERCISES
THREATEN THE NORDIC–BALTIC REGION**

The Swedish (2014) hunt for a Russian submarine…has real implications for the broader Nordic–Baltic region. The ASW operation outside Stockholm is merely the latest in a string of events and incidents over the last year. Stockholm was the target of a Russian exercise over Eastern Europe in 2013, when Russian bombers flew simulated attack runs against targets in and around the Swedish capital. Swedish and Finnish airspace have been violated on multiple occasions in recent times (photos of some of the incursions can be found on the Finnish air force's website), and a US RC-135 reconnaissance plane was chased into Swedish airspace by Russian fighter jets earlier this year. In early September, a Swedish–Finnish weather research vessel was buzzed by a Russian navy helicopter, while a Russian frigate maneuvered disturbingly close to the ship. This last incident occurred in international waters, but the research vessel may have gotten too close to a Russian submarine exercise. On the other side of the Baltic, an Estonian intelligence officer was snatched by Russian operatives and taken to Moscow for interrogation. The Baltic Sea region has also been the scene for some of Russia's largest military exercises in recent years. Finally, in response to the Ukraine crisis, NATO is increasing its own presence in the region, with several exercises intended to demonstrate the Alliance's ability to come to the defense of its members in the northeast, and the deployment of US forces to the Baltic states to reassure nervous allies (Nordenman 2014).

occurred just two days after President Barack Obama's visit to Estonia and announcement of a new 4000-man NATO early warning defense force in the Baltics.

10.1.2 The Arctic Theater

In 1996, the Baltic and Nordic countries with Russia and the United States formed a new organization, the Atlantic Council, for the purpose of resolving economic, political, security and ocean shipping issues in the Arctic Ocean before those issues led to hostilities (Lunde 2014). As a consequence of Russia's aggression in Georgia and Ukraine, the region faces a new and serious challenge: how to avoid confrontation with Russia on such issues as oil and gas production, fishing rights and Atlantic–Pacific shipping lanes in ice-free months. The Nordic countries of Norway, Denmark, Finland and Sweden have more to lose if hostilities occur in the Arctic than the Estonia, Latvia and Lithuania. Of all the European states, Norway is the most important state in the West's dealings with Russia for economic and geographic reasons. Norway and Russia have a common border in the North; Norway controls significant lands north of the Arctic Circle, operates extensive offshore oil production in Arctic waters and produces much of the World's farm-raised Atlantic Salmon. In 2013, the total of all types of seafood imported by Russia from Norway reach 6.6 million Norwegian kroner (844,000 US$ in 2014), an increase of 10 percent over the previous year. During the Ukraine crisis, Russia then banned all seafood imports from Norway in August of 2014 (Eurofish.com 2014). Norwegian maritime experience in the Arctic is also significant. It has explored much of the region, operates sea transport vessels in the Arctic, and its oil field service fleets also service Russian drilling facilities.

Denmark, while ostensibly not directly affected by disruptions in the Arctic, is indirectly affected because of its autonomous territory Greenland, which lies entirely above the Arctic Circle. Because of Greenland, Denmark plays a role in Arctic policy making. Should oil and gas be discovered on- or offshore in Greenland, it will be Denmark to establish a strong security presence in the region. Iceland, located just south of the Arctic Circle, is the second smallest nation with a marginal role in Arctic policy making. Iceland's major interests in the region are fishing and the recently identified potential for oil and gas production.

Finland, although it no longer has any direct access to the Arctic, is located between Russia and Sweden and has a strong strategic presence on the Baltic Sea. It also has deep cultural and language ties with Estonia. Because of this strategic importance, Finland began developing a comprehensive Arctic strategy in 2013. The problem facing that policy is the need to maintain a distinctly nonaligned policy while continuing to benefit from its extensive trade ties with Russia and political commitment to the EU. Although Finland is not a member of NATO, it does hold a strong observer status.

Sweden is another Arctic Council member without any direct access to the Arctic. It has maintained a nonaligned position along with Iceland. A member of the EU but not of NATO, Sweden has been one of Europe's strongest advocates for environmental protection in the Arctic and Baltic Sea region. However, the periodic incursion of Sweden's coastal water by real and suspected Russian Naval Forces has brought Sweden to developing closer ties with NATO Baltic/Nordic defense planners.

10.1.3 Russian Aggression in the Baltic States

After having suffered through nearly four years of an economic crisis deeper than the Great Depression of the 1930s, by 2013 and 2014, the Baltic states of Estonia, Latvia and Lithuania were back on the road to economic growth. Prior to the recession, growth rates in Estonia, Latvia and Lithuania had been some of the highest in the 28-nation EU. Much of that growth was the result of a strong real estate boom fueled by newly wealthy investors from Moscow acquiring underpriced properties in these three former Soviet republics. Russian investors have also purchased all or stakes in local businesses and industries, including increasing their participation in strategic industries. They are, therefore, increasing their power to influence the nations' economic and political policies. In Estonia and Latvia, large ethnic Russian minorities support Russia's soft power influence in the region. They have also agitated for an official recognition of Russian culture and acceptance of Russian language schools, with the objective of engaging more Russian participation in the national government policies toward Russia.

Russia has continued showing its willingness to do whatever was necessary to protect the well-being of those Russian residents of its former republics—the ethnic Russians who Putin describes as "Russia's compatriots." Acquiring Baltic real estate and purchasing Baltic state businesses, particularly in the energy and transport industries, and generous finding of Russian cultural events and organizations in the Baltic states are considered to be elements in Putin's strategy to eventually bring the lost republics back under Russian control. Table 10.1 displays several areas of Russia's interest in the Baltic states and indicates the level to which Russian and Baltic state foreign policies agree.

The three Baltic states had regained their independence from the disintegrating Soviet Union in 1991. They had then successfully dealt with the problems of rebuilding independent states with a strong commitment to democracy and market economies. Still, the future of the institutions of democracy in these strategically important small states remained tenuous. Non-Russian Baltic citizens seemed to be slipping deeper into ennui, whereas ethnic Russians that had migrated to the Baltics during the Soviet period were demanding more recognition of their rights. The weak commitment to democratic institutions is manifested by the Baltic state citizens' continuing very low trust in government and public authorities and low and continuing to decline levels of participation in elections and civic involvement. Moreover, they see declines in the already underdeveloped civil society and continuing corruption by scofflaws in both the public and private sectors. Nationalist pride was giving way to a weakening of civic engagement and acceptance of corruption that was similar to events in the 1930s that saw democratic government in the Baltics give way to autocratic rule and central control. They were thus ripe for annexation by the Soviets in the 1940s.

An October 2014 Atlantic Council report brought out the dangers the Baltic states face in light of Russia's resurgent aggressive foreign policy and willingness to employ its soft power:

> The Nordic-Baltic region may be emerging as the new 'soft spot' in the clash between the transatlantic community and a newly asser- tive Russia. The Baltic states are some of the weakest members of the (NATO) Alliance, and, due to their small size, would struggle to generate military power of any size no matter how much they spent on defense. Furthermore, all three Baltic states have significant Russian populations, are dependent on Russian energy supplies and struggle with the presence of Russian organized crime; all factors used by Moscow to great effect in both Georgia and Ukraine in the recent conflicts there.
>
> **M. Nordenman**
> *Atlantic Council, October 20, 2014*

Table 10.1 Selected Sources for Russia's Interests in the Baltic State Region

Interests	Importance for Russia	Ties with Baltic State Interests	Notes
As a source of energy and minerals supply and markets	Low (stable)	+	Minimal natural resources; Baltics remain 100% dependent upon Russian natural gas. Russia gaining greater ownership of domestic distribution agencies
As a transit area of transport	Declining in importance	+	Estonian and Latvian ports no longer important transit routes; Lithuania important for Russian transit to Kaliningrad Oblast; North Stream pipeline and new Russian ports reduce need for use of Baltic state ports
As a channel for providing access to the sea	High (declining)	+	New ports now meet Russia's import/export needs; access to Baltic Sea still important for Russian naval forces
As a military bridgehead or buffer zone	Low (perceived in 2014 as increasing)	–	Military threat seen as increasing since Russia's annexation of Crimea and support for separatists in Georgia and Ukraine
Foreign policy and political–military interests focused on the region	High (increasing)	+	View NATO expansion as a threat to Russian security and uses threats to dissuade further expansion. Russian policy goals are to gain as long a strategic warning as possible and to reduce NATO's potential and level of preparations for common defense.

Source: Puheloinen, A., *Russia's Geopolitical Interests in the Baltic Area*, Helsinki, Finland, National Defense College, 57–58, 1999.

The weaknesses in the Baltic states' democratic institutions were generating some apprehension that representative democracy in these new democracies may sooner or later give way again to authoritarian or despotic governments. Such a shift had happened in the 1930s during their first modern-era independence. Contributing to this possible outcome is a loss of belief in the promise of greater opportunity and a better life from renewed independence. These are resulting in a shrinking and aging population as the young and educated migrate in growing numbers. For others, the eroding faith in democratic institutions has raised the specter of erosion back to control by Russia. Indications are that either one or both of these phenomena have already occurred to varying degrees in Belarus, the Ukraine and former Central Asian republics.

Remaining free and independent is never going to be easy for the Baltic states, for as Grigore Pop-Eleches has noted,

> Countries trying to escape their past face an uphill battle in trying to develop well functioning democratic institutions. The optimistic 'possibilism' of the early transitions [must] be replaced by a more historically grounded realism about the prospects of political liberalism in the former Leninist countries ... with a thorough understanding of the relationship between legacies, institutions, and reform outcomes.

> **Pop-Eleches**
> *2007, pp. 924–925*

10.1.4 The Importance of the East Baltic

In his 1999 military, political and economic analysis of Russia for the Finish National Defense College, Ari Puheloinen identified these geostrategic regions in which Russia has particular interest, and which are of equal importance to Nordic–Baltic security planners: (1) Poland, and to a much lesser degree the relatively isolated Kaliningrad Oblast; (2) the passage between Finland and Estonia; (3) Gulf of Finland with the Aland Islands and Southern Finland; (4) the St. Petersburg area; and (5) the Straits of Denmark (Box 10.3).

Poland, situated at the western end of the great European Plain has long been the main invasion route into Russia and Russia's invasion route into Europe, giving it great land-based strategic importance. There are no important topographic barriers on this way into the Russian heartland. The passage between Finland and Estonia is Russia's access to the Baltic Sea and beyond, as well as a direct path for seaborne invasion of Russia. The Gulf of Finland and Aland Islands are in a position to restrict sea access to and from the passage and Russian oil ports, giving it great sea strategic value. St. Petersburg is Russia's second capital and the former capital city and important import/export hub and thereby has important land and sea strategic importance. The narrow Straits of Denmark are Russia's access to the Atlantic Ocean, giving it sea

BOX 10.3   RUSSIA'S ONGOING THREAT
FOR THE BALTIC AND NORDIC REGIONS

In a March 2001 meeting of the East European Studies group, recipient of a Wilson Center research grant Professor Martha Merritt included the following statement regarding post-Soviet Russia's foreign policy aims for the Baltic states:

> For the Russian Federation, the end of the Cold War meant loss of empire, loss of global advantage, loss of identity and loss of well-being. A key aspect of foreign policy strategy in the Putin administration has been the expansion of national security interests to include concerns more conventionally understood as domestic. In particular, Putin, unlike Yeltsin, has highlighted Russia's demographic crisis and portrayed it as a security threat. Many industrialized countries would have zero population growth or less without immigration, but Russia is dealing with a mortality crisis not seen outside of full-scale wartime in modern history. Life expectancy for men and women has fallen drastically in the last ten years, for men to less than 60 years of age.
>
> In his public remarks, Putin dwells not on the causes of this crisis—alcoholism and related accidents are prime contributors—but rather on the dangers of a low birth rate for Russia. Putin... insists upon language rights for Russian speakers outside Russia as a foreign policy concern, an area in which Putin's attention predates his presidency. The issue of citizenship and language rights in the Baltic states offer Russians a compelling example of a perceived assault on Slavic cultural norms, in some minds (and newspaper columns) a foreshadowing of the bombing campaign in the former Yugoslavia and of continued tension between east and west.

> **M. Merritt**
> *2011*

strategic value. For hundreds of years, Russia has attempted to control these strategic points and did so for all but the Denmark Straits during the Soviet era.

10.1.5 *Post-Soviet Transition*

Until 1991, the economies of the Baltic states were fully integrated into the social framework of the USSR. This resulted in formation of a deep layer of antidemocratic historical legacies in the form of the Russo–Soviet–style structural, cultural and institutional traditions. Although the three nations took advantage of Gorbachev-era reforms to proclaim their full sovereignty in the early 1990s, they could not erase these historical legacies overnight. In this sense, their full transformation will not take place, if ever, before at least another generation has passed.

Despite the great potential that exists for citizens of the Baltic states, the 2008–2010 years of economic trauma have had an impact on the way the people of these small nations interpret their future prospects. The citizens of these three countries know what it is like to live under a corrupt and inefficient government. The departing Soviets left behind a systematic ethos of bureaucratic corruption and heavy-handed exercise of power—traditions that limited opportunity and advancement. Under Soviet control, when advancement in a career often depended more upon being a member of the Communist Party than on merit. Additionally, as Russia continues to make forays into its former possessions such as Georgia and Ukraine, the apparent revanchist strategy of Putin has added to the worries of Baltic area citizens. The three states are each 100% dependent upon Russia for their oil and gas.

Independence saw widespread local theft of resources, strong-arm tactics of organized crime and deeply entrenched corruption of public officials were common in most of the former Soviet satellites during and immediately after departure of Soviet forces. They all suffered through a deep recession immediately after regaining their independence. Yet, their economies soon recovered, and they became some of the fastest-growing economies in the EU. But by 2008, they were caught up like much of the developed world in the real estate–cantered bubble economy. The result was a surge in citizens' confidence in their future as members in the EU. Despite the potential that the citizens believed existed for citizens of the Baltic states, the trauma following collapse of the economy in 2008 had a deep impact on the way the people saw their future prospects. Nostalgic calls for a return to the stable Soviet system were heard in the Baltic states and many of the other post-Soviet nations.

Putin encourages ethnic Russian minorities living in the Baltic states to continue to agitate for greater treatment by use of Russian-controlled media, sponsorship of groups and events designed to remind all Baltic state residents of the historical achievements, language and culture of Russia. By their open and often-voiced support of ethnic Russians in the Baltics, Putin's aim is to remind the non-Russian leaders of the states that their "flirt with democracy" must not cause a wider split with their former overlords. To achieve this goal, Russia employs a combination of hard and soft power tactics that are often subversive, "covert, implicitly coercive or of dubious legality" (Grigas 2012, p. 2).

One of the most disconcerting political phenomena in the Baltic states and elsewhere in Europe is declining citizen participation in political processes. There has been a steady decline in voter turnout in European elections. In the 1979 general election, voter turnout was nearly 62.0%; by the 2009 election, turnout had declined to 43.0% (Table 10.2). The Baltic states EU election turnouts, with Finland included as a reference, are also shown in Table 10.2. The most precipitous drop was recorded by Lithuania, where voter turnout dropped from 48% at the 2004 election to less than 21% in 2009.

Table 10.2   Average Voter Turnouts in European Elections, 1999–2009

	Year		
	1999	*2004*	*2009*
EU average	49.61%	45.47%	43.00%
Estonia	63.05%	45.14%	44.9%
Latvia	—	44.34%	53.7%
Lithuania	—	48.38%	20.98%
Finland	30.14%	39.43%	40.30%

Source: Malkopoulou 2011.

10.2 Future Regional Security Scenarios

Leery of Russia's long-term intentions for the Baltic and Nordic states, many local residents in the Baltic states are worried that regaining power over the Baltics is next on Putin's agenda. Russia's strategy has been to bring the former republics politically, militarily and economically into the Russian orbit through such means as the Eurasian Economic Union (EEU) and energy dependence. However, the EEU is still a work in progress, the success of which has been delayed by Russia's annexation of Crimea. The possible outcomes for any integrative action include the following four possible scenarios:

1. Russia regaining the right for providing all military security for the region with Russian-led forces. This includes eliminating all NATO connections.
2. Russia regaining greater, if not all, control over the economy of the Baltic states.
3. Recreating client state system by allowing local independence in a federal system, but shifting the states into *de facto* if not *de jure* bi-national Russian client states, with their foreign relations controlled from Moscow.
4. Total absorption of the Baltic states as local districts into the structure of the Russian Federation. This would entail Russian control of all political and economic spheres and eventual total Russification of the people, culture and places. Local ethnic identity to be eliminated and closed after schools.

10.2.1 Control of Regional Security

Russia discontinues use of peaceful negotiations and participation in regional organizations such as the Council of Baltic States and instead expands use of threats of armed incursions and eventual annexing of all or parts of the Baltic states. In this scenario, Russia hopes to replace NATO with a similar organization, controlled by the Russian military and using Russian weapons and tactics. Presence of Russian forces in Finland, Norway, Poland and Sweden are included as a way of block any further expansion of NATO into the Nordic/Baltic region and gaining compliance with Russian policies. Unless provoked, Russia stops short of military action in or territorial acquisition in the pro-Russian Nordic–Baltic bloc.

10.2.2 Peaceful Gaining of Economic Control

Russia accelerates its long-term method of regaining the ability to influence Baltic state foreign policy by using greater economic power to influence Baltic states' economic and security policies. The ability to offer energy supplies at low cost helps to ensure compliance with Russian foreign policies. States are left free to manage all other aspects of their own domestic governance. Russia uses profits from its vast energy supplies to gain controlling interest in local and regional energy distribution businesses and transportation systems, by favorable trade agreements, long-term government loans and by foreign direct investment in all sectors of regional economies. Implied threats of economic destabilization reinforce policy concurrence.

10.2.3 Creating Client States

Russia is able to use its energy sources and results of previous colonization policies to relatively inexpensively bring some former republics back under its wing as *client states* without any actual annexation of territory. The first two of the breakaway former Soviet republics to succumb to this siren song were Belarus and Kazakhstan, both of which have joined the Moscow-led Eurasian Economic Union. In 2014, the third former republic Kyrgyzstan accelerated its intent to join Russia's version of the EU when it accepted Russia's promise of financial and military aid (Ott 2014).

Russia uses several different tactics in its campaigns to recapture client states like the Baltic states, Ukraine and Belarus. These tactics include vast sums of money, supply of low-cost energy, economic investment acquisition of critical local industries, assistance with infrastructure development, subterfuge through abetting ethnic Russian minorities in separatist agitation and military assistance that morphs into military dependence. In Kyrgyzstan, for example, over a several-year period, Russia has written off more than half a million dollars of Kyrgyzstan's debt for a 15-year lease on a Russian air base in Kyrgyzstan, a promise to provide military equipment worth more than US$1 billion, pressured Kyrgyzstan to close a US air base for which it was receiving annual rent payments of $60 million, construction by the Russian state power company of a series of hydropower facilities and sold for a token one dollar Kyrgyzstan's complete natural gas network to the Russian natural gas monopoly Gazprom. In turn, Gazprom agreed to invest more than US$500 million to upgrade the system and to absorb Kyrgyzstan's debt of US$40 million. Rosneft, the Russian state–owned oil company, has agreed to purchase a controlling interest in the country's airport.

10.2.4 Territorial Expansion

Putin's underlying goal seems to be reestablishing a Russian Empire by annexing territories that until 1991 were part of the empire of the Soviet Union. The consensus among many analysts is that Russia's strategic goal is total annexation of at least the Baltic states. By its heavy-handed and intimidating actions in the Baltic states since 2000, Russia has shown that it is indeed seeking to reestablish greater influence in all of its former client states, including Latvia, Lithuania and Estonia. While Russia's foreign strategy was originally intentionally opportunistic rather than overtly aggressive, it has shown its willingness to use armed intervention and economic and cyber warfare to get its own way.

10.3 Changes in the West's View of Post-Soviet Russia

Conventional wisdom in the West long held that the overarching goal of Russia's foreign policy was focused on regaining influence over former satellite states, not on territorial expansion toward reestablishing the Soviet Empire. A typical opinion of the early 2000s was that the aim of Russian was to "exorcise past humiliation and dominate its 'near abroad'—not an ideologically driven campaign to dominate the globe" (Gates 2009). However, by the second decade of the century, this interpretation was discovered to be only partially true. Indeed, Putin has always wanted to erase the world's view of a post-Soviet Russia as an inconsequential failed state. However, Putin's statements and actions in Ukraine and Georgia, among others, have revealed that, more than becoming a regional power, his goal has been regaining Russia's status as a global superpower, equal in power to influence global affairs as the United States, EU and China.

The West's perception of that strategy is very different from the absolute control over all aspects of society once practiced by Soviet leaders. On the surface, it may have reinforced a desire for the West to believe that Russia did not have a single, rigid strategy for regaining its past glories. Analysis of the several interrelated strategies that appeared to focus on exercising ever-increasing influence in the politics of target states diverted the West's interest away from the larger foreign policy goal: revival of the Russian Empire. Until 2014, Russian foreign policy did not appear to include a territorial accretion by military conquest component. Instead, it appeared to be nothing more than a gradual but unswerving drive to eventually regain a level of influence short of outright dominance over the social, economic and political affairs of what were to again become economically dependent client states friendly to the Russian world view.

10.3.1 Policy Implementation

The tactical implementation of this policy began with gradual encirclement of smaller states, achieved by intimidation in a variety of forms such as energy dependence, economic warfare and riotous clashes by ethnic Russian minorities. Able to induce the fear of more aggressive action, Russia saw intimidation as a more cost-effective strategy in practice than overt military action. An added benefit was that it did not provoke active retaliatory measures by the EU or NATO. However, as Russia has demonstrated by the invasion of Georgian territory, there was always the threat present that Russian tanks might roll across the borders at any time.

Since the events in Georgia and Ukraine, leaders of other former Soviet territories must consider that Russia under Putin looks upon military invasion as a viable option for exercising control over its special interest states. The Baltic states have sought to counter this threat by becoming members of NATO. Others have also considered this defense since it is likely to be the only move that can prevent even a temporary Russian incursion into their territory. At a minimum, the countries' defense forces need to become strong enough to delay an invasion to give NATO time enough to confront an aggressor.

The real threat to the independence of Estonia and Latvia remains to be the array of creeping pressures to establish two-community states with the Russian language an official second language and Russian culture slipping again into dominance. Only the Estonians and Latvians can counter these pressures. Lending support on this issue is the point that the EU certainly does not want to welcome Russian as one of the official languages for the conduct of EU business.

Risks to Baltic states' security increase when the countervailing weight of the EU and NATO is weak. Estonia has been the only one of the three Baltic states to spend the NATO-agreed minimum of 2% of their annual budgets on defense. The military security of the states depends on the protective umbrella of the United States, the EU and NATO. Stronger European support, given a very cautious Germany and the US and UK involvement in the Middle East, is unlikely at the present. Under these circumstances, Baltic state leaders, while clearly retaining a commitment to Western collective security agreements, must avoid situations that could provoke a Russian economic or military reaction to bring down the established government and put a pro-Russian leadership in place.

The recent Russian invasion of Ukraine and annexation of Crimea shows that Russia is ready to use military force abroad to project what it considers to be indistinguishable from Russia's own domestic priorities. The value of the EU and NATO shield depends on other developments in the world and the political leadership in Europe. A promising sample of the power of this shield was the Council of Europe's February 2009 adoption of a resolution condemning Russia's occupation of Georgian territory and NATO's 2014 condemnation of Russia for its incursions in Ukraine. This Georgian resolution urged Russia to remove its recognition of South Ossetia. The resolution, according to Russian media, was seen as Russia's most serious diplomatic defeat in recent years. The NATO statement demanded that Russia give Crimea back to Ukraine and stop arming separatists.

Expanding economic cooperation between Russia and the Baltic states is subordinated to the current highly aggressive strategic political goals and increasingly bellicose stance of Russia. Greater economic cooperation requires a high degree of stability in international relations; this does not appear to be a high priority in Russian long-term foreign policies. Taken together, Russian actions are making Estonians, Latvians and Lithuanians very nervous indeed. They perceive Russian demands for greater influence as unjustified, dangerous and illegal.

10.4 Conclusion

When independence was regained by the Baltic states in 1991, the region suffered through widespread local theft of resources, strong-arm tactics by organized crime and deeply entrenched corruption of public officials. These actions were common in the rump Russian Federation and in most of the former Soviet satellites during and immediately after the collapse of Communist Party control. The new states all suffered through a deep recession immediately after regaining their independence. Yet, their economies soon recovered, and they became some of the fastest-growing economies in the EU.

Until 2009, the Baltic and Nordic states were caught up like much of the developed world in the real estate–cantered bubble economy. The result in the Baltics was a surge in citizens' confidence in their economic future as members in the EU. Despite the potential that citizens believed existed for citizens, the trauma following collapse of the economy in 2008 had a deep impact on the way the people saw their future prospects. Nostalgic calls for a return to the stable Soviet system were heard in the Baltic states and much of the other post-Soviet nations.

Although a return to economic growth since 2012 brought improved economic conditions, Russia's aggressive actions in the borderland states of Estonia, Georgia and Ukraine, triggered renewed concern over their security. The future of these reconstituted Baltic democracies and their Nordic supporters was again being threatened by a revanchist expansionist policy of Russia under Putin. The retrenchments suffered during the Great Recession saw many Baltic state residents begin questioning the economic benefits they expected from EU accession. The states also experienced citizens' declining faith in core democratic institutions. The Russian annexation of Crimea brought a halt to those atavistic thoughts. Concern for their security and stability returned to the political forefront. Increased participation in democratic institutions appears underway. What are more important for their security are the renewed interest in a common Baltic–Nordic security policy and commitment to increased spending for defense.

Chapter 11

Russian Foreign Policy after Putin

11.1 Introduction

In the years since the breakup of the Soviet Union, Russia-watchers in the West have seen the Russian Federation (RF) successor state evolve through a variety of foreign policy iterations as it struggled to find its way in the new political–economic world. Throughout the decade of the 1990s, Russia first appeared to be moving closer to the West. The formation of Russian foreign policy suffered without leadership from one "state of profound crisis" to another. By the end of President Boris Yeltsin's second term, it was clear that that rapprochement was dead, to be replaced by a policy that emphasized confrontation in place of cooperation (Shevtsova 2007a,b). This chapter reviews elements of the transition from the presidency of Boris Yeltsin to that of Vladimir Putin. It closes with a discussion of possible scenarios for the shape that Russia might take after Putin.

11.2 What Role for Russia?

The question of what role Russia was to take after dissolution of the USSR emerged early among the leadership of the Soviet Union successor state. In 1990, while still chairman of the Duma, Yeltsin announced that Russia was not interested in becoming the center of any new empire and would not seek any advantage over any of its former republics. In 1992, a few weeks after the formal breakup of the Union of Soviet Socialist Republics (USSR), Andrei Kozyrev, newly elected President Yeltsin's foreign minister, echoed those sympathies, asserting that relations with the family of former republics were then conducted as between equals; Russia did not seek any special position in the family. In February 1993, however, that spirit of equality was becoming shaky. Kozyrev announced a new policy when he reminded the West that Russia continued to have an interest in all armed conflicts in the territories of the former USSR. He then added that Russia retained a special responsibility in the region and called for all international organizations, including the United Nations, to grant Russia special powers as a guarantor of peace and stability in all former Soviet territories. According to Eduard Shevardnadze, one-time KGB and Communist Party official, Russian foreign minister from 1985 to 1990 and president of Georgia until 2005,

> The belief that we are a great country and that we should be respected for this is deeply ingrained in me, as in [every Russian]. But great in what? Territory? Population? Quantity of arms? Or the people's troubles? The individual's lack of rights? In what do we, who have virtually the highest infant mortality rate on our planet, take pride? It is not easy to answer the questions: Who are you and who do you wish to be: A country which is feared or a country which is respected; a country of power of a country of kindness?
>
> **J. Matz**
> *Constructing a Post-Soviet International Political Realty, 2001, p. 18*

11.2.1 A Smaller, Weaker Empire

Yeltsin's presidency was limited in what it could accomplish; some critics claim that he lacked a vision of where he wanted to take Russia after the collapse of the communist system (Donaldson and Nogee 2005). Yeltsin's handpicked successor Vladimir Putin was not burdened with that problem; he knew where he wanted Russia to go: a return to a proud, powerful, respected-if-not-feared empire and one of the three global superpowers (Eriksson 2007; Walker 2007). Sheer size reduction has much to say about Yeltsin's ability to influence world events, as Table 11.1 on population changes indicates. Governing the vast Eurasian reaches of the RF is an easier task today than it was as the USSR. The population of the RF today is only a little more than one-half of what it was during the last years of the Soviet

Table 11.1 The Population of the Soviet Union by Region and Ethnicity, 1989

	Soviet Union	Russia	Other Republics
Population in millions	285.7	147.0	138.7
Ethnic Russians	145.1	119.8	28.3
Ethnic non-Russians	140.7	27.2	113.4

Source: Anderson, B. A., *Population and Environment*, 23 (5): 437–464, 2005.

Union. In 1989, the population of the USSR was 285.7 million; the population of the Russia heartland was just 147 million. Table 11.1 includes a comparison of the ethnic composition of Russia and its other 14 republics as a single group at the 1989 collapse of the USSR.

11.3 The Putin/Medvedev Power Vertical

Under Putin's presidency, it has become increasingly important for the current political elite to reach agreement on a national idea that will preserve the gains that the country has achieved over the years of his administration. Casting the West once again as Russia's principal enemy has apparently turned out to be the idea that the public is most willing—and apparently most eagerly—to accept.

Many Russians equate the chaotic, insecure time of the decade before Putin with Yeltsin's failed attempt at introducing a democratic society. They look back at that period with justifiable dread of poverty, unemployment, disease and widespread criminal activity through which many suffered. They long for a return to the stability of the past and are, therefore, willing to allow Putin to continue Yeltsin's creation of a centralized dictatorship–like *power vertical* for the rule of law. After Yeltsin emasculated the parliament, he strengthened the power of the presidency. Putin has added to that powerbase so that today, all power radiates downward from a small group of former KGB officers and immensely wealthy oligarchs (hence the *power vertical* concept). Putin has reformed the judiciary and continues to increase state control. He has instituted a simplified tax system and exercised the power of the state to ensure that taxes are paid. He has made ownership of land and facilities more stable but allowed many former KGB and FSB officers to acquire or retain properties gained at artificially depressed prices. Putin's presidency is clearly the most stable Russian administration to appear in decades (Derluguian 2006).

What remains to be seen is what will happen after Putin. According to Richard Krickus (2014, p. 53),

> Kremlin-watchers agree that the days of the power vertical and Putin's rule are numbered, and Russian society is about to face significant internal political disruptions. The people running things in Russia, however, appear to be ill-prepared to deal with them...Russian-watchers predict the Kremlin leadership will prove incapable of imposing its will upon Russia's foreign rivals and, worse yet, may face a new internal crisis that results in a fate similar to that of the USSR.

In his first two four-year terms, Putin reinstituted centralized control, cemented relationships with China, modernized the military and warned Europe and the United States that Russia could no longer be ignored (Smyth 2005; Kuhar 2007; Smolchenko 2007; Kuchins and Zevelev 2012). He sat out as prime minister during the Dmitry Medvedev presidency then in 2012 was elected for a third term as president of Russia. When he first took office, he stated his intention to follow a policy of rapprochement with the West. However, subsequent events indicate that a distinct shift to a more aggressive effort is underway. Putin's apparent goal is reestablishment of the authority of the state and Russia's position as a global superpower (*New Europe* 2007; Krastev 2014). He has engineered a Russia that is capable of forcing its will on any or all of its former Soviet Empire territories. It is apparent that while also reestablishing its position as a world power, Russia has embarked once again on a path of reviving the Russian Empire (Motyl 1999).

Western political leaders appear to have forgotten that regaining Russia has embarked on a foreign policy aimed at regaining its status as a world power. It is doing so in calculated steps. The first step was to secure assurance of goodwill among its energy-poor neighbors on the Eurasian landmass by providing oil and gas at favorable prices. It then sought to regain influence over its border states by providing them with access to the large Russian consumer market; creation of a Eurasian common market was the tool employed. While dangling these incentives, Russia also engaged in small wars in selected border states, a policy that functions as an implied threat that the same could happen to states that refused to accept Russia's influence in their sovereignty.

11.3.1 Putin's Strengths

Since coming to power, Vladimir Putin has used heavy-handed aggression at least four times, first against ethnic minorities in the RF itself and then against its smaller neighbors. While doing so, he has also built a large public following; several polls taken in Russia after the annexation of the Crimea gave Putin an approval rating of more than 80%. He has built a strong cadre of supporters by rewarding trusted oligarchs with economic benefit. He has also strengthened the Soviet security forces, appointed many of his old KGB friends to important government positions, used arrests and more sinister actions to silence press critics and reversed the policy permitting residents to elect leaders in their administrative districts by making all those appointments from Moscow. He has used what his enemies in the West consider as illegal acts of aggressive diplomacy and domestic policy as the first steps in reconstituting the Russian Empire while also strengthening Russia's power position in the eyes of an increasingly timid Europe (Browning 2004). For example, Russia was threatened with what at first appeared to be only minor and inconsequential sanctions in retaliation for the annexation of the Crimea; subsequent events have revealed those sanctions to have been more effective than originally believed. In contrast, a consortium of nearly two dozen countries participated in the military retaliation against Saddam Hussein when Iraq invaded and annexed neighboring Kuwait.

The annexation of Crimea was not an arbitrary decision of simply another of Putin's experiments in regaining for Russia the land, people and influence in global affairs. Carefully preplanned, the invasion was a great public relations coup. The military scale in this second case was minimal and essentially bloodless. Russian President Putin's gamble paid off. Putin's territorial grab was costly from a geopolitical point of view. However, his objectives included (1) elimination of any threat to Russian naval bases in Crimea; (2) recognition in the West of the arrival of a different Russia run by a different, stronger leader; and (3) sending a message to other borderland states that Russia is not afraid to use armed aggression to maintain influence in the regions it considered to be of special interest. The annexation and recent military exercises in the Baltic Sea and Central Asia also sent the world new proof of the strength of Russia's partially reorganized and reformed military. In the face of a substantially weaker foe such as Georgia or Ukraine, Putin was able to gain tremendous personal glory at home as the architect of a new, once-again assertive Russia. Putin's strength was that he was competing for recognition as a regional power, if not yet a global superpower, from what appeared to be an unassailable base of a natural resource and energy–rich, nuclear-armed, secure political leader. He is apparently convinced that his actions have succeeded in having Russia again be recognized as one of the three or four global superpowers. Among his supporters, he is seen as the autocratic boss of a powerful nation even if outsiders do not yet award Russia its former superpower appellation he and his close followers long for.

11.3.2 Putin's Weaknesses

Putin's weaknesses include the greatly reduced and continuing-to-decline population of the RF, the old core of the Soviet Union (the RF population from 1980 to 2012 compared to other large nations is shown in Table 11.2); although increasing in size and capability, a military that is still not as technologically advanced as that of the West; an industrial infrastructure that remains relatively weak; and an economy that is too dependent upon commodity exports for economic growth. One of

Table 11.2   Population of Russia, the United States, China, India and Ukraine 1980–2012

	1980	*1990*	*2000*	*2012*
Russia (million)	139.0	148.3	146.3	143.5
China (million/billion)	981.2	1.135 b	1.263 b	1.351 b
India (million/billion)	699.0	868.9	1.042 b	1.237 b
United States (million)	226.5	249.6	282.2	313.9
Ukraine (million)	49.97	51.89	49.18	45.51

Source: World Bank, *Russian Economic Report,* available at http://www.worldbank
.org/en/news/press-release/2014/09/24/russia-economic-report-32, (accessed June 8, 2014).

Putin's greatest weaknesses has been Russia's lack of political credibility on all fronts and recognition of his increasing willingness to use of hard power along with his soft power tactic of withholding energy supply (Romanova 2007). His invasion of Ukraine and threats to borderlands Moldova and the Baltic states result in increased apprehension about Russia's belligerence and Putin's intentions (Fredén 2005).

The West's leaders have had to accept the idea that the Cold War security concerns have resurfaced and that they must strengthen their intelligence and counterespionage systems to be ready for renewed Cold War threats and armed and cyber conflict (Williamson 2012). Meanwhile, Putin continues his misleading, often contradictory and unexpected offers of energy price deals to European opponents. Caught off guard by Putin's increasing aggressiveness, the strongest and most affluent countries in the West have become uncertain and reluctant to face Russia's demonstrated or imagined might and power. The main reason for Europe's passive apprehension is more than the fear of war or other violent conflicts; they see a determined effort to rebuild the Russian Empire. Aggressive diplomacy is clearly working for Putin's Russia. To achieve his goals, he fluctuates between three foreign policy strategies.

11.4 Alternative Foreign Policy Strategies

Russia's continuing use of a saber-rattling and intimidation with its borderlands is just one of four possible foreign policy alternatives. The first is the policy that has been defined by a confidential informant as a *martial arts* or *judo approach to diplomacy*; it is aggressive by definition. The second is economic warfare centered on energy assets. The third is the heavy-handed intimidation over weaker neighbors; this intimidation has often been accompanied by arms and leadership support for ethnic Russian separatists in former republics and territorial annexation tactics in Finland and Ukraine. The fourth is a benign, friendly neighbor approach that stresses common security needs and mutually beneficial trade.

11.4.1 The Martial Arts Approach

Putin has been shown to be an accomplished judo expert. He is said to have integrated his physical, emotional and intellectual abilities of judo in his geopolitical power plays. The threat of increasingly aggressive actions reflects a flexible, often-only-tentative master stroke, one always aimed for the win at the lowest possible cost and effort. The rationale for continuing with this approach is technically incorrect, if it is focused on Russia's smaller, weaker former republics. It may be appropriate for describing some of Russia's actions against the United States.

As described by Yoffie and Kwak (2001, 2002), the judo approach is used by smaller opponents (countries or companies) to combat larger opponents. The strategy includes three elements: movement, balance and leverage. Movement entails the use of speed and agility by the smaller opponent; balance refers to absorbing and countering an opponent's actions; leverage is the use of the larger opponent's strengths against him. This explanation, correct or not, is only one of the empire-building alternatives available to Putin. Internal pressures and political disruption applied by ethnic Russians living in the former Soviet states are manifestations of this strategy. This may not be the best alternative, but it does describe some aspects of Putin's policy actions toward the EU, the United States and NATO to date.

11.4.2 Economic Warfare Approach

The second alternative is economic warfare in one or more versions. There is no particular reason why Putin would want to start a shooting war in his actions to build a greater Russia. Russia is considered to be technologically at least a decade behind the West, although this may be less appropriate for describing portions of Russia's military technology. There is no obvious advantage to begin hostilities against larger opponents. Moreover, Putin's own active service life is also necessarily limited. There is no guarantee that the current empire-building strategy will survive Putin's time as Russia's leader.

The alternative of a trade or economic war is thus more compatible with known Russian capabilities. For years to come, Russia will remain a regional supplier of raw materials and commodities to the West, particularly oil and natural gas. Russia has become as dependent upon existing markets as the nations in Europe and Asia are on the supply of Russia's fuels. To change this pattern of growth and competition takes not only time but also very major investments that Russia's potential enemies have thus far not been willing to make. Russia has been able to smooth over political disagreements with reductions in oil and gas exports.

Cutting off the supply of fuels has been employed as a foreign policy weapon against countries that resist greater Russian influence in their political or economic affairs. The problem is that those cuts have also adversely affected downstream customers. Increasingly, when pipelines across former Soviet states are cut, homes and businesses in the EU suffer the consequences. Thus, this option may be realistic from Russia's perspective, but it is not so to EU customers; Russia is increasingly branded as an unreliable supplier.

11.4.3 The Aggressive Diplomacy Approach

Only a generally comparative military strength is needed to back up a hard aggressive diplomacy that can scare a fearful balancing alliance of defenders. Taking the second option, the aggressor can use a flexible strategy to negotiate concessions, increased Russian influence and the eventual return of some nations of the Russian Empire. The targets of this option are Russia's borderlands, including Ukraine. They are the small nations now dependent on the defensive shield of the NATO and other alliances. At issue are the relative strengths of Russia and the weaknesses of the West (Graham 2007).

The third alternative has been the approach that seems to be most desirable by Putin. It has involved use of various degrees of hard power that range from military exercises that feign an invasion: overflights of bomber aircraft, cutting off imports from a target nation, implied and real threats of reductions in energy supplies or steep increases in energy prices, to armed invasions in support of Russian speaking minorities, to the so-far-most-severe territorial annexation. It allows for cooperation among major powers of Europe and Asia, does not endanger Russia and permits the rebuilding of the empire piece by piece, much in the way Putin has already begun. Putin employs this weapon at every chance he gets. However, annexation of Crimea may have been one use too many, as Russian economic difficulties that have occurred from US and EU sanctions and drops in energy prices attest. Russia has announced more than once that it will do whatever is necessary to "protect the rights" of foreign citizens residing in other countries. Moreover, as a matter of historical precedent, it maintains special minority or other rights and arrangements favorable to Russia in its former republics.

11.4.4 *The Friendly Neighbor Approach*

Putin's fourth policy choice is improved cooperation with the West with a show of increased willingness to engage in collaboration on the mutually important bilateral issues concerning the former Russian Empire. This approach was instituted by Gorbachev and Yeltsin but declined by Putin. This approach permits a large and flexible choice of negotiated relationship opportunities. It is unclear as to whether Putin has ever seen closer association with the West as a viable policy that could result in maintaining benign peace with its independent former republics or whether it might lead to a peaceful closer association of one or more republics in Central Asia and the Baltics. The relationship between Russia and Belarus suggests how this alternative might work. Should this allegedly friendlier approach yield benefits too slowly, a further cooling of relationships is likely (Kempe 2007; Strauss 2014). However, as a result of Russia's 2014 and earlier actions in Ukraine, the cooperative approach may not be acceptable to the West.

11.5 The Recurring Foreign Policy Aim

Events in the Russian borderlands since 2000 have shown that a salient strategy of Putin's foreign policy is to take advantage of every opportunity to match the empire-building successes of Peter the Great. As a practical matter, doing so calls for an ideology that is strong enough to unite the many nationalities that extend across the Eurasian land mass (Russia's *sacred* mission), economic and technological resources, as well as formidable modern military power. However, collapse of the Soviet Union left Russia devoid of a unifying ideology; despite its vast resources, Russia's economy is overwhelmingly dependent upon income from oil and gas exports; the once-formidable military force of more than 4 million men that today is less than 1 milllion strong is a mere shadow of its former military strength; moreover, continuing negative population growth and declining income from depressed oil and gas prices make that force unlikely to improve significantly in the future.

The outcomes of Russia's little wars in Chechnya, Georgia and Ukraine show that despite its problems, the Russian army is strong enough to ultimately deal with internal and external discord in its borderlands. In its dealings with its smaller and weaker former republics, Russia does have the ability and intent to employ intimidation in its international negotiation processes. This aggressive diplomacy magnifies the fears of aggression and war among the borderlands of Russia, from Finland on the Baltic Sea and Ukraine on the Black Sea. In the Crimean situation, aggressive diplomacy was used to maximum effect to limit the defense or resistance to the annexation by the Ukrainian and Tatar opponents. The annexation of Crimea was justified largely by several augments that are often repeated in Russia. These included the historical memory of conquest and previous possession of an area of strategic importance for the defense of *Mother Russia*, the interests and rights of a now-predominately-assertive Russophone colonist population and the promised financial and military support of Russia's *compatriot* members of the Russian diaspora.

The social structures and shared willingness among Russians to applaud Putin's foreign policy initiatives are defined by shared understandings, expectations and knowledge among the elite that are involved in carrying out his foreign policy. A shared national identity as children of Mother Russia and a common external enemy in the shape of a combined United States, EU and NATO are examples. Social structures involve the availability of material resources such as valuable natural resources, currency reserves and modern armaments. Russia's strong economy based on high energy prices and close existence of the EU as an apparent captive market for Russian oil, gas and other natural resources gives Putin the elbow room to make autocratic decisions (Mau 2007). His large nuclear arsenal and million-man army with modern weapons enable Putin to exercise strong power.

These factors have meaning when they become part of the shared knowledge and understanding. Social structures exist not in actors' heads nor in their capabilities but in the actions taken and the practices and processes that are manifestations of the shared knowledge and understanding. The lesson for constructionist foreign policy analysts, then, is to look at actions, not assertions. Russia's absorption of the Crimea and its recent wars with its former subjects are expressions of actions enough.

The *protecting-compatriots* justification Putin gives for his aggressive adventures is the long-stated determination to use any means necessary to protect Russians living outside of the RF as legal as approved by Russian authorities for use in Russia.

Thus, Russia has used and will continue to use this distorted or false defense argument for an action against universal norms of sovereignty. The Russian-provoked and -executed invasions of Georgia and Ukraine are good examples of the moral superiority that aggressors feel. They are convinced that their regular and irregular forces have the privilege to cross any virtually undefended border uninvited, as was executed against Baltic state border guard stations in 1940 and in Ukraine in 2014.

As recently as 2009, Russia's foreign policy was described as "most likely [to] remain...opportunistic rather than overtly aggressive" (King and McNabb 2009). At that time, US Secretary of Defense Robert Gates said that Russia's military strategy in Georgia was the result of a "desire to exorcise past humiliation and dominate its near abroad, [not an] ideologically driven campaign to dominate the globe." Along with Secretary Gates, the consensus was that Russia's then-existing foreign policy did not include military conquest but, rather, was a gradual but unswerving drive to eventually regain dominance over the social, economic and political affairs of what are to become entirely dependent client states (King and McNabb 2009, p. 39).

Events then have proven that consensus to be patently incorrect. In 2013 and 2014, it became abundantly clear that Russia's leaders are driven by the same expansionist dreams that motivated the tsars and leaders of the Soviet Union. Russia under Putin has the same expansionist goals as his Soviet and Romanov predecessors: Their long-term goal continues to be reestablishing the Russian empire. Imperial status does not only necessarily entail territorial absorption; it can also mean using economic, political or militarial dominance over ostensibly independent satellite states. Putin's desires to reestablish Russia's reputation as a global power worthy of respect have led him to follow what appears to be the use of energy supply as a promise or a threat direct in Europe, together with the threat of providing military support to separatists as the *wild card* in foreign relations.

11.6 Implications for the West

Western observers of Russian foreign policy were wrong when they concluded that Putin was not likely to use military force to carry out its policy goals. Not only has he done so more than once, it also appears as if he is willing to do so again and again. Some foreign policy observers liken Putin's actions in the Crimea and the West's tepid reaction to his use of armed force to similar unwillingness to stop Hitler from taking over the Sudetenland in 1938 (Cohen 2014; Lo 2014), and the brutal aftermath of that mistake.

Russian foreign policy clearly took a distinctly revanchist, outward-looking turn with the ascendency of Putin. Over his first two terms as president of the RF, Putin and a band of former KGB and FSB power elite, a number of whom were with Putin in the St. Petersburg security forces, attempted to address each of the

Yeltsin-era crisis points. In the process, they also took significant first steps in an effort to reestablish Russia's reputation as a geopolitical great power status. The very high prices for oil and gas exports that existed for a number of years helped make it possible for Russia to make giant strides toward reestablishing Russia as a geoeconomic superpower, including upgrading and rearming its military. Repercussions resulting from Russia's annexation of Crimea have severely limited the opportunity of continuing on this path.

Now in his third four-year term as president of Russia, "apparently until 2024, Putin seems to have one overriding objective: the re-establishment of Soviet Russia's empire" (Tisdall 2011). To achieve this goal, Russian foreign policy under President Putin has brought the world closer to, if not to another Cold War, at least to what has been described as a *Cold Wave* (Arbatov 2007; Janco 2007). It is manifestly apparent that Russia's policies during several centuries of expansionism and world power influence have not been shelved. Rather, Russia's reliance on armed diplomacy actions in the Crimea and elsewhere indicate that the policies of coercion are once again front and center. Not the least factor crying for greater attention to be paid to Russia's aggressive foreign policy is the existence of thousands of nuclear warheads and the weapons to deliver them that remain in Russian hands (Kaplan 1954). Along with completely rebuilding the nation's military forces, Putin is also rebuilding and upgrading much of Russia's aging nuclear arsenal.

With the caveat that the range of coercive diplomacy options is exceedingly large, Byman and Waxman (2002) identified five coercive strategies that have been used by modern nations as elements of their foreign policy: air strikes (which appear to be an instrument of first resort rather than last), including the increasing use of drones; invasions by land forces; land grabs; the threat of nuclear attack and other weapons of mass destruction; sanctions and international isolation (without the use of military means); support for an insurgency, including support for one or more ethnic minorities; and combinations of these and other instruments. Military action against minority populations within a nation's boundaries such as Putin's wars in Chechnya is an exercise of internal police actions, not invasion of a sovereign nation.

Putin's policy against Ukraine began with an armed incursion by a small number of masked special forces with the mission of protecting Russian naval and other military bases after the overthrow of the pro-Russia government. Ethnic Russian citizens also played a classic subversion role (Diez 2004). This quickly evolved into a combination of armed invasion and land grab options. Putin justifies this action by calling the invasion necessary to protect the large body of ethnic Russians living in the Crimea—in a sense preempting the need for supporting friendly ethnic groups. The United States and EU responded with weak political sanctions that include the banning of travel by some Russian oligarchs, limited economic sanctions such as freezing a few individual and bank assets and the weak threat of future political isolation.

11.7 Russia's Relations with the West

Russia's reaction to the May 1, 2004 admission of ten new members to the EU and the admission of many Eastern European nations to NATO reflects its return to a more aggressive approach to foreign policy. This expansion brought the EU to the borders with Russia as new members included the Czech Republic, Estonia, Hungary, Latvia, Lithuania, Poland, Slovakia and Slovenia. Accordingly, Russia feels that this eastward expansion of the EU and NATO forces her once again on the *geopolitical defensive* (Kuchins and Zevelev 2012). In reaction to this perceived encirclement, Russia has begun to modernize and rearm its military.

11.7.1 Relations with NATO

At their 2014 summit session, NATO ministers endorsed a strong denunciation of Russia's annexation of Crimea and continued support of ethnic Russian separatists in eastern Ukraine. They upgraded NATO force and surveillance levels in the Baltic states and Poland. They also concurred with the several levels of sanction against Russia by the United States and the EU. Putin reacted to those actions in a December 2014 press conference by declaring NATO's actions a military threat to Russia and declaring NATO's buildup of military infrastructure as Russia's greatest military threat. Putin announced an upgrading of the 2010 Russian military doctrine. Putin then reaffirmed Russia's decision to use nuclear weapons in retaliation to similar use or other mass destruction weapons against Russia or its allies by any nation. Nuclear weapons would also be used to deter any use of conventional weapons that "threaten the very existence" of the Russian state. The upgraded doctrine now states that Russia could use precision weapons (i.e., tactical nuclear weapons) as elements in a deterrence strategy.

11.7.2 Relations with Former Possessions

One of the trouble spots of Russia's current foreign policy for years since the breakup has been deciding on what attitude to adopt toward its former republics, particularly the Baltic states (Estonia, Latvia and Lithuania), Georgia, Moldova and Ukraine. During the Yeltsin presidency, much of the country's foreign policy involved forging new ways for coming to terms with new relationships with these border states. Yeltsin administration policy makers also focused on dealing with instabilities in the northern and southern Caucasus regions while also building new relations with the United States and Europe. The Caucasus includes the post-Soviet states of Georgia, Armenia and Azerbaijan plus such Russian political hotspots as Chechnya.

After the independence of the former Soviet republics that occurred during the Yeltsin presidency, the attitude of the new states fell into two categories (Gorenburg and Gaffney 2006): The first group included the states that remained suspicious of Russia and believed that it would try to regain control of their countries through overt or covert means. This particularly applied to the Baltics, Georgia and Ukraine. The second category includes those states that were not ready for independence and therefore retained strong economic ties to Russia. Among the second group are Azerbaijan, Belarus, Moldova and, to a degree, Georgia. During the Yeltsin presidency, Russia attempted to move the former group toward the second by emphasizing its economic power, control over energy resources and pressures on their large Russian minorities residing in the Baltics (Nordberg 1999). Russia took issue with Latvian and Estonian citizenship laws, which they charged discriminated against ethnic Russians living within their borders. When the three Baltic countries joined NATO and the EU, the situation became even more exacerbated. Russian appeals to the EU resulted in some easing of the citizenship laws thus easing tensions somewhat.

With a compliant political infrastructure in place and docile opponents unwilling to block his actions, Putin was able to exercise his newfound muscles. The path that his exercise would take has been spelled out for anyone to see: Every move was telegraphed in the Ministry of Foreign Affairs' publication of Russia's foreign policy goals and standards to 2020. The latest version of that conceptual document was approved by President Putin on February 12, 2013.

11.8 Scenarios for a Russia after Putin

In a May 2014 publication of the US Army's Strategic Studies Institute, Professor Richard J. Krickus described four possible outcomes for Russia after Putin no longer rules the country, along with the prospects that each scenario holds for a return to balanced US–Russia relationship. Two of the possible outcomes were described as benign and two as malignant. The two benign outcomes were continuation of the system with little change (*Status Quo*) and a return of the policy of westernization and a revitalized democracy movement begun under Gorbachev and Yeltsin (the *Western Path to Development*). The malignant possible outcomes include greater exercise of the restrictions on the media, arrests of political opponents, state ownership of the energy sector and strict control over civil society, which has appeared during Putin's presidency (*Stalin Lite*). The most severe possible outcome—what Krickus terms *Russia in Chaos*—is a collapse of the economy and of the existing *power vertical* system that is now governing Russia. While considered to be the least plausible of the four scenarios, this last outcome would represent a return to Cold War relations between the United States and Russia while also resulting in serious repercussions in terms of global security.

11.8.1 Status Quo

With annexation of the Crimea, control of violence in Chechnya and a successful holding of the Winter Olympics, Putin is enjoying unprecedented popularity at home. He is exceptionally popular among everyday Russians, enjoying an increase from the 60% approval rating he received in 2012 to 81% in late 2014. At just 62 years of age and reelected to a third term as president, he is likely to remain in control of the RF at least until 2020. He has erected a tight system of wealthy oligarchs and former members of several Soviet security agencies to carry out his plans with little question. Governors of all the more than 80 districts are now appointed by the president; many are former KGB operatives or military officers. He has instilled strict restrictions over electronic and print media and limited access to opposition Internet sources. Not only has he reasserted Russia's place in the world through liberal use of populist rhetoric, he has also used income from very high oil and gas sales to increase benefits for the growing middle class and rural population and raised pay and benefits, including housing, of the military. His plan to invest billions in reorganizing and rearming the Russian military has won him the acquiescence of senior military officers. More importantly, his harsh treatment of protestors has all but silenced effective opposition from those who would have greater freedom and Western-style prosperity in Russia. If he has a weak spot, it is twofold. The first is the *petro-state* nature of the Russian economy; more than half of the government's annual budget is in the form of profits from oil and gas exports; prices for both of these commodities are subject to global geopolitical pressures. The second is the endemic corruption that permeates Russian business and government, including the dysfunctional legal system.

In this scenario, little freeing of the restrictions imposed is likely to occur under whoever replaces Putin. Hence, Russia and the West will work together when conditions warrant and continue to accuse each other of failing to adjust to a changed world. Once sanctions over Russia's land grab in Crimea are resolved and Russia's economy recovers, the world will see a continuation of the existing system verbal warfare. Relations between the United States and Russia will not improve unless Putin receives the cooperation and concessions that he believes are merited by Russia. On the other hand, they are not likely to get much worse than they are today, particularly as conditions over Ukraine become less a problem. According to Krickus (2014, p. 22),

> [Putin] knows Russia will never enjoy the power that the soviet leaders did.... He has no intention of taking on the West in a serious showdown because his most urgent foreign policy goal is regional, not international—although the region in question, the former Soviet space, is massive. Specifically, he wants to re-integrate former Soviet entities back into Russia's clutches and to deny the West the capacity to integrate them into the EU and NATO. Using this measuring stick, Putin's foreign policy agenda shows promise as many analysts in Eastern Europe remind their American counterparts.

In conclusion, this scenario is not likely to change much from now to 2020 unless the EU and US economic sanctions cause significant uproar in Russia. On the other hand, Krickus reports that there are signs that the status quo may be moving to the Soviet Lite outcome—one of the more malign scenarios.

11.8.2 The Path to the West

The once-small but vociferous democratic contingent may return should economic sanctions and a weak drop in export income result in a collapse of Putin's power vertical coalition. If that occurs, a revolution similar to what brought Yeltsin to power in 1991 may see a greater interest among the Russian parliament and Putin's successors in diversifying the Russian economy, democratic freedom with greater pluralism in government, a serious effort to control corruption among the economic oligarch and governing class and less foreign policy belligerence. The pro-democracy movement that flourished after the collapse of the Soviet Union has had to retreat underground (Baker and Glasser 2007).

11.8.3 Stalin Lite

In this scenario, the increased police state measures adopted by Putin during the global recession of the first decade of the new century and the steep drop in export income that followed will not only continue, they also are likely to increase. The government's income from gas and oil exports fell during the recession; deep cuts were necessary in government workers' salaries, pensions and other entitlements, along with delaying of military reforms that included plans to improve benefits, including housing, to serving military. Tighter controls were initiated over business, the economic system and commerce. Ethnic protestors and separatists, leftists including Communist party leaders, nationalists and other liberals were arrested; several journalists were murdered. Putin, responding to the unrest, included a call for a return to spirituality a turning away from pro-Western though and patriotism in his 2012 state of the nation address.

As oil and gas prices improved, so did Putin's popularity and his imperial inclinations. He ratcheted up his criticism of the West, particularly against what he called the unipolar foreign policy actions of the United States in the Middle East. This was also when Russia accelerated its efforts to regain its lost influence in the former republics. Under Russian leadership, former republics would allow complete control of their domestic affairs, but foreign affairs would have to be consistent with Russian policies. These "imperialistic utterances from Moscow" and subsequent events in the borderlands resulted in resistance from the former republics that had gained accession to the EU and those that desired membership, including Azerbaijan, Georgia and Ukraine.

11.8.4 Chaos in Russia

Chaos is the worst-case scenario of what might happen to Russia after Putin. While considered to be the least plausible of the four scenarios, this last of four possible outcomes would represent a return to Cold War relations between the United States and Russia while also resulting in serious repercussions in terms of global security. Although some regions such as Chechnya are likely to continue to push for autonomy, the possibility that Russia will break apart along the lines of diverse nationalities as did the USSR, while considered remote, could result in a number of "ethnic, religious, regional, and economic fiefdoms" replacing centralized authority (Krickus 2014, p. 65). China, with long borders with Russia and a population of more than a billion, would quickly move in to consolidate power over the region, giving it access to the vast energy and mineral resources.

Putin has taken steps to alleviate the possibility of further division of the empire. Recognizing the possibility of Balkanization, in 2004, he removed the opportunity for citizens in regional districts to elect their own governors, all of whom are now appointed by the president. He has also sought to bring the former republics together in a federalized Eurasian Economic Union much like the EU. After some initial success, his interest in joining such a union with Russia has waned; in 2014, only Belarus and Kazakhstan remain in the customs union.

11.8.5 The Most Probable Scenario

For the United States and the EU, a return to a Western form of government after Putin is the most desirable scenario but not necessarily the most likely Russia of the future. A solid core of pro-democracy advocates remains in Russia despite Putin's crackdown on liberals. However, for self-interest and the sustainability of the existing power elite, the most likely outcome is continuation of the movement toward a police state, *Soviet Lite*. That will mean continuation of worrisome times for the borderland states and renewal of Cold War–like relations between Russia and the West, as current events suggest.

11.9 Conclusion

There is little doubt that Russian armor can roll almost unmolested across the borders of all her former republics and Cold War client states. This is particularly true of the borders with all of Northern and Central Europe.

The allegedly least aggressive foreign policy option combined with misleading data leads to distortions of truth and prevents constructive agreements. This leads to actual misunderstandings and concessions by the West. Such concessions weaken Russia's borderland states and eventually the larger West. This is the most dangerous aspect of Russia's aggressive diplomacy. Therefore, to guard the freedom of the borderland states and the West in general, it is necessary to maintain NATO—the thin red line of defense.

Four possible scenarios have been proposed for Russia after Putin's eventual demise: Status Quo, Movement Toward the West, Soviet Lite and Return to Chaos. The West must be prepared to deal with Russia in any of these possible outcomes and particularly be prepared if Scenario 4 includes a return to nuclear posturing and Cold War diplomacy. Should that happen, Western security planners will find themselves forced to

Si vis pacem, para bellum.

Appendix: US Department of Defense Cyberspace Definitions

Computer network attack: A category of files employed for offensive purposes in which actions are taken through the use of computer networks to disrupt, deny, degrade, manipulate or destroy information resident in the target information system or computer networks or the systems/networks themselves. The ultimate intended effect is not necessarily on the targeted system itself but may support a larger effort, such as information operations or counterterrorism, e.g., altering or spoofing specific communications or gaining or denying access to adversary communications or logistics channels.

Computer network exploitation: Enabling operations and intelligence collection capabilities conducted through the use of computer networks to gather data about a target or adversary automated information systems or networks. See also *computer network attack*.

Counter-cyber (CC): A mission that integrates offensive and defensive operations to attain and maintain a desired degree of cyberspace superiority. CC missions are designed to disrupt, negate and/or destroy adversarial cyberspace activities and capabilities before and after their employment.

Critical cyber system/asset/function: An information system is considered to be vital if a physical or cyber incident affecting the confidentiality, integrity and availability of the system, asset or function would have significant negative impact on the national security, economic stability, public confidence, health or safety of the United States.

Cyber attack: A hostile act using computer or related networks or systems and intended to disrupt and/or destroy an adversary's critical cyber systems, assets or functions. The intended effects of cyber attack are not necessarily limited to the targeted computer systems or data themselves—for instance, attacks on computer systems that are intended to degrade or destroy infrastructure. A cyber attack may use intermediate delivery vehicles including peripheral devices, electronic transmitters, embedded code or human operators. The activation or effect of a cyber attack may be widely separated temporally and geographically from the delivery.

Cyber Defense: The integrated application of Department of Defense (DoD) or US government cyberspace capabilities and processes to synchronize in real time the ability to detect, analyze and mitigate threats and vulnerabilities and outmaneuver adversaries in order to defend designated networks, protect critical missions and enable the United States freedom of action. Cyber Defense includes

- *Proactive Network Operations*: e.g., configuration control, information assurance measures, physical security and secure architecture design, intrusion detection, firewalls, signature updates, encryption of data at rest.
- *Defensive counter-cyber (DCC)*: Includes the following: (1) military deception via honeypots and other operations and (2) redirection, deactivation or removal of malware engaged in a hostile act/imminent hostile act.
- *Defensive countermeasures.*

Cyber incident: Level 1 or Level 2 incident on the Cyber Risk Alert Level system. A cyber incident is likely to cause, or is causing, harm to critical functions and services across the public and private sectors by impairing the confidentiality, integrity or availability of electronic information, information systems, services or networks and/or threatening public health or safety, undermining public confidence, having a negative effect on the national economy or diminishing the security posture of the nation.

Cyber-operational preparation of the environment (C-OPE): Non-intelligence-enabling functions within cyberspace conducted to plan and prepare for potential follow-on military operations. C-OPE includes but is not limited to identifying data, system/network configurations or physical structures connected to or associated with the network or system (to include software, ports and assigned network address ranges or other identifiers) for the purposes of determining system vulnerabilities and actions taken to assure future access and/or control of the system, network or data during anticipated hostilities.

Cybersecurity: All organizational actions required to ensure freedom from danger and risk to the security of information in all its forms (electronic, physical) and the security of the systems and networks where information is stored, accessed, processed and transmitted, including precautions taken to guard against crime, attack, sabotage, espionage, accidents and failures. Cybersecurity risks may include those that damage stakeholder trust and confidence, affect customer retention and growth, violate customer and partner identity and privacy protections, disrupt the ability to conduct or fulfill business transactions, adversely affect health and cause loss of life and adversely affect the operations of national critical infrastructures.

Cyberspace: Domain characterized by the use of electronics and the electromagnetic spectrum to store, modify and exchange data via networked systems and associated physical infrastructures.

Cyberspace operations: The employment of cyber capabilities where the primary purpose is to achieve objectives in or through cyberspace. Such operations include computer network operations and activities to operate and defend the Global Information Grid.

Cyberspace superiority: The degree of dominance in cyberspace by one force that permits the secure, reliable conduct of operations by that force and its related land, air, sea and space forces at a given time and sphere of operations without prohibitive interference by an adversary.

Cyber warfare: An armed conflict conducted in whole or in part by cyber means. Military operations conducted to deny an opposing force the effective use of cyberspace systems and weapons in a conflict. It includes cyber attack, cyber defense and cyber-enabling actions.

Defensive counter-cyber (DCC): All defensive countermeasures designed to detect, identify, intercept and destroy or negate harmful activities attempting to penetrate or attack through cyberspace. DCC missions are designed to preserve friendly network integrity, availability and security and protect friendly cyber capabilities from attack, intrusion or other malicious activity by proactively seeking, intercepting and neutralizing adversarial cyber means that present such threats. DCC operations may include the following: military deception via honeypots and other operations; actions to adversely affect adversary and/or intermediary systems engaged in a hostile act/imminent hostile act; and redirection, deactivation or removal of malware engaged in a hostile act/imminent hostile act.

Information assurance: Actions that protect and defend information systems by ensuring availability, integrity, authentication, confidentiality and nonrepudiation. This includes providing for restoration of information systems by incorporating detection, protection and reaction capabilities.

National Military Strategy for Cyberspace Operations (NMS-CO): The comprehensive strategy of the US Armed Forces to ensure US military superiority in cyberspace. The NMS-CO establishes a common understanding of cyberspace and sets forth a military strategic framework that orients and focuses DOD actions in the areas of military, intelligence and business operations in and through cyberspace.

Network operations: Activities conducted to operate and defend the DOD's Global Information Grid.

Offensive counter-cyber (OCC): Offensive operations to destroy, disrupt or neutralize adversary cyberspace capabilities before and after their use against friendly forces but as close to their source as possible. The goal of OCA operations is to prevent the employment of adversary cyberspace capabilities prior to employment. This could mean preemptive action against an adversary. It differs from the generic use of *cyber attack* in that the latter can be used to affect noncyber systems, including but not limited to infrastructure, transportation and other networks, etc., and is not specifically tied to imminent or ongoing of hostilities.

Offensive cyberspace operations: Activities that, through the use of cyberspace, actively gather information from computers, information systems or networks or manipulate, disrupt, deny, degrade or destroy targeted computers, information systems or networks. This definition includes C-OPE, OCC, cyber attack and related electronic attack and space control negation.

References

Ambrosio, T. 2005. *Challenging America's Global Preeminence*. Aldershot, UK: Ashgate Publishing.

Armstrong, R. 2012. What are Russia's relations with its former "sister republics"? Internet essay. Available at http://www.allrussias.com/essays/2012/Armstron.pdf (retrieved April 14, 2014).

Anderson, B. A. 2005. Russia faces depopulation? Dynamics of population decline. *Population and Environment*, 23 (5): 437–464.

AP World History. 2011. Eastern Europe and Russia. In P. N. Sterns, S. B. Schwartz, M. B. Adas, and M. J. Gilbert. 2007. *World Civilizations, the Global Experience*, 5th ed. New York: Pearson Higher Education. Available at http://easterneuroperussiawhap2.weebly.com/important-maps1.html.

Arbatov, A. G. 2004. Military reform: From crisis to stagnation. In S. E. Miller and D. Trenin, eds., *The Russian Military*. Cambridge, MA: MIT Press, 95–120.

Arbatov, A. G. 2007. Is a new cold war imminent? *Russia in Global Affairs*, 5 (2). Available at http://eng.globalaffairs.ru/number/n_9127 (retrieved June 8, 2014).

Arms Control Association (ACA). 2012. The Conventional Armed Forces in Europe (CFE) Treaty and the Adapted CFE Treaty at a Glance. Available at http://www.armscontrol.org/factsheet/cfe (retrieved March 9, 2014).

Ashmore, W. C. 2007. Impact of alleged Russian cyber attacks. Ft. Leavenworth, KS: U.S. Army School of Advanced Military Studies. Available at http://www.dtic.mil/cgi-bin/GetTRDoc?AD=ADA504991 (retrieved April 15, 2015).

Ashmore, W. C. 2009. *Impact of Alleged Russian Cyber Attacks*. Ft. Leavenworth, KS: U.S. Army Command and General Staff College.

Aybet, G. 2010. The NATO strategic concept revisited: Grand strategy and emerging issues. In G. Aybet and R. R. Moore, eds. *NATO: In Search of a Vision*. Washington, DC: Georgetown University, 35–50.

Backus III, O. P. 1954. Was Muscovite Russia imperialistic? *American Slavic and East European Review*, 13 (4): 522–534.

Baev, J. 2003. *The Organization and Doctrinal Evolution of the Warsaw Pact (1955–1969)*. Paper presented at an international conference at Spitzbergen Island, Norway and published in Bulgaria.

Baev, P. K. 2004. The trajectory of the Russian military: Downsizing, degeneration, and defeat. In S. E. Miller and D. V. Trenin, eds. *The Russian Military: Power and Policy*. Cambridge: MIT Press, 43–72.

Baker, P. and S. Glasser. 2007. *Kremlin Rising: Vladimir Putin's Russia and the End of Revolution*. Washington: Potomac Books.

Beauvois, D. 1999. Russia, Belarus, and Ukraine: Can the "Slavic core" of the Community of Independent States lay claim to historical legitimacy? In M. P. Lewis and G. Lepesant, eds. *What Security for Which Europe?* New York: Peter Lang, 33–42.

Biography.com. 2014. Vladimir Putin. The biography channel website. Available at http://www.biography.com/people/vladimir-putin-9448807 (retrieved March 8, 2014).

Bishku, M. B. 2011. The South Caucasus republics and Russia's growing influence: Balancing on a tightrope. *MERIA Journal*, 15 (1): 1–11.

Blank, S. 2006. Reading Putin's military tea leaves. *Eurasia Daily Monitor*, 3 (98): 117–120. Johnson's Russia List (JRL) E-Mail Newsletter (May 19). Available at http://www.cdi.org/russia/johnson/2006-117-20.cfm (retrieved September 4, 2013).

Boersma, T., T. Mitrova, G. Greving, and A. Galkina. 2014. Business as usual: European gas market functioning in times of turmoil and increasing import dependence. Washington, DC: Brookings Energy Security Initiative Policy Brief 14-05. Available at http://www.brookings.edu/~/media/Research/Files/Papers/2014/10/european-gas-market-import-dependence/business_as_usual_final_3pdf?la=en (retrieved December 20, 2014).

Bohlen, A. 1966. Changes in Russian diplomacy under Peter the Great. *Cahiers du Monde russe et soviétique*, 7 (3): 341–358.

Borger, J. 2015. US and Russia in danger of returning to an era of nuclear rivalry. *The Guardian* online (January 4). Available at http://www.theguardian.com/world/2015/jan/04/us-russia-era-nuclear-rivalry (retrieved January 8, 2015).

Browning, C. S. 2004. The EU as a foreign policy actor: The limitations of territorial sovereignty. In S. Guzzini and D. Jung, eds. *Contemporary Security Analysis and Copenhagen Peace Research*. London: Routledge, 167–179.

Bushkovitch, P. 2009. Poltava's consequences: Local autonomy in the Russian Empire during the reign of Peter I. *Harvard Ukrainian Studies*, 31 (1/4): 135–158.

Byman, D. and M. Waxman. 2002. *The Dynamics of Coercion*. Cambridge: Cambridge University.

Cartwright, J. E. 2013. *Joint Terminology for Cyberspace Operations*. JCS Memorandum with Cyberspace Operations Lexicon. U.S. Department of Defense, August 28. Available at https://publicintelligence.net/dod-joint-cyber-terms/ (retrieved January 3, 2015).

Cassidy, J. 2014. Putin's Crimean history lesson. *The New Yorker* (March 18). Available at http://www.newyorker.com/news/john-cassidy/putins-crimean-history-lesson (retrieved August 19, 2014).

Chafetz, G. 1996. The struggle for a national identity in Post-Soviet Russia. *Political Science Quarterly*, 111 (4): 661–668.

CIA. 1965. Warsaw pact military strategy: A compromise in Soviet strategic thinking. (Document reference title: Caesar XXVI, released June 2007). Langley, VA: Central Intelligence Agency.

CIA.gov. 2013. Map of Russia. Available at http://www.cia.gov/library/publications/cia-maps-publications/ (retrieved August 19, 2014).

Clackson, A. 2014. The Russia-China counter-alliance to US-NATO aggression. Global Research: Center for Research on Globalization. Available at http://www.globalresearch.ca/the-russia-china-counter-alliance-to-us-nato-aggression (retrieved August 24, 2014).

Clarke, R. and R. K. Knake. 2010. *Cyber War*. New York: HarperCollins.

Cohen, A. 1997. *The "Primakov Doctrine": Russia's Zero-Sum Game with the United States*. Washington, DC: The Heritage Foundation. Available at http://www.heritage.org/research/reports/1997/12/the-primakov-doctrine-russias-zero-sum-game-with-the-united-states (retrieved August 21, 2014).

Cohen, R. 2014. Putin forces us to reconsider poor Neville Chamberlain. *Washington Post* (March 10). Available at http://www.washingtonpost.com/opinions/richard-cohen -ukraine-carries-the-echoes-of-sudetenland/2014/03/10/36ba5b6c-a873-11e3-8599 -ce7295b6851c_story.html (retrieved March 19, 2014).

Comey, D. D. 1962. Marxist-Leninist Ideology and soviet policy. *Studies in Soviet Thought*, 2 (4): 301–320.

Commission on Security and Cooperation in Europe (CSCE). 2014. About the Helsinki Process. Available at http://www.csce.gov/index.cfm?FuseAction=AboutHelsinkiProcess .OSCE (retrieved November 23, 2014).

Cooper, W. H. 2012. *Russia's Accession to the WTO and its Implications for the United States.* Congressional Research Service, the U.S. Library of Congress Report for Congress (July 17). Available at http://www.fas.org/sgp/crs/row/R42085.pdf (retrieved June 8, 2014).

Cordell, K. and S. Wolff. 2007. A foreign policy analysis of the German question: Ostpolitik revisited. *Foreign Policy Analysis*, 3 (3): 255–271.

COSD. 2014. The beginning of the Cold War. (Canada), Online Learning Resources. Available at https://eschoolbc.sd23.bc.ca/mod/book/view.php?id=23449&chapterid=9948 (retrieved June 10, 2014).

Curtis, G. E., ed. 1992. *The Warsaw Pact.* Washington, DC: Federal Research Division of the Library of Congress. Available at http://www.shsu.edu/~his_ncp/WarPact.html (retrieved June 5, 2014).

Curtis, G. E., ed. 1996. *Russia: A Country Study.* Washington, DC: Federal Research Division of the Library of Congress. Available at http://www.shsu.edu/~his_ncp/Muscovy.html (retrieved November 17, 2014).

Curtiss, J. S. 1979. *Russia's Crimean War.* Durham, NC: Duke University.

Darczewska, J. 2014. The anatomy of Russian information warfare: The Crimean operation, a case study. Warsaw: Centre for Eastern Studies. Available at http://www.osw .waw.pl/sites/default/files/the-anatomy-of-russian-information-warfare.pdf (retrieved May 8, 2014).

Dash, P. L. 1999. Twilight of Yeltsin years. *Economic and Political Weekly*, 34 (37): 2639–2641.

Deloitte CIS. 2014. *2014 Russian Oil & Gas Outlook Survey.* Moscow: Deloitte CIS.

Demurin, M. 2005. Russia and the Baltic States: Not a case of "flawed" history. *Russia in Global Affairs*, 3 (3): 130–139.

Derluguian, G. 2006. The fourth Russian Empire? *PONARS* policy memo 411. Available at http://www.csis.org/media/csis/pubs/pm_0411.pdf (retrieved June 4, 2014).

DeWilde, J. H. 2004. Fears into fences: The isolationist pitfall of European federalism. In S. Guzzini and D. Jung, eds. *Contemporary Security Analysis and Copenhagen Peace Research.* London: Routledge, 180–192.

Diez, T. 2004. The subversion of borders. In S. Guzzini and D. Jung, eds. *Contemporary Security Analysis and Copenhagen Peace Research.* London: Routledge, 128–140.

Dinerstein, H. S. 1958. The Soviet employment of military strength for political purposes. *Annals of the American Academy of Political and Social Science*, 318 (July): 104–112.

Diuk, N. 2014. Euromaidan: Ukraine's self-organizing revolution. *World Affairs* online (March/April). Available at http://www.worldaffairsjournal.org/article/euromaidan -ukraine%E2%80%99s-self-organizing-revolution (retrieved December 27, 2014).

Donaldson, R. H. and J. L. Nogee. 2005. *The Foreign Policy of Russia*, 3rd ed. Armonk, NY: M. E. Sharpe.

Donnelly, A. S. 1975. Peter the Great and Central Asia. *Canadian Slavonic Papers*, 17 (2/3): 202–217.

Dutertre, G. 2011. Historical map of Ukraine. Available at http://www.google.com/url?sa=i&rct=j&q=&esrc=s&source=images&cd=&cad=rja&uact=8&docid=NSNmUCIHlm7mGM&tbnid=2o8ee3B95WJQ6M:&ved=0CAQQjB0&url=http%3A%2F%2Fgillesenlettonie.blogspot.com%2F2011_08_01_archive.html&ei=U9eVU-r0G8TyoATgnoKQCQ&bvm=bv.68445247,d.cGU&psig=AFQjCNGY_EcckYDe0HYFpxQ91MuNqX0HvA&ust=1402415075217995 (retrieved June 9, 2014).

East, W. G. 1951. The new frontiers of the Soviet Union. *Foreign Affairs*, 29 (4): 591–607.

Ebel, R. E. 2009. *The Geopolitics of Russian Energy: Looking Back, Looking Forward.* Washington, DC: Center for Strategic and International Studies.

Economist. 2007a. Putin's people (August 25). 384 (8543): 5.

Economist. 2007b. The making of a neo-KGB state (August 25). 384 (8543): 25–28.

Economist. 2014. Russia and Ukraine: A brief intermission. (September 13). Available at http://www.economist.com/node/21617016/print (retrieved October 15, 2014).

Energy Information Administration (EIA). 2015. Today in energy: Crude oil prices down sharply in fourth quarter of 2014. Available at http://www.eia.gov/todayinenergy/detail.cfm?id=19451 (retrieved April 15, 2015).

Entous, A. and J. Barnes. 2014. Russian buildup stokes worries. *Wall Street Journal* (March 24), 1, A8.

Eriksson, J. 2007. Power disparity in the digital age. In O. F. Knudsen, ed. *Security Strategies, Power Disparity and Identity: The Baltic Sea Region.* Aldershot, UK: Ashgate Publishing, 123–148.

Etkind, A. 2011. *Internal Colonization: Russia's Imperial Experience.* Malden, MA: Polity Press.

Eurofish.com. 2014. European fishing report. Available at http://www.eurofish.dk/index.php?options=com_content&view=article&id-119&3Anorway&catid=37&Itemid=27 (retrieved April 16, 2015).

Eurostat. 2014. Energy dependence of EU member states, 2001–2012. Available at http://www.eia.gov/countries/cab.cfm?fips=rs (retrieved October 16, 2014).

Evans, R. 2014. Moscow signals concern for Russians in Estonia. *Reuters Service* (March 19). Available at http://www.reuters.com/article/2014/03/19/us-russia-estonia-idUSBREA2I1J620140319 (retrieved August 20, 2014).

Fedorov, Y. 2013. State armament program 2020: Current state and outlook. *Trialogue Club International.* Available at http://www.pircenter.org/media/content/files/11/13781899761.pdf (retrieved October 29, 2014).

Fedotov, G. and N. Zhurnal. 1953. The fate of empires. *Russian Review*, 12 (2): 83–94.

Fedyszyn, T. R. 2012. Renaissance of the Russian navy? *U.S. Naval Institute Proceedings Magazine* (March). Available at http://www.un=sni.org/print/24042 (retrieved October 28, 2014).

Fenger, M. 2007. Welfare regimes in Central and Eastern Europe: Incorporating post-communist countries in a welfare regime typology. *Contemporary Issues and Ideas in Social Sciences*, 3 (2): 1–30.

Feygin, V. 2007. Are the energy majors in decline? *Russia in Global Affairs*, 5 (1): 25–31.

Foucher, M. 1999. Geopolitical reorganization between the Baltic Sea and the Black Sea. In M. P. Lewis and G. Lepesant, eds. *What Security for Which Europe?* New York: Peter Lang, 43–48.

Fox-Brewster, T. 2014. "State sponsored" Russian hacker group linked to cyber attacks on neighbours. *The Guardian* (October 29). Available at http://www.theguardian.com/technology/2014/oct/29/russian-hacker-group-cyber-attacks-apt28 (retrieved December 24, 2014).

Fredén, L. 2005. Shadows of the past and the Baltic countries. *Russia in Global Affairs*, 3 (3): 122–129.

Freeze, G. L. 2009. *Russia: A History*, 3rd ed. Oxford: Oxford University.

Gabrielsson, R. and Z. Sliwa. 2013. Baltic region energy security—The trouble with European solidarity. *Baltic Security and Defense Review*, 15 (1): 144–184.

Galeotti, M. and A. S. Bowen. 2014. Putin's empire of the mind. *Foreign Policy* (online). Available at http://foreignpolicy.com/2014/04/21/putins-empire-of-the-mind/ (retrieved May 20, 2014).

Gidadhubli, R. G. 2007. Boris Yeltsin's controversial legacy. *Economic and Political Weekly*, 42 (20): 118–1820.

Global Fire Power. 2014. Russia military strength. (August 27). Available at http://www .globalfirepower.com/country-military-strength-detail.asp?country_id=russia (retrieved October 29, 2014).

Globalfirepower.com, 2015. Defense budget by country. Available at http://www.globalfirepower .com/defense-spending-budget.asp (retrieved May 21, 2015).

Global Security. 2014. Russian navy—Fleet modernization 2000s. Available at http://www .globalsecurity.org/military/world/russian/mf-reform.htm (retrieved October 28, 2014).

Godzimirski, J. M. 2008. Putin and Post-Soviet identity. *Problems of Post-Communism*, 55 (5): 14–27.

Goel, S. 2011. Cyberwarfare: Connecting the dots in cyber intelligence. *Communications of the ACM*, 54 (8): 132–140.

Golts, A. 2004. The social and political condition of the Russian military. In S. E. Miller and D. V. Trenin, eds. *The Russian Military: Power and Policy*. Cambridge: MIT Press, 73–94.

Goncharenko, R. 2014. Russia's slow invasion of Ukraine. *Deutsche Welle* (March 4). Available at http://www.dw.de/russias-slow-invasion-of-ukraine/a-17706523 (retrieved July 9, 2014).

Gorenburg, D. 2010. Russia's state armaments program 2010: Is the third time the charm for military modernization? Available at http://www.ponarseurasia.org/sites/default/files /policy-memis-pdf//pepm_125.pdf (retrieved October 29, 2014).

Gorenburg, D. 2011. The Russian military's manpower problem. Available at http://russia mil.worldpress.com/2011/07/29/the-russian-militarys-manpower/problem (retrieved July 7, 2014).

Gorenburg, D. 2014. Russian military reform: Tracking developments in the Russian military. Reassuring the Baltic states (October 1). Available at http://russiamil.worldpress .com/ (retrieved October 15, 2014).

Gorenburg, D. and H. H. Gaffney. 2006. Great promise unfulfilled: How Russia lost its way after independence. *PONARS* working paper 26. Available at http://www.csis.org/files /media/csis/pubs/ruseur_wp_026.pdf (retrieved June 8, 2014).

Gotkowska, J. 2014. Russia's game in the Baltic Sea region: A Polish perspective. *European Council on Foreign Relations* commentary (December 16). Available at http://www.ecfr .eu/article/commentary_russias_game_in_the_baltic_sea_retgion_a_polish_perspec tive381 (retrieved December 29, 2014).

Graham, T. 2007. The dialectics of strength and weakness. *Russia in Global Affairs*, 5 (2). Available at http://eng.globalaffairs.ru/number/n_9138 (retrieved November 13, 2014).

Grigas, A. 2012. Legacies, coercion and soft power: Russian influence in the Baltic states. London: Chatham House briefing paper. Available at http://www.chatham house.org /research/Russia-eurasia (retrieved November 13, 2014).

Guseinov, V., A. Denisov, and A. Goncharenko. 2007. The evolution of the global energy market. *Russia in Global Affairs*, 5 (1): 8–24.

Guzzini, S. and D. Jung, eds. 2004. *Contemporary Security Analysis and Copenhagen Peace Research*. London: Routledge.

Hajda, L. A., ed. 1999. *Ukraine in the World: Studies in the International Relations and Security Structure of a Newly Independent State.* Cambridge, MA: Ukrainian Research Institute of Harvard University.

Halsall, P. 1997. *Modern History Sourcebook: The Brezhnev Doctrine, 1968.* Speech reported in *Pravda*, September 25, 1968; translated by Novisti, Soviet Press Agency. Reprinted in L. S. Stavrianos. 1971. *The Epic of Man.* Englewood Cliffs, NJ: Prentice Hall, 46–66. Available at http://www.fordham.edu/halsall/mod/1968brezhnev.asp (retrieved June 10, 2014).

Halperin, C. J. 2006. Ivan IV and Kyiv. *Harvard Ukrainian Studies*, 28 (1/4): 461–469.

Hamilton, D. S., A. Simonyi, and D. L. Cagan, eds. 2014. *Advancing U.S.-Nordic-Baltic Security Cooperation.* Baltimore, MD: Center for Transatlantic Relations at Johns Hopkins University. Preface, ix–xxiv. Available at http://transatlantic.sais-jhu .edu/publications/books/Advancing_U.S.-Nordic-Baltic_Security_Cooperation /Advancing_U.S.-Nordic-Baltic_Security_Cooperation (retrieved January 2, 2015).

Heilprin, J. 2014. UN says death toll in eastern Ukraine up to 4707. Available at http:// www.seattlepi.com/news/world/article/UN-says-death-toll-in-eastern-Ukraine-up-to -4-707-5957525.php (retrieved December 16, 2014).

Heinzig, D. 1983. Russia and the Soviet Union in Asia: Aspects of colonialism and expansionism. *Contemporary Southeast Asia*, 4 (4): 417–450.

Herman, R. G. 1996. Identity, norms, and national security: The Soviet foreign policy revolution and the end of the Cold War. In P. J. Katzenstein, ed. *The Culture of National Security.* New York: Columbia University Press, 271–309.

Herzog, S. 2011. Revisiting the Estonian cyber attacks: Digital threats and multinational responses. *Journal of Strategic Security*, 4 (2): 49–60.

Hill, F. and P. Jewett. 1994. Back in the USSR: Russia's intervention in the internal affairs of the former Soviet republics and the implications for United States policy towards Russia. Harvard University Ethnic Conflict Project. Available at http://search.aol .com/aol/search?s_it=topsearchbox.search&s_chn=prt_ct15&v_t=comsearch&q=Back +in+the+USSR%3A+rUSSIA%27S+INTERVENTION (retrieved April 14, 2015).

Hollis, D. 2011. Cyberwar case study: Georgia 2008. Small Wars Foundation: smallwarsjournal .com. Available at http://smallwarsjournal.com/blog/journal/docs-temp/639-hollis.pdf (retrieved August 5, 2014).

Holquist, P. 2010. "In accord with state interests and the people's wishes": The technocratic ideology of imperial Russia's resettlement administration. *Slavic Review*, 69 (1): 151–179.

Hooper, C. V. 2014. The double standards of Crimean cold-war diplomacy. Available at http://historynewsnetwork.org/article/154970 (retrieved March 8, 2015).

Hopf, T. 1996. Russian identity and foreign policy in Estonia and Uzbekistan. In C. A. Wallander, ed. *The Sources of Russian Foreign Policy After the Cold War.* Boulder, CO: Westview Press, 147–171.

Hosking, G. 2007. Russians in the Soviet Union: Rulers and victims. *Open Democracy*, August 21, np. Available at http://www.opendemocracy.net.globalization-institutions _government/russians_soviets_3670.jsp (retrieved April 13, 2014).

Hugh, G. 2013. *History in the News*: Timeline and chronology for the history of Russia, AD 200-2013. Available at http://archive.awesomestories.com/biography/stories/ivan_terrible /images/muscovy.gif (retrieved June 9, 2014).

Hughes, L. 1998. *Russia in the Age of Peter the Great.* New Haven: Yale University.

Hydrocarbons Technology. 2013. NordStream gas pipeline (NSGP), Russia-Germany. Available at http://www.hydrocarbons-technology.com/projects/negp (retrieved June 3, 2014).

Iaccino, L. 2014. Ukraine crises: Who are Russia's biggest allies? *International Business Times* (March 5). Available at http://www.ibtimes.co.uk/ukraine-crisis-who-are-russias-biggest-allies-1439028 (retrieved June 2, 2014).

Ikenberry, G. J. 2014. The illusion of geopolitics. *Foreign Affairs*, 93 (3): 80–90.

International Institute for Strategic Studies (IISS). 2007. *The Military Balance 2007.* London: Oxford University Press.

Jackson, W. D. 2002. Encircled again: Russia's military assessed threats in a post-Soviet world. *Political Science Quarterly*, 117 (3): 373–400.

Janco, G. J. 2007. Avoiding a new Cold War: Managing US-Russian relations. *Russia Profile. org.* Available at www.eurasiacenter.org/.../2007/Cold%20War%20Brief%20EC.pdf (retrieved June 8, 2014).

Järvenpää, P. 2014. Challenges to the Nordic-Baltic region after Crimea: A Baltic view. In D. S. Hamilton, A. Simonyi, and D. L. Cagan, eds. *Advancing U.S.-Nordic-Baltic Security Cooperation.* Baltimore, MD: Center for Transatlantic Relations at Johns Hopkins University, 77–90. Available at http://transatlantic.sais-jhu.edu/publications/books/Advancing_U.S.-Nordic-Baltic_Security_Cooperation/Advancing_U.S.-Nordic-Baltic_Security_Cooperation (retrieved January 2, 2014).

Järvenpää, P. 2014. *Zapad 2013: A View from Helsinki.* Available at http://www.jamestorn.org/uploads/media/Zapad_2013-View-From-Helsinki_-_Fall.pdf (retrieved April 16, 2015).

Joenniemi, P. 2004. A Deutschian security community? Nordic peace reframed. In S. Guzzini and D. Jung, eds. *Contemporary Security Analysis and Copenhagen Peace Research.* London: Routledge, 143–152.

Johnson, K. 2014. Putin aims his energy weapon at Ukraine. Available at http://www.foreignpolicy.com/articles/2014.04/09/putin_aims_his_energy_weapon_at_ukraine (retrieved October 8, 2014).

Kambara, T. 2007. *China and the Global Energy Crisis.* Cheltenham, UK: Edward Elgar.

Kanet, R. E. 2006. The superpower quest for empire: The Cold War and Soviet support for "wars of national liberation". *Cold War History*, 6 (3): 331–352.

Kanet, R. E. 2010a. The "new" members and future enlargement: The impact of NATO-Russia relations. In G. Aybet and R. R. Moore, eds. *NATO: In Search of a Vision.* Washington, DC: Georgetown University, 153–174.

Kanet, R. E. 2010b. Projections about a post-Soviet world—Twenty-five years later. *International Journal on World Peace*, 27 (3): 31–42.

Kanevskaya, N. 2014. How the Kremlin wields its soft power in France. *Radio Free Europe/ Radio Liberty.* Available at http://www.rferl.org/articleprintview/25433946.html (retrieved November 24, 2014).

Kaplan, F. I. 1954. The decline of the Khazars and the rise of the Varangians. *American Slavic and East European Review*, 13 (3): 1–10.

Kaplan, R. D. 2013. *The Revenge of Geography.* New York: Random House.

Karatnycky, A. 2005. Ukraine's orange revolution. Available at http://www.foreignaffairs.com/articles/60620/adrian-karatnycky/ukraines-orange-revolution (retrieved November 28, 2014).

Karp, R. 2007. The conditionality of security integration: Identity and alignment choices in Finland and Sweden. In O. F. Knudsen, ed. *Security Strategies, Power Disparity and Identity: The Baltic Sea Region.* Aldershot, UK: Ashgate Publishing, 45–72.

Katzenstein, P. J. ed. 1996. *The Culture of National Security.* New York: Columbia University Press.

Keeping, J. 2006. Where law does not rule: The Russian oil and gas sector. *International Journal*, 62 (1): 69–80.

Kempe, I. 2007. Beyond bi-lateralism. Adjusting EU-Russian relations. Centrum für Angewandt Politikforschung working paper 11. Available at http://www.cap.lmu.de /download/2007/CAP-Aktuell-2007-12.pdf (retrieved June 8, 2014).

Kennan, G. (as author "X"). 1947. The sources of Soviet conduct. *Foreign Affairs*, 25 (4): 566–582.

King, G. J. and D. E. McNabb. 2009. Crossroads dynamics in foreign policy: The case of Latvia. *Problems of Post-Communism*, 56 (3): 29–41.

King, G. J. and D. E. McNabb. 2014. *Imperium Reconditum: Russia's Small War in Ukraine.* Unpublished white paper. Tacoma, WA: Pacific Lutheran University.

Kipp, J. W. 1999. Russia's northwest strategic direction. *Military Review*, 79 (4): 52–65.

Kireeva, A. 2012. Russia's East Asia policy: New opportunities and challenges. *Perceptions*, 17 (4): 49–78.

Kissinger, H. 1994. *Diplomacy.* New York: Simon and Schuster.

Klein, M. and K. Pester. 2014. Russia's armed forces on modernization course: Progress and perspectives of military reform. Shiftung Wisssenschaft und Politik (German Institute for International and Security Affairs). *SWP Comments 9* (January). Available at http:// www.swp-berlin.org/en/publications/swp-comments-en/swp-aktuelle-details/article /russias_military_reforms.html (retrieved October 26, 2014).

Knudsen, O. F. 2007a. An overall perspective on regional power strategies. In O. F. Knudsen, ed. *Security Strategies, Power Disparity and Identity: The Baltic Sea Region.* Aldershot, UK: Ashgate Publishing, 1–8.

Knudsen, O. F. 2007b. Looking to the future: Security strategies, identity and power disparity. In Olav F. Knudsen, ed. *Security Strategies, Power Disparity and Identity: The Baltic Sea Region.* Aldershot, UK: Ashgate Publishing, 177–186.

Knudsen, O. F., ed. 2007c. *Security Strategies, Power Disparity and Identity: The Baltic Sea Region.* Aldershot, UK: Ashgate Publishing.

Knudsen, O. F. and C. Jones. 2007. Events and ideas in the region: An overview 1980–2000s. In O. F. Knudsen ed. *Security Strategies, Power Disparity and Identity: The Baltic Sea Region.* Aldershot, UK: Ashgate Publishing, 29–44.

Kollmann, N. S. 2009. Muscovite Russia, 1450–1568. In G. I. Freeze, ed. *Russia: A History*, 3rd ed. Oxford: Oxford University, 31–62.

Koslowski, R. and F. V. Kratochwil. 1994. Understanding change in international politics: The Soviet Empire's demise and the international system. *International Organization*, 48 (2): 215–247.

Krastev, I. 2008. Russia and the Georgia war: The great power trap. ODR (Open Democracy, August 31). Available at http://www.opendemocracy.net/article/russia-and-the-georgia -war-the-great-power-trap (retrieved March 11, 2014).

Krastev, I. 2014. Russian revisionism: Putin's plan for overturning the European Order. *Foreign Affairs.* Available at http://www.foreignaffairs.com/articles/140990/ivan -krastev/russian-revisionism (retrieved March 11, 2014).

Krickus, R. J. 2014. *Russia after Putin.* U.S. Army War College Strategic Studies Institute. Available at http://www.strategicstudiesinstitute.army.mil/pubs/download.cfm?q=1200 (retrieved December 18, 2014).

Kuchins, A. and I. A. Zevelev. 2012. Russian foreign policy: Continuity in change. *The Washington Quarterly*, 35 (1): 147–161.

Kuhar, I. 2007. Russia builds up its military. *Voice of America News (newsVOA.com)*, (August 27). Available at http://www.voanews.com/englisnh/2007-08-27-voa29.cfm (retrieved September 4, 2013).

Kumar, A. 2013. *Russian Military Reforms: An Evaluation*. India: Institute for Defense Studies and Analyses. Available at http://www.idsa.in/issuebrief/RussianMilitaryReforms_amit_230513.html (retrieved October 15, 2014).

Kuzio, T. 1999. Return to Europe—Ukraine's strategic foreign policy agenda. In M. P. Lewis and G. Lepesant, eds. *What Security for Which Europe?* New York: Peter Lang, 49–64.

Lally, K. 2014. Russian forces in Ukraine: What does the Black Sea Fleet in Crimea look like? *Washington Post* (March 1). Available at http://www.washingtonpost.com/world/europe/russia-decides-to-send-troops-into-crimea-what-does-the-black-sea-fleet-look-like/2014/03/01/38cf005c-a160-11e3-b8d8-94577ff66b28_story.html (retrieved July 9, 2014).

Laqueur, W. 2014. After the fall: Russia in search of a new ideology. *World Affairs*, March/April. Available at http://www.worldaffairsjournal.org/article/after-fall-russia-search-new-ideology (retrieved November 23, 2014).

Lavrov, S. 2012. Russia in the 21st-century world of power. *Russia in Global Affairs*, 2012 (4). Available at http://eng.globalaffairs.ru/print/number/Russia-in-the-21st-Century-World-of-Power-15809 (retrieved December 28, 2012).

LeDonne, J. P. 2009a. Poltava and the geopolitics of Western Eurasia. *Harvard Ukrainian Studies*, 31 (1/4): 177–191.

LeDonne, J. P. 2009b. The territorial reform of the Russian Empire, 1775–1796. II: The borderlands. *Harvard Ukrainian Studies*, 31 (1/4): 177–191. *Cahiers du Monde russe et soviétique*, 24 (4): 411–420.

Legvold, R. 2014. Managing the new cold war. *Foreign Affairs*, 93 (4): 74–84.

Lenin, V. I. 1963. *Collected Works*. Moscow: Progress Publishers (open source). Available at http://www.marxists.org/archive/lenin/works/1916/imp-hsc/index.htm (retrieved August 23, 2014).

Lepesant, G. 1999. Introduction: Unity and diversity of Europe's Eastern marches. In M. P. Lewis and G. Lepesant, eds. *What Security for Which Europe?* New York: Peter Lang, 1–32.

Levada Center. 2013. Russian public opinion, 2005–2013. Available at http://www.levada.ru/print/18-06-2013/vneshnepoliticheskie-vragi-i-druzya-rossii (retrieved June 3, 2014).

Lewis, D. W. P. 1999. The eastern border of an enlarged European Union. In M. P. Lewis and G. Lepesant, eds. *What Security for Which Europe?* New York: Peter Lang, 169–178.

Lewis, D. W. P. 1999. Conclusion: A new map requires fresh thinking. In M. P. Lewis and G. Lepesant, eds. *What Security for Which Europe?* New York: Peter Lang, 179–194.

Lewis, D. W. P. and G. Lepesant, eds. 1999. *What Security for Which Europe?* New York: Peter Lang.

Lewitter, L. R. 1958. Peter the Great, Poland and the Westernization of Russia. *Journal of the History of Ideas*, 19 (4): 493–506.

Libicki, M. 1999–2000. Rethinking war: The mouse's new roar? *Foreign Policy*, 117: 30–43.

Lieven, A. 1994. *The Baltic Revolution: Estonia, Latvia, Lithuania and the Path to Independence*. New Haven: Yale University.

Light, M. 2006. Gassy issues. *The World Today*, 62 (11): 20–22.

Lloyd, J. 2014. Ukraine's future lies with the West, but there is much suffering ahead. *Reuters blogs* (September 19). Available at http://blogs.reuters.com/john-lloyd/2014/09/19/ukraines-future-lies-with-the-west-but-there-is-much-suffering-ahead/ (retrieved December 25, 2014).

Lo, B. 2003. *Vladimir Putin and the Evolution of Russian Foreign Policy*. London: Blackwell.

Lo, B. 2014. Crimean secession: A Russian remake of the 1938 Sudeten Crisis? *The Irish Examiner* (March 19). Available at http://www.irishexaminer.com/analysis/Crimean-secession-a -russian-remake-of-the-1938-sudeten-crisis-26393.html (retrieved March 19, 2014).

Longworth, P. 2005. *Russia's Empires: Their Rise and Fall from Prehistory to Putin.* London: John Murray.

Lukin, A. 2014. What the Kremlin is thinking. *Foreign Affairs*, 93 (4): 85–93.

Lunde, L. 2014. High North-increasing tension? A Nordic perspective. In D. S. Hamilton, A. Simonyi, and D. L. Cagan, eds. *Advancing U.S.-Nordic-Baltic Security Cooperation.* Baltimore, MD: Center for Transatlantic Relations at Johns Hopkins University, 189–198. Available at http://transatlantic.sais-jhu.edu/publications/books/Advancing _U.S.-Nordic-Baltic_Security_Cooperation/Advancing_U.S.-Nordic-Baltic _Security_Cooperation (retrieved January 2, 2015).

Lynch, M. 2003. The emancipation of the Russian Serfs, 1861: A charter of freedom or an act of betrayal? *History Today.* Available at http://www.historytoday.com/michael-lynch /emancipation-russian-serfs-1861-charter-freedom-or-act-betrayal (retrieved November 7, 2014).

Madariaga, I. de. 1990. *Catherine the Great.* New Haven: Yale University.

Mahaptra, L. 2013. Who are Russia's allies and enemies? Here's how Russians view other countries. *International Business Times* (September 21). Available at http://www .ibtimes.com/who-are-rissias-allies-enemies-heres-how-russians-view-other-countries -infographic-1409150/ (retrieved June 3, 2014).

Mandelbaum, M. 2014. Why they fought: How war made the state and the state made peace. *Foreign Affairs*, 93 (6): 154–157.

Manilov, V. 1997. National security of Russia. Occasional paper in Strengthening Democratic Institutions Project, Belfer Center for Science and International Affairs, Harvard University. Available at http://belfercenter.ksg.harvard.edu/publication/3029 /national_security_of_russia.html (retrieved March 7, 2014).

Mankoff, J. 2014. Russia's latest land grab. *Foreign Affairs*, 93 (3): 60–68.

Martin, J. 1983. Muscovy's northeastern expansion: The contest and a cause. *Cahiers du Monde russe et soviétique*, 24 (4): 459–470.

Martin, J. 2009. From Kiev to Muscovy: The Beginnings to 1450. In G. I. Freeze, ed. *Russia: A History*, 3rd ed. Oxford: Oxford University, 1–30.

Matthews, O. and B. Powell. 2014. As in the Cold War, Russia is vulnerable on energy. *Newsweek Global* (April 18), 162 (15): 31–40.

Matz, J. 2001. *Constructing a Post-Soviet International Political Reality.* Uppsala: Uppsala University Press.

Mau, V. 2007. Strengths and weaknesses of the Russian economy. *Russia in Global Affairs*, 5 (1): 98–116.

Mazitans, K. 2014. Russian armed forces military reforms and capability developments (2008–2012). *Baltic Security & Defense Review*, 16 (1): 5–45.

McFaul, M. A. 2007a. Ukraine imports democracy: External influences on the Orange Revolution. *International Security*, 32 (2): 45–83.

McFaul, M. A. 2007b. A revival of Russia's military power. Interviewed on *National Public Radio* (NPR) by Neal Conan (August 22). Available at http://www.carnegieendown ment.org/publications/index.cfm?fa=print (retrieved June 8, 2014).

Medvedev, D. 2008. Interview given to Television Channel One, Russia, NTV. Available at http:// archive.kremlin.ru/eng/text/speeches/2008/08/31/1850_type82912type82916_206003 .shtml (retrieved June 14, 2014).

Merritt, M. 2001. Constructing threat in Russia's foreign policy: Ethnicity, apocalypse, and Baltic warriors. *Wilson Center Global Europe Program Meeting Report Paper 231.* Available at http://www.wilsoncenter.org/publication/231-constructing-threat-in-russias -foreign-policy (retrieved October 23, 2014).

Metais, R. 2013. Ensuring energy security in Europe: The EU between a Market-based and a geopolitical approach. *EU Diplomacy Papers March.* Bruges, Belgium: College of Europe.

Michell, R. 1872. Summery statistics of the Russian Empire. *Journal of the Statistical Society of London*, 35 (3): 341–372.

Miller, D. B. 1967. The coronation of Ivan IV of Moscow. *Jahrbücher für Geschichte Osteuropas*, 15 (4): 559–574.

Miller, S. 2004. Moscow's military power: Russia's search for security in an age of transition. In S. E. Miller and D. V. Trenin, eds. *The Russian Military: Power and Policy.* Cambridge: MIT Press, 1–42.

Ministry of Foreign Affairs of the Russian Federation (MFA). 2013. Concept of the Foreign Policy of the Russian Federation. Approved by President V. Putin on February 12, 2013. (Unofficial English translation). Available at http://www.mid.ru/brp_4.nsf/0 /76389FEC168189ED44257B2E0039B16D (retrieved April 14, 2015).

MIR. 2013. Rossotrudnichestvo to open offices in over 100 countries. MIR press release. Moscow: Russkiy Mir Foundation. Available at http://www.russkiymit.ru.ruskiymir /en/news/common/news6562.html (retrieved January 1, 2015).

Morozov, V. 2004. Inside/outside Europe and the boundaries of Russian political community. *PONARS* working paper 23. Available at http://www.csis.prg/media/csis/pubs /ruseur_wp_023.pdf (retrieved June 8, 2014).

Morozov, V. 2008. Energy dialogue and the future of Russia. In P. Aalto, ed. *The Russian Energy Dialogue: Europe's Future Energy Security.* Aldershot, UK: Ashgate, 43–62.

Mosely, P. E. 1948. Aspects of Russian expansion. *American Slavic and East European Review*, 7 (3): 197–213.

Motyl, A. J. 1999. Why empires reemerge: Imperial collapse and imperial revival in comparative perspective. *Comparative Politics*, 31 (2): 127–145.

Mouritzen, H. 2004. Initiating a security community: General theory, history, and prospects for Baltic-Russian relations. In S. Guzzini and D. Jung, eds. *Contemporary Security Analysis and Copenhagen Peace Research.* London: Routledge, 154–166.

Mueller, J. 2009. War has almost ceased to exist: An assessment. *Political Science Quarterly*, 124 (2): 297–321.

Muzalevsky, R. 2009. Russia's strategy in Central Asia: An analysis of key trends. *Yale Journal of International Affairs*, 4 (1): 26–42.

NATO (North Atlantic Treaty Organization). 2014. Wales Summit Declaration. http:// www.nato.int/cps/en/natohq/official_texts_112964.htm (retrieved June 11, 2015).

Natural Gas Europe. 2014. The death of the south Stream project: Russia's desperation and Turkey's challenge. Available at http://www.neurope.eu/article/trans-anatolia-nabucco -and-south-stream-pipelines-bet-turkey (retrieved December 3, 2014).

New Europe. 2007. Putin vows to make Russia a military power and then some. *New Europe: The European Weekly*, Issue 744 (August 24). Available at http://www.neurope.eu/article /putin-vows-make-russia-military-power-and-then-some (retrieved June 8, 2014).

New York Times. 1998. Russia cutting oil exports through Latvia. April 10, A10.

Newman, C. 2014. After Ukraine crisis, why Crimea matters. *National Geographic* (February 24). Available at http://news.nationalgeographic.com/news/2014/02/140224-ukraine -crisis-yanukovych-black-sea-coup-russia/ (retrieved August 15, 2014).

Nichol, J. 2011. Russian military reform and defense policy. Report 7-5700 (August 24). Washington DC: Congressional Research Service.

Nordberg, M. 1999. Energy, interdependence and security in Belarus and Ukraine. In M. P. Lewis and G. Lepesant, eds. *What Security for Which Europe?* New York: Peter Lang, 125–138.

Nordenman, M. 2014. Russia's mysterious hunt for Russian submarine and its significance for Nordic-Baltic security. Atlantic Council, October 20. Available at http://www.atlanticcouncil.org/blogs/natosource/sweden-s-mysterious-submarine-hunt-and-its-significance-for-nordic-baltic-security (retrieved November 29, 2014).

Noreen, E. 2007. Threat images and socialization: Estonia and Russia in the new millennium. In O. F. Knudsen, ed. *Security Strategies, Power Disparity and Identity: The Baltic Sea Region.* Aldershot, UK: Ashgate Publishing, 97–122.

Nurick, R. and M. Nordenman. 2011. *Nordic-Baltic Security in the 21st Century: The Regional Agenda and the Global Role.* Washington, DC: Atlantic Council.

Nye, J. 2004. *Power in the Global Information Age: From Realism to Globalization.* London: Routledge.

Odia, R. 2014. Russian rearming program, Ukraine crisis just tip of the iceberg. *Prophecy News Watch* (March 4). Available at http://www.prophecynewswatch.com/7014/March04/042.html (retrieved October 29, 2014).

Oliner, S. P. 1982. Soviet nationalities and dissidents: A persistent problem. *Humboldt Journal of Soviet Relations,* 10 (1): 19–61.

Orttung, R. 2006. Causes and consequences of corruption in Putin's Russia. *PONARS* policy memo 430. Available at http://www.csis.org/media/csis/pubs/pm_0430.pdf (retrieved June 8, 2014).

Ott, S. 2014. Russia tightens control over Kyrgyzstan. *The Guardian* (September 15). Available at http://www.theguardian.com/world/2014/sep/18/russia-tightens-control-over-kyrgyzstan (retrieved November 10, 2014).

Özkan, G. 2012. Spoils of war: Impact of Georgia-Russia war on Russian foreign and security policies in the "near abroad." *Journal of Gazi Academic View,* 6 (11): 34–64.

Paksoy, H. B. 1991. "Basmachi": Turkistan national liberation movement 1916–1930s. In P. D. Steeves, ed. *Modern Encyclopedia of Religions in Russia and the Soviet Union.* Vol. 4. Gulf Breeze, FL: Academic International Press, 5–20.

Pannier, B. 2009. New Turkmen-China pipeline breaks Russia's hold over central Asian gas. *Radio Free Europe* (December 14). Available at http://www.rferl.org/articleprintview/1903108.html (retrieved December 4, 2014).

Parsons, R. 2006. Russia: New bill on national identity generating protests. *Radio Free Europe/Radio Liberty* (March 9). Available at http://www.rferl.org/content/article/1066546.html (retrieved June 8, 2014).

Paul, M. C. 2004. The military revolution in Russia, 1550–1682. *The Journal of Military History,* 68 (1): 9–45.

Pelenski, J. 1983. The emergence of the Muscovite claims to the Byzantine-Kievan "Imperial Inheritance." *Harvard Ukrainian Studies,* 7 (1983): 520–531.

Perry, C. M., M. J. Sweeny, and A. C. Winner. 2000. *Strategic Dynamics in the Nordic-Baltic Region.* Dulles, VA: Institute for Foreign Policy Analysis.

Petersen, A. and K. Barysch. 2011. *Russia, China and the Geopolitics of Energy in Central Asia.* London: Centre for European Reform.

Pikayev, A. A. 2005. A velvet divorce. *PONARS* policy memo 369. Available at http://www.csis.org/media/csis/pubs/pm_0369.pdf (retrieved June 8, 2014).

Pillalamarri, A. 2014. India and Russia reinforce ties. *The Diplomat* (July 25). Available at http://thediplomat.com/2014/07/india-and-russia-reinforce-ties/ (retrieved August 23, 2014).

Pipes, R. 1964. *The Formation of the Soviet Union.* Cambridge: Harvard University.

Pollard, N. and A. Scrutton. 2014. Sweden says credible reports of foreign submarine in its waters. *Reuters News Agency* (October 20). Available at http://www.reuters.com/article/2014/10/19/us-sweden-deployment-idUSKCN0I80T320141019 (retrieved October 20, 2014).

Pool, P. 2013. War of the cyber world: The law of cyber warfare. *International Lawyer,* 47 (2): 299–325.

Puheloinen, A. 1999. *Russia's Geopolitical Interests in the Baltic Area.* Helsinki, Finland: National Defense College.

Putin, V. W. 2007. Speech at the 43rd Munich conference on security policy (February 10). Translated from Russian. Available at http://www.opendemocracy.net/full_text_vladimir_putins_amazing_speech_at_munich_security_conference_0 (retrieved June 8, 2014).

Radchenko, S. 2014. Russia's elusive quest for influence in Asia. *The Diplomat.* Available at http://thediplomat.com/2014/05/russias-elusive-quest-for-influence-in-asia/ (retrieved August 23, 2014).

Richardson, J. 2009. Denial-of-service: The Estonian cyberwar and its implications for U.S. national security. *International Affairs Review,* 18 (1). Available at http://www.iar-gwu.org/none/65 (retrieved August 5, 2014).

Rollinson, S. J. 2010. Maps of Russia. Available at http://www.drshirley.org/geog/geog31.html (retrieved June 13, 2014).

Romanova, T. 2007. Energy partnership—A dialog in different languages. *Russia in Global Affairs,* 5 (1): 32–45.

Romanova, T. 2008. Energy dialogue from strategic partnership to the regional level of the northern dimension. In P. Aalto, ed. *The EU-Russian Dialogue: Europe's Future Energy Security.* Aldershot: Ashgate, 63–92.

Rosendahl, J. 2014. Finland says Russian navy interfered with Baltic Sea research vessel. *Reuters News Agency* (October 11). Available at http://uk.reuters.com/article/2014/10/11/uk-finland-vessel-russia-idUKKCN0I00KH20141011 (retrieved October 20, 2014).

Royan, H. 1980. *Catherine the Great.* Trans. Joan Pinkham. New York: Dutton.

Russia Today (RT). 2014. Sanctions and weaker oil prices could cost Russia 4% of GDP—Official. Available at http://rt.com/business/190628-sanctions-gdp-russia-oil-price/ (retrieved October 14, 2014).

Rühl, C. 2010. Global energy after the crisis: Prospects and priorities. *Foreign Affairs,* 89 (2): 63–75.

Rumer, E. B. and A. F. Stent. 2009. *Repairing US-Russian Relations: A Long Road.* Washington: INSS-CERES.

Rynning, S. 2004. The new NATO: Europe's continued security crisis. In S. Guzzini and D. Jung, eds. *Contemporary Security Analysis and Copenhagen Peace Research.* London: Routledge, 193–204.

Safranchuk, I. 2008. The competition for security roles in Central Asia. *Russia in Global Affairs,* 6 (1): np.

Schneider, D. A. 2008. The Shanghai cooperation organization. *American Diplomacy.* Chapel Hill: University of North Carolina. Available at http://www.unc.edu/depts/diplomat/item/2008/0709/comm/schneider_shanghai.html (retrieved August 20, 2014).

Scott, M. 2014. Russian hackers used a bug in Microsoft Windows for spying, report says. *New York Times* international business (October 14). Available at http://www.nytimes .com/2014/10/15/business/international/russian-hackers-used-bug-in-microsoft-win dows-for-spying-report-says.html (retrieved October 16, 2014).

Shackelford, S. J. 2010. Estonia three years later: A progress report on combating cyber attacks. *Journal of Internet Law*, 13 (2): 22–29.

Shelley, L. I. 1999. Organized crime and corruption: Security threats. In M. P. Lewis and G. Lepesant, eds. *What Security for Which Europe?* New York: Peter Lang, 149–168.

Shevtsova, L. 2007a. Post-communist Russia: A historic opportunity missed. *International Affairs*, 83 (5): 891–912.

Shevtsova, L. 2007b. Anti-Westernism is the new national idea. *The Moscow Times* (August 7). Available at http://www.carnegieendowment.org/publications/index.cfm?fa=print (retrieved August 27, 2013).

Shlapentokh, D. 2013. The death of the Byzantine Empire and construction of historical/ political identities in late Putin Russia. *Journal of Balkan and Near Eastern Studies*, 15 (1): 69–96.

Shuster, S. 2014. The Maidan's last stand: Ukraine's protesters resist police crackdown. *Time* online (February 18). Available at http://time.com/8128/kiev-protests-maidan -europe-yanukovych/ (retrieved December 27, 2014).

Singer, P. W. and A. A. Friedman. 2014. *Cybersecurity and Cyberwar.* New York: Oxford University.

Smith, D. L. 1993. Muscovite logistics, 1462–1598. *The Slavonic and East European Review*, 71 (1): 35–65.

Smith, M. A. 2010. NATO-Russia relations: Will the future resemble the past? In G. Aybet and R. R. Moore, eds. *NATO: In Search of a Vision.* Washington, DC: Georgetown University, 99–129.

Smolchenko, A. 2007. Russia air show: Flexing military might? *Business Week* electronic version, August 21. Available at http://www.businessweek.com/print/globalbiz/content /aug2007 (retrieved September 4, 2013).

Smyth, R. 2005. Maintaining control: Putin's strategy for holding power past 2008. *PONARS* policy memo 397. Available at http://www.csis.org/media/csis/pubs/pm_0397.pdf (retrieved June 8, 2014).

Snyder, J. 1996. Democratization, war and nationalism in the post-communist states. In C. A. Wallander, ed. *The Sources of Russian Foreign Policy After the Cold War.* Boulder, CO: Westview Press, 21–40.

Snyder, R. S. 2005. Bridging the realist/constructionist divide: The case of the counterrevolution in soviet foreign policy at the end of the Cold War. *Foreign Policy Analysis*, 1 (1): 55–71.

Sommerville, J. P. 2014. *Russia and the Great Northern War.* Available at http://faculty .history.wisc.edu/sommerville/351/351-152.htm (retrieved June 17, 2014).

Sorokin, P. A. 1967. The essential characteristics of the Russian nation in the twentieth century. *Annals of the American Academy of Political and Social Science*, 370 (1): 99–115.

Spinka, M. 1926. The conversion of Russia. *The Journal of Religion*, 6 (1): 41–57.

Stapleton-Gray, R. and W. Woodcock. 2011. National internet defense-small states on the skirmish line. *Communications of the ACM*, 54 (3): 50–55.

Statiev, A. 2009. Soviet ethnic deportations: Intent versus outcome. *Journal of Genocide Research*, 11 (2/3): 243–264.

Stavridis, J. 2014. Former NATO commander explains Ukraine crisis. Available at http:// mashable.com/2014/03/04/nato-commander-ukraine/ (retrieved July 8, 2014).

Steblsky, I. 2014. The Crisis in Crimea and Eastern Ukraine *Encyclopaedia Britannica* online. Available at http://www.britannica.com/EBchecked/topic/612921/Ukraine/320746 /The-crisis-in-Crimea-and-eastern-Ukraine (retrieved July 9, 2014).

Stegen, K. S. 2011. Deconstructing the "energy weapon": Russia's threat to Europe as a case study. Available at http://www.sciencedirect.com/science/article/pii/S0301431511 005866 (retrieved June 8, 2014).

Strategypage.com. 2013. Russia: Rebuilding the empire has not been easy. Available at http:// www.strategypage.com/and/russia/20131222.aspx (retrieved June 8, 2014).

Stratfor. 2014a. Russia: Putin's annual speech marks dramatic shift. (December 4). Available at http://www.stratfor.com/sample/geopolitical-diary/russia-putins-annual-speech-marks -dramatic-shift (retrieved December 17, 2014).

Stratfor. 2014b. Russia puts the brakes on South Stream. Available at http://www.stratfor .com/geopolitical-diary/russia-puts-brakes-south-stream (retrieved December 3, 2014).

Strauss, R. L. 2014. A chill in the air. *Stanford*, 43 (3): 60–68.

Strayer, R. 2001. Decolonization, democratization, and communist reform: The Soviet collapse in comparative perspective. *Journal of World History*, 12 (2): 375–406.

Sunderland, W. 2000. The "colonization question:" Visions of colonization in later Imperial Russia. *Jahgbücher für Geschichte Osteuropas, Neue Folge*, 48 (2): 210–232.

Suny, R. G. 2000. Nationalities in the Russian Empire. *Russian Review*, 59 (4): 487–492.

Surowiecki, J. 2014. Putin's power play. *The New Yorker* financial page (March 24). Available at http://www.newyorker.com/magazine/2014/03/24/putins-power-play (retrieved October 15, 2014).

Szporluk, R. 2006. Lenin, "Great Russia" and Ukraine. *Harvard Ukrainian Studies*, 28 (1/4): 611–626.

Taagepera, R. 1980. Soviet collectivization of Estonian agriculture: The deportation phase. *Soviet Studies*, 32 (3): 379–397.

Taylor, A. 2014. To understand Crimea, take a look back at its complicated history. *Washington Post* online (February 27). Available at http://www.washingtonpost.com/blogs/world views/wp/2014/02/27/to-understand-crimea-take-a-look-back-at-its-complicated-history/ (retrieved December 17, 2014).

Tebbe, G. 1999. Baltic Sea regional cooperation after 1989. In M. P. Lewis and G. Lepesant, eds. *What Security for Which Europe?* New York: Peter Lang, 105–112.

Thornton, R. 2011, Military modernization and the Russian ground forces. U.S. Army Strategic Studies Institute. Available at http://www.strategicstudiesinstitute.army.mil /pdffiles/PUB1071.pdf (retrieved April 15, 2015).

Tikk, E., K. Kaska, K. Rünnimeri, M. Kert, A.-M. Talihärm, and L. Vihul. 2008. *Cyber Attacks Against Georgia: Legal Lessons Identified*. Tallinn, Estonia: Cooperative Cyber Defense Centre of Excellence. Available at http://www.carlisle.army.mil/DIME/docu ments/Georgia%201%200.pdf (retrieved August 5, 2014).

Tisdall, S. 2011. Putin prepares the Russian empire to strike back. *The Guardian* (December 1). Available at http://www.theguardian.com/commentisfree/2011/dec/01/putin-prepares -russian-empire.print (retrieved March 7, 2014).

Tishkov, V. A. 1991. The Soviet empire before and after perestroika. *Theory and Society*, 20 (5): 603–629.

Torke, H.-J. 2009. From Muscovy towards St Petersburg, 1598–1689. In G. I. Freeze, ed. *Russia: A History*, 3rd ed. Oxford: Oxford University, 63–99.

Transparency International. 2014. Corruption ratings by country: Russia, 2013. Available at http://www.transparancy.org/country#RUS (retrieved June 6, 2014).

Troyat, H. 1980. *Catherine the Great*. Joan Pinkham, Trans. New York: Dutton.

Tsygankov, A. P. 1997. From international institutionalism to revolutionary expansionism: The foreign policy discourse of contemporary Russia. *Marshon International Studies Review*, 41 (2): 247–268.

Tsygankov, A. P. 2013. *Russia's Foreign Policy: Change and Continuity in National Identity*, 3rd ed. Lanham, MD: Rowman and Littlefield.

Tulun, M. O. 2013. Russification policies imposed on the Baltic people by the Russian empire and the Soviet Union. *Ulusararasi Suçlar ve Tarih*, 14 (1): 139–160.

TV-Novosti (RT). 2015. Russia-China trade hits record $59 billion in first half of 2014. Available at http://rt.com/business/197516-russia-china-trade-half-2014 (retrieved January 5, 2014).

US Energy Information Administration (USEIA). 2014 (updated March 12). Overview of Russia's 2013 Oil Production by Region. Available at http://www.eia.gov/countries/cab.cfm?fips=rs (retrieved April 15, 2015).

US Navy. 2014. *Unconventional Cyber Warfare: Cyber Opportunities in Unconventional Warfare*. Monterey, CA: Naval Postgraduate School.

Van der Oye, D. S. 2010. *Russian Orientalism*. New Haven: Yale University.

Vasudevan, H. 1993. Russia's presidency. *Economic and Political Weekly*, 28 (51): 2823–2828.

Victorov, I. 2014. The legacy of tandemocracy. *Baltic Worlds*, 7 (2–3): 14–21.

Volkov, V. 2005. Will the Kremlin revive the Russian idea? *PONARS* policy memo 370. Available at http://www.csis.org/media/csis/pubs/pm_0370.pdf (retrieved June 8, 2014).

Walker, M. 2007. Russia v. Europe: The energy wars. *World Policy Journal*, 24 (1): 1–8.

Walker, S. G. 2007. Generalizing about security strategies in the Baltic Sea region. In O. F. Knudsen, ed. *Security Strategies, Power Disparity and Identity: The Baltic Sea Region*. Aldershot, UK: Ashgate Publishing, 149–171.

Wallander, C. A. 1996. The sources of Russian conduct: Theories, frameworks, and approaches. In C. A. Wallander, ed. *The Sources of Russian Foreign Policy After the Cold War*. Boulder, CO: Westview Press, 1–19.

Wallwork, L. 2014. Will the Trans-Caspian pipeline ever be built? Available at http://exclusive.multibriefs.com/content/will-the-trans-caspian-pipeline-ever-be-built (retrieved December 3, 2014).

Weinstein, A. 2007. Russian phoenix: The collective security treaty organization. *Whitehead Journal of Diplomacy and International Relations*, 8 (Winter/Spring): 167–180.

Weir, F. 2007. Russia's resurgent military. *Christian Science Monitor* (August 17). Available at http://www.csmonitor.com/2007/0817/p01s06-woeu.html (retrieved June 8, 2014).

Weitz, R. and V. Zimmerman. 2014. Modernization leaves Russia's military improved but limited. *World Politics Review* (April 15). Available at http://www.worldpoliticsreview.com/articles/print/13705 (retrieved July 2, 2014).

Wendt, A. 1998. Constructing international politics. In M. E. Brown, O. R. Coté, S. M. Lynn-Jones, and S. E. Miller, eds. *Theories of War and Peace*. Cambridge, MA: MIT Press, 416–426.

Westphal, K. 2008. Germany and the EU-Russia energy dialogue. In P. Aalto, ed. *The EU-Russian Dialogue: Europe's Future Energy Security*. Aldershot: Ashgate, 93–118.

Williams, C. J. 2014. Ukraine separatist leaders plot strategy with Russian lawmakers. *Los Angeles Times* (November 10). Available at http://www.latimes.com/world/europe/la-fg-ukraine-russia-separatists-moscow-visit-20141110-story.html (retrieved December 26, 2014).

Williamson, M. I. 2012. *The Cyber Military Revolution and the Need for a New Framework of War.* Unpublished master's degree thesis. Norfolk: VA: National Defense University Joint Warfighting School. Available at http://oai.dtic.mil/oai/oai?verb=getRecord&metadataPrefix=html&identifier=ADA562392 (retrieved August 25, 2014).

Wilson, A. 2014. Belarus wants out. *Foreign Affairs* (March 20). Available at http://www.foreignaffairs.com/articles/141048/andrew-wilson/belarus-wants-out (retrieved August 6, 2014).

Wilson, E. J. 2008. Hard power, soft power, smart power. *Annals of the American Academy of Political and Social Science*, 616 (March): 110–124.

Windsor, P. 2002. *Strategic Thinking.* Boulder, CO: Lynne Rienner.

World Bank. 2014. *Russian Economic Report.* Available at http://www.worldbank.org/en/news/press-release/2014/03/26/russian-economic-report-31 (retrieved June 8, 2014).

Yerofeyev, I. A. 2014. Ukraine: The Maidan protest movement. Available at http://www.britannica.com/EBchecked/topic/612921/Ukraine/314882/The-Maidan-protest-movement (retrieved December 27, 2014).

Yoffie, D. B. and M. Kwak. 2001. *Judo Strategy: Turning Your Competitor's Strength to Your Advantage.* Cambridge: MA: Harvard Business School.

Yoffie, D. B. and M. Kwak. 2002. Judo strategy: 10 techniques for beating a stronger opponent. *Business Strategy Review*, 13 (1): 20–30.

Young, A. 2014. Global defense budget seen climbing in 2014; first total increase since 2009 as Russia surpasses Britain and Saudi Arabia continues its security spending spree. *International Business Times* (February 6). Available at http://www.ibtimes.com/global-defense-budget-seen-climbing-2014-first-total-increase-2009-russia-surpasses-britain-saudi (retrieved July 7, 2014).

Youngs, R. 2014. A new geopolitics of EU energy security. Carnegie Europe. Available at http://carnegieeurope.eu/publications/?fa = 56705 (retrieved October 15, 2014).

Zamiatin, D. 2008. The territory of nostalgia: Russia's geographic image and problems of linguistic identity in the former Soviet republics. *Russian Politics and Law*, 46 (6): 59–71.

Zasenko, O. E. 2014. Ukraine: The Maidan protests. *Encyclopaedia Britannia* online. Available at http://www.britannica.com/EBchecked/topic/612921/Ukraine/314882/The-Maidan-protest-movement (retrieved December 27, 2014).

Zielonka, J. 2005. Europe as empire: The nature of the enlarged European Union. Paper presented at the Wilson Center, September 21. Available at http://www.wilsoncenter.org/publications/326-europe-empire-the-nature-of-the-enlarged-european-union (retrieved October 16, 2014).

Zolotarev, P. 2007. Russian and U.S. defense policies in the era of globalization. *Russia in Global Affairs*, 5 (2): 33–46.

Index

A

ABM treaty, *see* Anti-Ballistic Missile treaty
Agents of Russification, 88
Aggressive diplomacy, 11, 181–182
All-volunteer army, transition to, 98
Anarchy, as nature of world politics, 44
Anti-Ballistic Missile (ABM) treaty, 48
Antisocialist action, 76
Armed diplomacy, 5, 15
Atlantic Council, 15, 165
Atlantic-wide security policy, 55

B

Baltic and Nordic states, Russian intimidation
  in, 159–174
  Arctic theater, 163–164
  changes in the West's view of post-Soviet
    Russia, 172–174
    membership of Baltic states in, 173
    policy implementation, 173–174
    target states, politics of, 172
  Finland's observer status in NATO, 164
  future regional security scenarios, 170–172
    control of regional security, 170–171
    creating client states, 171–172
    local ethnic identity, 170
    peaceful gaining of economic control, 171
    possible scenarios, 170
    recreating client state system, 170
    territorial expansion, 172
  importance of the east Baltic, 167–168
  intercepted spy planes, 162
  NATO and Baltic/Nordic defense, 162–163
    anarchy, 162
    reconnaissance plane, 163
    Russia's aggressive military exercises, 163
    submarine exercise, 163

NATO fighter jets, 162
Nordic–Baltic–US security cooperation, 161
post-Soviet transition, 168–169
  citizenship and language rights, 168
  flirt with democracy, 169
  real estate–cantered bubble economy, 169
  Russia's ongoing threat, 168
  traditions, 169
  years of economic trauma, 169
Russian aggression in the Baltic states,
    164–167
  Atlantic Council report, 165
  corruption by scofflaws, 165
  emerging new "soft spot," 165
  ethnic Russians, 165
  nationalist pride, 165
  "Russia's compatriots," 165
  weak commitment to democratic
    institutions, 165
underwater testing of coastal defenses, 162
Berlin Wall, removal of, 3
Brezhnev Doctrine, 76–79
  changing strategic doctrines, 77–78
  Czechoslovakia revolt, 76
  preventive diplomacy initiatives, 79
  renouncing of, 3
  Russia's European alliances 1970–1989, 79
  status quo of borders, 79

C

Catherine the Great
  age of, 28–31
  wars with Ottoman Empire, 146
CFE, *see* Conventional Armed Forces in Europe
Chechnya insurgencies, effects of, 97–98
China
  defense budget, 96
  population, 179, 190

as superpower, 44
treaties with, 30
CIS, *see* Commonwealth of Independent States
Coercive diplomacy, 141, 185
Cold War
    NATO and Warsaw Pact countries in, 75
    relations, return to, 187
    renewal of, 11–12
    Russia's loss of, 9
Collapse and rebirth of the Soviet empire, 3–15
    armed diplomacy, 5
    Atlantic Council, objective of, 15
    autocratic leadership, 5
    Berlin Wall, removal of, 3
    Brezhnev Doctrine, renouncing of, 3
    collapse of the Soviet Union (1991), 5
    elements of workable foreign policy, 4
    ending ties with the West, 11
        aggression as a tool of diplomacy, 11
        NATO membership, 11
    glasnost, 3
    Great Depression, 3
    incursion, 5
    perestroika, 3
    rebuilding a nation, 5–8
        authoritarian political system, 6
        immediate post-Soviet era, 7
        quest for a new national identity, 7
        Russia is back, 7–8
        system established by Yeltsin, 6
    regaining status lost, 10–11
    renewal of the Cold War, 11–12
        communist ideology, key points of, 11
        Marxist–Leninist state of Russia, 11
    revanchism, 9
    rise of the phoenix, 9–10
        expansion of NATO, 9
        resource-based economy, 10
    shaping Putin's foreign policy, 8–9
    special-interest neighbors, resurrecting
        relations with, 12–15
        borderland states, 14
        government struggles, 14
        NATO, Ukraine's desire for closer ties
          with, 13
        regaining respect, 13–15
    Western-style democracy, transition to, 5
Collective Security Treaty Organization
    (CSTO), 80, 84
Colonization in conquered territories, 86–90
    agents of Russification, 88
    for economic growth, 88–89

Estonian example, 87
fiefdoms, 88
forced deportation, 87
imperial building, 88
indigenous societies, 86
landlords, 88
Mongol invasions, 89
in Muscovite Russia, 87
peasant settlers, 86
progress and modernization, 88
in Romanov empire, 88–90
for security, 89–90
serfs, 88
Siberian labor camps, 87
Soviet-era deportations, 89–90
Commonwealth of Independent States (CIS),
    6, 80
Communist Party
    –approved organizations, 162
    authoritarian approach, 44
    autocratic government, transition from, 5
    domination, ascendancy of, 19
    Eastern European regimes, 76
    ideology, key points of, 11
    reduced power of, 6
Consolidation, Putin-era foreign policy of,
    57–71
    derzhavnichestvo, 58
    evolution of consolidation policy, 57–58
    foreign policy goals, 61–65
        against all enemies, 63–65
        by force if necessary, 62–63
        country most antagonistic to Russia, 64
        criticism of US and NATO actions in
          Iraq and Afghanistan, 62
        human rights and freedoms, 61
        regaining superpower status, 62
    Putin-era foreign relations, 58–61
        aggressive approach to foreign policy, 59
        annexation of Crimea, 58
        cordon sanitaire, 59
        geopolitical defensive, 59
        geostrategic objectives, 60
        relations with former republics, 60–61
        relations with the West, 59–60
    Russia's use of soft power, 65–69
        building friendly networks, 68–69
        compatriots living abroad, 67
        cultural centers, 67
        House of Moscow, 67
        influencing public opinion, 66
        internal critics, 65, 66

nascent civil society, 65
Rossotrudnichestvo, 67
special-interest small states, 66
spiritual ties, 67
Ukio Bank, 68
Constructionist foreign policy theory, principles of, 42
Conventional Armed Forces in Europe (CFE), 59
Conversion of the Military to Contract Service, 98
Corruption perception index (CPI), 48
CPI, *see* Corruption perception index
CSTO, *see* Collective Security Treaty Organization
Cyber wars, Russia's undeclared, 109–121
    attack on NATO websites, 119
    comparison of cyber warfare in post-Soviet states, 110
    cyber and shooting war with Georgia (2009), 118–119
    cyber skirmishing, 121
    cyber tactics, 111–112
    cyber war with Estonia (2007), 112–116
        denial-of-service programs, 113
        Europe's most wired country, 115
        IP spoofing, 113
        logic bomb, 113
        marginalization of ethnic identity, 114
        paperless government, 115
        permanent denial-of-service programs, 113
        polymorphic malicious programming, 113
        SQL injection, 113
        zombie, 113
    cyber war with Lithuania (2008), 116–117
    cyber war with Ukraine, 119–120
    Kyrgyzstan under cyber attack (2009), 117–118
    propaganda, 109
    verbal reprimands, 109
    victims of Soviet labor camps, 116
Czechoslovakia
    invasion of, 76
    land taken from, 32
    "people power," 148
    satellite membership in NATO, 74

D

DDoS attacks, 117, 119
Defense, *see* Reforming and rearming Russia's military

Defensive barriers, building of, 73–91
    Brezhnev Doctrine, 76–79
        changing strategic doctrines, 77–78
        Czechoslovakia revolt, 76
        preventive diplomacy initiatives, 79
        Russia's European alliances 1970–1989, 79
        status quo of borders, 79
    building barriers in the East, 79–86
        alliances in East, South and Southeast Asia, 82–83
        counteralliance to NATO, 85
        economic strengths, 84
        Iron Triangle alliance, 85
        liberal empire concept, 80
        maintaining Russia's East Asian policy, 83–86
        military forces, 85–86
        Shanghai Five, 81
        strategic aims in Central Asia, 82
        strategic alliances, 84–85
        treaties, 84
    building barriers in the West, 74–79
        antisocialist action, 76
        Brezhnev Doctrine, 76–79
        counterweight to NATO, 74
        NATO and Warsaw Pact countries in the Cold War, 75
        people's democracies, 74
        satellite governments, 74
        Warsaw Pact, 74
    colonization in conquered territories, 86–90
        agents of Russification, 88
        for economic growth, 88–89
        Estonian example, 87
        fiefdoms, 88
        forced deportation, 87
        imperial building, 88
        indigenous societies, 86
        landlords, 88
        Mongol invasions, 89
        in Muscovite Russia, 87
        peasant settlers, 86
        progress and modernization, 88
        in Romanov empire, 88–90
        for security, 89–90
        serfs, 88
        Siberian labor camps, 87
        Soviet-era deportations, 89–90
    geography, expansionist policies and, 73
    problem ethnic groups, mass deportation of, 73

Denial-of-service (DoS) programs, 113
Deportation
    in conquered territories, 86–90
    Estonian example, 87
    mass, 47, 73
    Soviet-era, 89–90
Derzhavnichestvo, 58
Diplomacy
    aggressive, 11, 178, 181
    armed, 5, 15
    coercive, 141, 185
    judo approach to, 180
    martial arts approach to, 180
    preventive initiatives, 79
    resolving problems through, 43
DoS programs, *see* Denial-of-service programs

E

Economic warfare foreign policy approach, 181
EEU, *see* Eurasian Economic Union
Empire revival (Russian aggression in Ukraine),
        145–158
    history of Russian–Ukraine relations,
            145–150
        beating death of journalist, 149
        Maidan protests, 149–150
        official annexation of Ukraine, 146
        Orange Revolution, 147
        Ottoman Empire, Catherine the Great's
            wars with, 146
        "people power," 148
        Ukrainians protest Russian language
            law, 147–150
    Putin's revenge, 150–156
        continuing war, 153–156
        importance of Crimea, 151–153
        little war with Ukraine, 153
        prolonged deployment, 156
        takeover of Crimea, 154–156
        treaty, 154
    Slavic Core, 145
    what happens next, 156–158
        economic warfare, 158
        national pride, 157
        NATO demands, 158
        NATO's reaction to Russia's intervention
            in Ukraine, 157, 158
        near-sacred memories, 157
Energy weapon in Russia's foreign policy, 123–141
    acquiescence of target countries, 139–141
    coercive diplomacy, 141

energy resources, state control of, 124–126
    decentralized production, 125–126
    gas production areas, 125
    oil production areas, 125
energy weapon, means for implementing,
        132–139
    basing an economy on a single
        commodity, 135
    cutoffs in Ukraine (2014), 139
    employing the energy weapon, 135–139
    gas crisis (2006), 135–137
    gas crisis (2009), 137–139
    geopolitical weapon, oil and gas as, 133
    problems and pitfalls, 133–135
transit routes and modes, control of, 126–132
    alternative sources of supply, 127
    EU Energy Security Strategy (2014), 130
    liquefied natural gas imports, 132
    Nord Stream natural gas pipeline, 128
    Southern Gas Corridor, 128
    southern pipeline proposals, 127–128
    South Stream pipeline, 128–129
    Trans-Anatolia pipeline, 128
    Trans-Caspian Pipeline, 128, 129
    Turkmenistan–China pipeline, 129–132
    Turkey's role in Russia–EU gas wars, 140
Estonia
    cyber war with (2007), 112–116
    deportation and collectivization in, 87
EU Energy Security Strategy (2014), 130
Eurasian Economic Union (EEU), 170
Europe's most wired country, 115

F

Federal Security Service (FSB), 41, 46
Fiefdoms, 88
Flirt with democracy, 169
Foreign policy, elements of 4
Friendly neighbor foreign policy approach, 182
Friendly networks, building of, 68–69
FSB, *see* Federal Security Service

G

Geography, expansionist policies and, 73
Geopolitical defensive, 52, 59
Geopolitical weapon, oil and gas as, 133
Georgia
    cyber and shooting war with (2009),
            118–119
    impact of war with, 99

Glasnost, 3
Gorbachev, Mikhail, 3
    friendly neighbor approach, 182
    idea of establishing Iron Triangle alliance,
        85
    KGB-led coup against (1991), 46
    openness policies of, 12
    rapprochement sought with the West under,
        67
    reform attempts by, 97
    revitalized democracy movement begun
        under, 187
    socioeconomic crises under, 40
Great Depression, 3
Great Russia, 26

H

House of Moscow, 67
Human rights, 61, 79

I

IDC, *see* Institute of Democracy and
        Cooperation
Identity
    authoritarian, 58
    ethnic, 114, 170
    liberalist, 43
    loss of, 168
    post-Soviet, 45
    quest for new, 7
    shared, 42, 183
    statist, 43
Innovator's innovator, 27
Institute of Democracy and Cooperation
    (IDC), 66
International Security Assistance Force (ISAF),
    121
Internet, delivery of propaganda using, 109
Intimidation, *see* Baltic and Nordic states,
    Russian intimidation in
IP spoofing, 113
Iron Triangle alliance, 85
ISAF, *see* International Security Assistance
    Force
Ivan IV of Moscow, coronation of, 18

J

Journalists, murdered, 149, 189
Judo approach to diplomacy, 180

K

KGB
    former, 39, 41
    friends, 178
    -led coup, 46
    official (Shevardnadze), 7, 176
    reinvented, 45
Kievan Rus empire, 19–23
Kyrgyzstan under cyber attack (2009), 117–118

L

Landlords, 88
Liberal empire concept, 80
Liberalist identity, 43
Liquefied natural gas (LNG) imports, 132
Lithuania, cyber war with (2008), 116–117
LNG imports, *see* Liquefied natural gas
        imports
Logic bomb, 113

M

Malicious programming, 113
Manchuria, special interests in, 33
MAP, *see* Membership Action Plan
Martial arts foreign policy approach, 180–181
Marxist–Leninist state of Russia, 11
Medvedev, Dmitry, 41
    appointment of Putin by, 41
    defense industry problems of, 105
    number of contract personnel under, 98
    power vertical, 177
    principles of Russian foreign policy, 12
Membership Action Plan (MAP), 53
Military, *see* Reforming and rearming Russia's
        military
Missiles, military reforms including, 103
Mongol invasions, 89
Mother Russia, defense of, 183
Muscovite Empire, 23–25

N

NATO, *see* North Atlantic Treaty
        Organization
Nazi Germany, 34, 87, 157
Nordic–Baltic–US security cooperation, 161
Nordic states, *see* Baltic and Nordic states,
    Russian intimidation in
Nord Stream natural gas pipeline, 128

North Atlantic Treaty Organization (NATO), 5
  accusation of "illegal and illegitimate
      annexation of Crimea," 158
  actions in Iraq and Afghanistan, criticism
      of, 62
  as common enemy, 183
  Communist authoritarian approach and, 44
  Cooperative Cyber Defense Centre of
      Excellence, 118
  cosmetic sanctions from, 51
  counteralliance to, 85
  counterweight to, 74
  cyber defense, policy on, 115
  efforts in Afghanistan, main logistic center
      supporting, 117
  expansion, 9, 14
  fighter jets, 162
  Finland's observer status in, 164
  Germany's membership in, 68
  –led invasion, defense against, 74
  liberalist identity tied with, 43
  member countries in the Cold War, 75
  membership of Baltic states in, 159, 173, 187
  possible scenario, 170
  Putin's railing against extending, 48
  reaction to Russia's intervention in Ukraine,
      157, 158
  reaction to Russia's missile deployment, 103
  Russia's attitude regarding expansion, 52
  Turkey's membership in, 140
  Ukraine's desire for closer ties with, 13
  verbal reprimands, 109
  websites, attack on, 119
Nuclear submarines, military reforms
      including, 103
Nuclear warheads, 185
Nuclear weapons, reductions in number of, 49

O

Operational Strategic Commands (OSCs), 101
Orange Revolution, 147
Organization for Security and Cooperation in
      Europe (OSCE), 79
Orthodox Church, 23, 47
Orthodox Russians, 28
OSCE, *see* Organization for Security and
      Cooperation in Europe
OSCs, *see* Operational Strategic Commands
Ottoman Empire, 34
  Catherine the Great's wars with, 146
  way to save, 45

P

Paperless government, 115
Path to the West scenario, 189
PDoS programs, *see* Permanent denial-of-service
      programs
People's democracies, 74
Perestroika, 3
Permanent denial-of-service (PDoS) programs,
      113
Petro-state nature of Russian economy, 188
Polymorphic malicious programming, 113
Power vertical concept, 177, 187
Professionalization of armed forces, 98
Prolonged deployment, 156
Propaganda, 109
ProrussianTV, 66
Public opinion, use of soft power to influence,
      66

R

Rebirth of the Soviet empire, *see* Collapse and
      rebirth of the Soviet empire
Reforming and rearming Russia's military,
      95–107
  all-forces personnel reductions, 104–105
  military reforms (2000–2008), 97–99
    all-volunteer army, transition to, 98
    Conversion of the Military to Contract
        Service, 98
    edict requiring professionalization of
        armed forces, 98
    effects of Chechnya insurgencies,
        97–98
    impact of war with Georgia, 99
    little war, 99
    objections to proposed reform, 97
  military reforms (2008–2015), 99–104
    command-and-control and
        organizational changes, 101
    fleet reorganization, 104
    land forces reorganization, 102–103
    missiles, 103
    nuclear submarines, 103
    objectives of reforms, 100–104
    Operational Strategic Commands, 101
    reorganizing the Russian Air Force, 102
    reorganizing the Russian Army, 100–101
    reorganizing the Russian Navy, 103
    US and NATO reaction to Russia's
        missile deployment, 103

need for reforms, 95–97
    conscription, 95
    contract soldiers, 96
    military budgets, 96–97
    plans influencing Russia's strategic
        thinking, 95
    rearming the Russian military, 105–107
Revanchism, 9
Romanov Empire, 25–31
Rossotrudnichestvo, 67
Russia in Chaos scenario, 189–190
Russian Federation successor state, 175
Russian foreign policy after Putin, 175–191
    alternative foreign policy strategies, 180–182
        aggressive diplomacy approach, 181–182
        economic warfare approach, 181
        friendly neighbor approach, 182
        martial arts approach to diplomacy,
            180–181
    implications for the West, 184–185
        coercive diplomacy, 185
        military actions against minority
            populations, 185
        nuclear warheads, 185
        sanctions, 185
        subversion role of ethnic Russians, 185
    Putin/Medvedev power vertical, 177–180
        aggressive diplomacy, 178
        annexation of Crimea, 178
        centralized dictatorship, 177
        failed attempt at introducing democratic
            society, 177
        KGB friends, 178
        Putin's strengths, 178–179
        Putin's weaknesses, 179–180
        status as a world power, regaining, 178
    recurring foreign policy aim, 182–184
        common enemy, 183
        little wars, outcomes of, 183
        Mother Russia, defense of, 183
        shared national identity, 183
    role for Russia, 175–177
        population of the Soviet Union, 176
        request to grant Russia special powers,
            176
        smaller, weaker empire, 176–177
        Yeltsin announcement, 175
    Russia's relations with the West, 186–187
        exacerbated situation, 187
        nuclear weapons, 186
        relations with former possessions,
            186–187

        relations with NATO, 186
        sanctions, 186
        upgraded doctrine, 186
    scenarios for a Russia after Putin, 187–190
        desirable scenario, 190
        interest in revolution, 189
        journalists murdered, 189
        malignant possible outcomes, 187
        most probable scenario, 190
        nuclear posturing, 191
        petro-state nature of Russian economy,
            188
        power vertical system, 187
        repercussions in terms of global security,
            190
        restrictions over electronic and print
            media, 188
        revitalized democracy movement, 187
        Russia in Chaos, 189–190
        Stalin Lite, 189
        Status Quo, 187–189
        Western Path to Development, 189
        Winter Olympics, 187
    "state of profound crisis," 175
Russian Revolution (1917), 19
Russification, agents of, 88

S

SAPs, *see* State Armament Plans
SCO, *see* Shanghai Cooperation Organization
Serfs, 88
Shanghai Cooperation Organization (SCO),
    51, 80, 84
Shanghai Five, 81
Siberian labor camps, 87
Slavic Core, 145
Sociocultural identity device, 45
Soft power, Russia's use of, 65–69
    building friendly networks, 68–69
    compatriots living abroad, 67
    cultural centers, 67
    House of Moscow, 67
    influencing public opinion, 66
    internal critics, 65, 66
    nascent civil society, 65
    Rossotrudnichestvo, 67
    special-interest small states, 66
    spiritual ties, 67
    Ukio Bank, 68
SORT, *see* Strategic Offensive Reductions
    Treaty

Southern Gas Corridor, 128
Soviet Union
    collapse of (1991), 5
    disestablishment of (1989), 19
    emergence of civil society following breakup
        of, 65
    population of, 176
Special-interest neighbors, resurrecting relations
    with, 12–15
Spy planes, intercepted, 162
SQL injection, 113
SSI, *see* US Army Strategic Studies Institute
Stages in the building of a Russian empire,
    17–35
    Catherine the Great, age of, 28–31
        growth after Catherine, 29–30
        Orthodox Russians, 28
        partitioning of Poland, 28
        peace treaty, 29
        setback in the Crimean war, 30–31
        wars against the Ottoman Empire, 29
    coronation of Ivan IV of Moscow, 18
    creeping reimperialization, present policy
        of, 17
    disestablishment of the Soviet Union (1989),
        19
    end of the Soviet Union, 32
    Kievan Rus empire, 19–23
    Muscovite Empire, 23–25
        expansion under Ivan IV, 24–25
        principality of Moscow, transformation
            of, 23
        territorial expansion, 24–25
    Romanov Empire, 25–31
        Bering Strait, 29
        Catherine the Great, age of, 28–31
        consolidation under the Romanovs, 31
        Cossack lands, 25
        geopolitical events, 25
        Great Russia, 26
        growth after Catherine, 29–30
        innovator's innovator, 27
        setback in the Crimean War, 30–31
    Russian Empire's expansion into the East,
        acceleration of, 18
    Soviet Empire, 31–35
        expansionism, 32
        geopolitical conditions, changes in, 34
        growing impossibility of growth, 34
        Ottoman Empire, 34
        special interests in Manchuria, 33

Suez Canal crisis, 34
    WWII, 32, 33, 34
    trade treaty, 22
State Armament Plans (SAPs), 105
Statist identity, 43
Status quo of borders, 79
Status Quo scenario, 187–189
Strategic Arms Reductions treaties (START I
    and II), 49
Strategic Offensive Reductions Treaty (SORT),
    49
Suez Canal crisis, 34
Superpower
    geopolitical, Russia's reputation as, 41
    status, regaining, 62
    unipolar model of, 48

T

TCP, *see* Trans-Caspian Pipeline
Trans-Anatolia pipeline, 128
Trans-Caspian Pipeline (TCP), 128, 129
Transition of Russia's foreign policy, 39–55
    coalition, 39
    factors shaping post-Soviet foreign policy,
        39–42
        common external enemy, 42
        constructionist foreign policy theory,
            principles of, 42
        effects of socioeconomic crises, 40–42
        identification of the West, 40
        ideological foundation shift, 40
        policy aim of choice, 42
        Putin's elected replacement, 41
        Russia's reputation as geopolitical
            superpower, 41
        social structures, 42
        Yeltsin-era crisis points, 41
    new role for Russia, 43–45
        achievements in science and industry, 44
        anarchy, as nature of world politics, 44
        anti-Western group, 44
        authoritarian approach, 43
        Communist authoritarian approach, 44
        as counterbalance to power centers in
            the West and East, 44
        liberalist identity, 43
        Pan-Slav movement, 45
        post-Soviet identity question, 45
        reinvented KGB, 45
        sociocultural identity device, 45

statist identity, 43
Yeltsin's liberalist identity tied with
NATO, 43
rebuilding the state, 45–51
Anti-Ballistic Missile treaty, 48
armed intervention to protect Russian
minorities, 50
controlling corruption, 48
corruption perception index, 48
cosmetic sanctions from NATO, 51
dictatorship of law, 46–47
failed attempt at introducing democratic
society, 47
feelings of betrayal, 46
forging new alliances, 48–50
KGB-led coup, 46
mass deportation of whole nationalities,
47
nuclear weapons, reductions in number
of, 49
Orthodox Church, destruction of, 47
Ottoman Empire, way to save, 45
Putin's railing against extending NATO,
48
rebuilding Russia's armed forces, 51
recentralization of political system, 46
relations with former Soviet possessions,
50–51
Shanghai Cooperation Organization, 51
souverenaya democratiya, 47–50
Strategic Arms Reductions treaties, 49
Strategic Offensive Reductions Treaty,
49
Treaty on the Non-Proliferation of
Nuclear Weapons, 50
unipolar model of single superpower, 48
universal character, agreements having,
50
Russia, the EU and NATO, 52–54
annexing of Crimea, 55
Atlantic-wide security policy, 55
geopolitical defensive, 52
Membership Action Plan, 53
Russia's attitude regarding NATO
expansion, 52
testing, 53–54
Warsaw Pact, 52
Treaty on the Non-Proliferation of Nuclear
Weapons, 50
Turkey, role in Russia–EU gas wars, 140
Turkmenistan–China pipeline, 129–132

U

Ukio Bank, 68
Ukraine, *see also* Empire revival (Russian
aggression in Ukraine)
cutoffs of natural gas in, 139
cyber wars with, 119–120
desire for closer ties with NATO, 13
driven back under protective umbrella of
Russia, 158
NATO's reaction to Russia's intervention in,
157, 158
official annexation of, 146
protest of Russian language law, 147–150
Unipolar model of single superpower, 48
United States
businesses hacked, 120
counteralliance to, 85
as country most antagonistic to Russia, 64
defense budget, 96
desirable scenario for, 190
economic and military rise of, 40
population, 179
reaction to Russia's missile deployment, 103
return to Cold War relations, 187
sale of Alaska to, 18
sanctions by, 185
September 11, 2001 terrorist attack on, 48
SORT agreement, 49
as superpower, 44
Yeltsin's rapprochement with, 5
Universal character, agreements having, 50
US Army Strategic Studies Institute (SSI), 97
US Dept. of Defense cyberspace definitions,
193–196

W

Warsaw Pact (WP), 52, 60, 74
Western Path to Development scenario, 189
Western-style democracy, transition to, 5
Winter Olympics, 187
World War II, 32, 33, 34
WP, *see* Warsaw Pact

Y

Yeltsin, Boris, 5
administration policy makers, 186
attitude of new states under, 186
crisis points, 41

cyber capabilities under, 109
edict requiring professionalization of armed
    forces, 98
failure of economic policies, 12
foreign minister under, 43
foreign policy under, 50
friendly neighbor approach, 182
handpicked successor, 9
legacy, 6
military reform proposals killed under, 105
political environment under, 45

privatization under, 48
rapprochement sought with the West under,
    67
revitalized democracy movement begun
    under, 187
socioeconomic crises under, 40
system established by, 6

Z

Zombie, 113